D1293153

WEST AFRICA PARTITIONED

Also by John D. Hargreaves

A LIFE OF SIR SAMUEL LEWIS

PRELUDE TO THE PARTITION OF WEST AFRICA

WEST AFRICA : THE FORMER FRENCH STATES

FRANCE AND WEST AFRICA (*editor*)

NATIONS AND EMPIRES (*co-editor with R. C. Bridges, Paul Dukes and William Scott*)

WEST AFRICA PARTITIONED: Volume I, THE LOADED PAUSE, 1885–1889

THE END OF COLONIAL RULE IN WEST AFRICA

ABERDEENSHIRE TO AFRICA

West Africa Partitioned

Volume II

The Elephants and the Grass

JOHN D. HARGREAVES

MACMILLAN

First published 1985

Published by
THE MACMILLAN PRESS LTD
Houndmills, Basingstoke, Hampshire RG21 2XS
and London
Companies and representatives
throughout the world

Printed in Hong Kong

British Library Cataloguing in Publication Data
Hargreaves, John D.
West Africa partitioned.
Vol II: The elephants and the grass
1. Africa, West—History—19th century
I. Title
966 DT476.2
ISBN 0-333-19224-9

Contents

List of Maps

List of Abbreviations

AE	Archives Etrangères, Paris (all references to the series *Memoires et Documents* unless otherwise stated)
AM	Archives de la Marine, Paris
ANS	Archives Nationales du Senegal
ANSOM	Archives Nationales, Section d'Outre-mer, Paris
BCAF	*Bulletin du Comité de l'Afrique française*
C of C	Chamber of Commerce
CEA	*Cahiers d'Etudes Africaines*
CFAO	Compagnie française de l'Afrique occidentale
CHJ	*Cambridge Historical Journal*
CMS	Church Missionary Society
CO	Colonial Office
CP	Confidential Print
DDF	*Documents Diplomatiques français, 1e série, 1871–1900*
Econ. HR	*Economic History Review*
ED, IX	*Etudes Dahoméennes*, IX (1953)
EHR	*English Historical Review*
FO	Foreign Office
GP	Die Grosse Politik der Europaïschen Kabinette
HJ	*Historical Journal*
IFAN	*(Bulletin de l') Institut français {fondamentale} de l'Afrique noire*, Dakar
JO	*Journal Officiel*
JAH	*Journal of African History*
JHSN	*Journal of the Historical Society of Nigeria*
JICH	*Journal of Imperial and Commonwealth History*
MAE	Ministre des Affaires Etrangères
MMC	Ministre de la Marine et des Colonies
NALB	Native Affairs Letter Book (Sierra Leone National Archives)
PP	*Parliamentary Papers*
PQ	Parliamentary Question

PRO	Public Record Office, London
RFECE	*Revue française de l'étranger et des Colonies et Exploration*
RFHOM	*Revue française d'histoire d'Outre-mer*
RNC	Royal Niger Company
SCOA	Société Commerciale de l'Ouest Africaine
SLA	National Archives of Sierra Leone
SLS	Sierra Leone Studies
SMA	Archives, Société des Missions Africaines, Rome
SSEC	Sous-Secretaire d'Etat pour les Colonies

No place of publication is included in references to English-language works published in London, nor to French-language works published in Paris.

Preface

When in the 1950s I began to study the European partition of West Africa I hoped to combine the approaches of a new African and an older Imperial school of historiography. My primary intention was to use the insights of what was still an experimentally Afrocentric approach to illuminate those encounters between Africans and Europeans which culminated in the establishment of colonial rule. At the same time I hoped to help resolve debates about the "new imperialism" of the later nineteenth century by more conventional studies of decisions taken by European governments, seen in the context of the economic, social and political development of their states and of the international environment. I had no preconceived intention to develop either a "peripheral" or a "metropolitan" theory of imperialism – these concepts had not yet been formulated; it simply seemed that both sorts of study were needed to explain what had happened.

Since then work by fellow-historians, and the course of history itself, have made this design seem rather naive. Theoretical debates and historical monographs combine to suggest a much more complex relationship between West African colonialism and the general phenomenon of the "new imperialism". Any general theory of the latter, it now seems clear, must adopt a world-wide view, paying at least as much attention to China, South America, Eastern Europe and the Middle East as to areas directly subject to colonial partition. On the other hand, an understanding of the specific conditions in which colonial rule was established in West Africa remains of considerable importance for West Africans themselves. Many monographs of the last twenty years have described aspects of the Afro-European relationship in great detail and with deep insight into the historical identity of the particular African societies involved. As far as my own project is concerned, the effect has been to demonstrate the naivety of youth, and thereby perhaps to encourage a certain lethargy of middle age. While demonstrating the impracticality of re-examining the whole story through the archival evidence (as I once dreamed of doing) this new wealth of secondary literature makes it feasible to attempt a general interpretative narrative of a texture which was inconceivable twenty-five years ago. Earlier volumes of this study have already acknowledged extensive debts to other scholars; parts of the present volume are essentially a work of synthesis to which my own archival researches have contributed relatively little.

For the 1880s, the focus of my study has been diffuse, concentrating on ways in which particular relationships in Africa were affected by a new instability in the international economy and the European state system. The events of these years were still perceived by most Europeans and Africans against essentially local horizons. While some Africans were, and increasingly felt themselves to be, part of a world Islamic community, and a few were beginning to understand something of their new involvement with Europe, most still saw relations with their neighbours in the context of regional networks created by common kinship, culture, or interests. Similarly Europeans, even when appealing to London, Paris or Berlin for a gunboat, were more concerned with specific interests than with any Imperial cause. In the 1890s however pressures from the European states became more purposeful; local conflicts are perceived as part of some wider international process, and a Eurocentric approach becomes more useful than an Afrocentric one for a historian who seeks to describe what happened.

Changes in actual relationships between Africans and Europeans were reflected in the ways in which Europeans conceptualized them. During much of the nineteenth century, disciples of Charles Darwin might have described West African societies by reference to his celebrated "tangled bank". The laws of historical evolution seemed to be producing a wide variety of social formations – "so different from each other, and dependent upon each other in so complex a manner" – each adapting to the environment produced through the gradual advance of Christianity, civilization and commerce in different ways, and with varied success. Though most Caucasian observers would have regarded colonial enclaves like Saint Louis or Freetown as representing "the higher animals", they could still see some place within the scheme of things for African societies capable of adapting, institutionally and culturally, to the new environment.

During the 1890s a much cruder view of the "struggle for survival" than Darwin's own came to characterize both the writings of "Social Darwinians" and the actual behaviour of European governments. Armed with the Maxim gun and other specimens of improved technology, they began to behave as though survival on the tangled bank depended on the competitive application of superior force. To some degree this change was influenced by reports of observers with some African experience, but essentially it seems to reflect the self-doubt of European nations in a more competitive economic and political climate. As between themselves, Europeans tried to prevent their exertions in Africa leading to armed conflict; their own struggle culminated in the ritualized though potentially lethal sporting contests popularly dubbed as "steeplechases". But the obstacles to be overcome were not merely natural hazards but African polities whose "carefully constructed forms" had not adequately prepared them to deal with sudden incursions of armed foreigners.

Many years later Jomo Kenyatta would publicize an African metaphor for this period: "when elephants fight, it is the grass that gets trampled". Africans were not always quite such passive victims as this implies. Even at the height of the invasion some were able to bargain with the elephants, others to penetrate their hides; there are still books to be written about the politics of survival on this trampled, tangled bank. But from the mid-1890s Afro-European relations have to be discussed in a different context from that in which this study originated.

This changing pattern of events is reflected in what some may find the asymmetrical structure of this volume. Chapter 7 reviews some of the forces governing Afro-European relations around 1890 and identifies, as expediting European penetration of the continent, the growing political effectiveness of relatively small pressure groups in Germany, and especially

France. The next three chapters narrate the advances of the colonial powers on certain West African frontiers within the period 1890–4, and attempt to establish inter-relationships between these several campaigns. Although by 1892 the British government had conceded hegemony to France in much of the south-western quarter of the region, the Ijebu campaign of 1892 is shown to initiate a new readiness to accept military and political commitments in the interest of future commercial expansion; and the French conquest of Dahomey opened the way for the celebrated steeplechase towards the middle valley of the Niger. Chapter 11, which is not based on archival research to the same extent as its predecessors, deals much more briefly with the final European rivalries. Since it was in the years 1894–8 that West African problems made their strongest impact on European diplomacy they have already been fairly intensively studied from this point of view; because the scope for African statecraft to affect the outcome was now much more restricted I have felt justified in compressing my account of this final phase of the partition. In a concluding chapter I attempt to assess the significance of the whole process in relation to the wider problem concerning imperialism with which I began.

* * *

There are as usual a number of debts of gratitude which it is a pleasant duty to recall. The overseas archival research would not have been possible without generous assistance from the British Academy (both a West European Grant and further assistance from the Small Grants Fund) and from the University of Aberdeen. I am equally grateful for a grant from the Twenty-Seven Foundation towards the cost of preparing the manuscript for publication. The sometimes puzzling task of doing this was undertaken, with her usual perceptive and cheerful efficiency, by Mrs Margaret Anderson. For assistance with the maps I am again grateful to my daughter Sara.

The long list of libraries and archives whose staff have assisted my research must begin with the Library of the University of Aberdeen. In Paris I again thank Marie-

Antoinette Ménier and the staff of the *Archives Nationales, Section d'Outre-Mer;* M. Audouy and the staff of the *Service Historique de la Marine;* and the staff of the *Archives Etrangères*. In Rome, Father Noel Douau, archivist of the *Missions Africaines*, was helpful beyond the line of duty. In Dakar I enjoyed the co-operation of M. Saliou Mbaye, director of the National Archives of Senegal, and in Freetown of Mrs Gladys Jusu-Sheriff, then in charge of the Sierra Leone National Archives at Fourah Bay College. Over the years there is perhaps a tendency to take for granted the efficient support of the staffs of the Public Record Office, the British Library, and the Royal Commonwealth Society; I am glad to take this opportunity to re-affirm my sincere gratitude.

When working in Paris I have enjoyed the hospitality as well as the advice and shrewd judgement of Marc and Timée Michel, and in London that of Robert Smith. I cannot list all the other friends and colleagues in Africa, Europe and America whose work and advice have been of direct or indirect assistance, though I sadly recall my friendship with the late Yves Person. But the help of my colleague Roy Bridges, which has included a shrewdly critical reading of most of the manuscript, requires an expression of particular thanks. So above all does the loving support which I have received over many years from my family, and especially my wife Sheila. I fear she may not find the finished work an adequate recompense for all she has had to tolerate and forgo.

J.D.H.

7 The Gathering Storm

CONTINENTAL CONFRONTATION?

And we are here as on a darkling plain
Swept with confused alarms of struggle and flight
Where ignorant armies clash by night.

Twenty years after "Dover Beach" Arnold's uncertainties had become more widely and crudely shared by Europeans who felt their security threatened by economic depression or the extension of the franchise; and one manifestation of this was a loss of confidence in the prospects for the peaceful modernization of Africa by commerce, Christianity and civilization alone. At Berlin in 1884–5 the European powers had tried to stabilize their own rivalries by drafting rules which would allow their subjects maximum opportunities to trade in Africa with a minimum of government control. But African responses to change were in many places threatening to upset the illusory equilibrium which existed; and those social and political forces within western European states which had for some time been making for more active uses of state power (vol. I, pp. 15–30, 201–2) were about to organize themselves more effectively.

Europeans active in Africa found several reasons for anxiety. The prospects for *s'occidentalisation* (vol I, pp. 6–10) seemed to be diminishing. Disappointment was increasingly expressed about the performance of western-educated Africans in Church and government office; but when African leaders like Jaja did hold their own within the modern political economy their mentors were no better pleased. Nor was much faith placed in the prospects of collaboration with "strong native governments" thrown up by the "African partition"; savagery was taking precedence over nobility in European images of Africa. Asante had been decisively out of British favour since 1873; Dahomey had never seemed an attractive partner; the military oligarchy of Ibadan appealed only to those prejudiced against its neighbours in Ijebu or Abeokuta. But the deepest cause of European unease in the 1880s was anti-Muslim prejudice, rejuvenated by the rise of Mahdism in the Nile valley; Gordon's death at Khartoum, coinciding with the closing stage of the Berlin Conference, seemed to falsify hopes of gradual and peaceful adjustment in relations between the two continents.

This sense of a coming confrontation between Christian civilization and evil forces led by Muslims grew most strongly in eastern and central Africa, where Christian missionaries in Buganda and Malawi felt themselves under deliberate threat from "Arab" slave-traders. Alexander Mackay, applying medical analogies to the condition of Africa as observed from Kampala, believed surgical intervention was necessary "to remove the present dead weight of oppression lying on its heart".

> It is no cure for a deep-seated abscess merely to plug up the mouth of the wound by which the fetid pus finds an exit. . . . The horrid, chronic bloodshed and cruelty, practised in inner Africa, cannot be ended by gunboats catching prizes on the ocean. . . . Let the powers of Europe divide the interior between them, i.e. from the lakes to the coast, not for annexation, but for friendly negotiation with the natives, and peaceful supervision.[1]

Distant observers whose geography was impressionistic sometimes assumed that the Muslim trading network which supplied the Indian Ocean slave-trade extended throughout the continent; one Irish MP, possibly confusing Samori with Tippu Tip, was worried lest firearms might be reaching East African Arabs through Liberian ports.[2]

It is difficult to assess how strongly this sense of a global threat from African Islam was felt by Europeans working on the western side of the continent. Certainly, it was sometimes exaggerated by proconsuls anxious to justify their own aggressive policies, as in much alarmist talk by French military officers about the perils of a great "Tijani League" (vol. I, pp. 64, 84). Goldie, too, using his authority as self-appointed expert on the Central Sudan, may have exaggerated his fears in order to discourage Christian missionaries from intruding into his sphere, when he declared:

> It is impossible to ignore the uneasy (when not actually hostile) attitude towards Christendom now prevailing among the Mahommedan rulers or dominant castes throughout Central Africa. . . . This tension of feeling is, no doubt, primarily due to the late general advance of European powers into Africa, and to the hostilities which have in some instances occurred between Christians and Moslems.

But when Goldie went on to speak of the influence of "large bands of fanatical pilgrims and dervishes", referring to a proclamation in the name of the Mahdi recently posted in Bida,[3] it was not all invention. There were many Mahdist sympathizers to the west of Lake Chad: Rabih Fadlallah, the former lieutenant of Zubair Pasha who had emerged from the wreck of the Egyptian empire to establish a predatory hegemony over the middle Chari basin, would benefit from their support during his conquest of Bornu in 1893. And to the north-east the influence of the Sanusiyya was becoming established in Wadai.[4] There was little to justify specific fears that any West African ruler was planning to attack the rights and privileges of Europeans as hitherto understood. But when new demands were presented, involving changes in economic relationships or the concession of political or military guarantees, refusal to concede could be interpreted as evidence of unregenerate commitment to an order based on fanaticism and slavery. Africans' defence of their sovereign independence was increasingly used to provide ideological charters for further European expansion.

An element of genuine humanitarian concern, ill-informed and ethnocentric though it may have been, continued to influence European attitudes. Ever since the Congresses of Vienna and Verona had registered a great reversal of Christian morality, action against slavery had been proclaimed a subject for concern by the concert of Europe. While this change arose partly from perceptions of the interest of advanced commercial and industrial nations in opening new African markets, it was also grounded in a muddled sense of collective moral obligation. Yet in the last resort this European vision could only be enforced militarily through the agency of national states. In 1889–90 a new manifestation of this high-minded internationalism ended by expediting competing invasions of Africa by British, French and Germans.

* * *

Although in 1884–5 the governments conferring at Berlin had been generally unwilling to exercise political or military power beyond the African coastline, their vague affirmations about combating the slave trade and promoting African welfare had provided handles for future use. On 1 July 1888 these were grasped by Charles Lavigerie, Cardinal Archbishop of Algiers, who echoed the agonies of Christian missionaries in Eastern and Central Africa in a resounding sermon in the Parisian church of Saint-Sulpice. With the approval of Pope Leo XIII, Lavigerie appealed to international opinion – *la vraie reine du monde d'aujourd' hui* – to undertake "a great crusade of faith and humanity" against the continuing slave-trade on the African mainland.[5] His high-minded initiative became quickly politicized; the effective response to this international clarion-call was the formation of more *national* anti-slavery committees, each seeking to influence a government whose priorities were inevitably determined by the short-term expediency of national interest. Lavigerie himself, aware that relations between the Church and the Third Republic had reached a critical stage, recognized these constraints; a few weeks after his Saint-Sulpice sermon he declined to address a congress of German Catholics for fear of offending French nationalist sentiment.[6]

Lavigerie's challenge was taken up by British abolitionists who, though no longer so militant as formerly, still commanded broad sympathy among influential sections of society. The British and Foreign Anti-Slavery Society organized a meeting for Lavigerie in London on 31 July, with the septuagenarian Earl Granville in the chair; Cardinal Manning, sharing the platform with Quakers and evangelical Anglicans, declared that British opinion had been "stagnant

[only] because it has not consciousness of the facts". The Society now attempted to enlighten it. There were questions in the Commons, a leader in *The Times,* a formal visit by Lavigerie to Lord Salisbury.[7] V. Lovett Cameron, explorer of the Congo basin, told Sir John Kirk of his intention.

> to get up an agitation and then if we can raise the money to establish boats and stations from Mouth of Shire to North of Tanganyika. The Archbishop of Canterbury is in for it, and so is Dick Burton.

To this improbable couple Cameron hoped to add Manning, the proconsul Euan Smith, and Sir Robert Fowler, MP; but he failed to recruit Kirk, who commented drily "there is no use crusading in a country you cannot keep after you have conquered it".[8]

The Foreign Office, while sharing Kirk's scepticism, responded with some concern for what would now be called its "public image", at home and abroad. Sir Clement Hill of the African department noted that the Berlin Act would justify a tentative diplomatic initiative, "though it would probably be of more use for a Blue Book than to the Africans". Salisbury, anxious to embark on no course which could not be sustained by some substantial "public impulse", invited his Under-Secretary, Sir James Fergusson, to assess opinion in the Commons. When he reported concern extending beyond the core of anti-slavery veterans, Salisbury agreed to take soundings about an international conference, which Leopold II of Belgium, whose international acceptability as an African power still rested on a humanitarian reputation as well as on neutrality in the European power balance, might be invited to convene.[9]

The scope of the programme of such a conference remained debatable. Fergusson (who as Governor of Bombay had personal knowledge of atrocities connected with the Indian Ocean slave-trade) was willing to consider sponsoring Lavigerie's suggestion of an international volunteer force, which Hill thought might attempt

> the organisation of native tribes so as to enable them to

> resist the Slave Trade, affording them armed assistance where necessary. They would be the pioneers of the civilisation spreading inland from the coast through the enterprise of the Governments or Chartered Companies.

But his superior Lister quickly dismissed any such "dreadful innovation", while Salisbury added drily, "It is not an entire innovation. The Crusades furnish a precedent, but it was not an encouraging one."[10] Neither philanthropy nor interest would yet justify military commitments in the African interior; international action could be effective only on the Indian ocean or the East African littoral.

Here however Bismarck had his own reasons to seek international co-operation. In August 1888 the Arab notable Abushiri ibn Salim al-Harthi raised a widespread revolt in German East Africa; and in November Salisbury agreed to join an Anglo-German blockade of the coast. Though essentially this was intended to protect their colonial interests, both governments found it expedient to present it as part of their confrontation with slave-traders; for Bismarck this was a particularly useful way to disarm opposition to his colonial policy from Windthorst and the Centre Party.[11] And although the immediate effect of the Abushiri revolt was to delay any wider diplomatic initiative it did underline the practical advantages of international co-operation to restrict the export of slaves and the import of firearms. By March 1889 Salisbury was ready to encourage the postponed Commons debate, and to renew his approach to Leopold, with German support. When a conference of seventeen nations eventually opened in Brussels on 18 November 1889 it was not only a response to the moral pressure which Lavigerie's campaign had generated throughout Western Europe, but a means of providing international sanction for measures by Britain and Germany.[12]

This seemed all too evident to the French. Etienne feared that humanitarian language masked political designs which, unless France made the most of her own claims in the West, would upset the African balance to her disadvantage.

> Britain's continual encroachments in southern Africa, her

> measures to extend the influence of the Cape up to the Zambezi in contempt of Portuguese rights . . . the formation of territorial companies which are preparing the way for official annexation – all these facts, which probably form part of a comprehensive plan, are so many indications of the expansionist projects of British policy in these regions. . . . If the result of these deliberations is to be a sort of amicable partition of the African continent among the various colonizing powers, a large share could not be denied to that nation which, through the seniority and size of her African establishments, has more claim than any other to make her voice heard. We are well placed to create in the future a large and powerful empire on the West Coast, and the success of our enterprises depends on the energy with which we can successfully defend ourselves against the encroachments which other powers may try to make in the zone which has come down to us.[13]

The Foreign Ministry however did not share this paranoia and their delegates at Brussels proved quietly co-operative on practical issues;[14] the British responded by not pressing too hard such sensitive matters as their naval "right of visit" to suspected slavers flying a French flag. The Conference produced no dramatic political crises; at first sight the General Act to which the participants finally agreed on 2 July 1890 seemed confined to implementing their professed "firm intention of putting an end to the crimes and devastations engendered by the trade in African slaves . . . and of securing for that vast continent the benefits of peace and civilisation".[15]

Closer study of the hundred Articles does however suggest an expectation that these admirable purposes would not be achieved without territorial partition. The opening articles, declaring the most effective means of counteracting the slave trade to be "progressive organisation of the administrative, judicial, religious and military services in the African territories placed under the sovereignty or protectorate of civilized nations", and the construction of modern means of communication, reflected Leopold II's desire to obtain international sanction for more active policies by the Congo Free State, and for the increased taxation necessary to finance them. Other governments might not be quite so ready to expand their colonial commitments, but the rhetoric of Brussels pointed in this direction. On the very eve of the General Act Britain and Germany signed the Agreement which finally delimited their spheres of influence in eastern Africa.

In West Africa too the new humanitarianism could be used to justify expansion. On 26 March 1889, during the Parliamentary debate on the slave trade, Sir Walter Barttelot called for intervention at Salaga, where 20 000 slaves captured by a Muslim potentate called King Jaberima were being sold each year. This was a garbled version of a report by ex-Inspector Firminger and, when visiting Salaga, had himself received exaggerated reports about Samori;[16] but it fuelled fears about the West African future. As Sir John Kennaway, a former President of the Church Missionary Society, put it in the same debate: "We cannot find that outlet for our manufactures which is so necessary to our commercial existence in communities which have been deprived of all their inhabitants."[17] Less publicly, Etienne briefed the Foreign Ministry on the recent revival of slave-raiding in Dahomey (which he well knew to be a response to new European demands), hoping to justify his own projected forward policy.[18] Increasingly the intense hostility to slavery revived by Lavigerie's crusaders was used by Europeans to justify the subjection of those African peoples whose "savagery" they held responsible.

The Brussels Act also facilitated this subjection by providing international regulation over the import of firearms – a subject on which France and Britain had several times failed to reach agreement in West Africa. Articles VIII to XIII provided that all imported firearms and ammunition should be deposited in "a public warehouse"; while flint-lock muskets and percussion guns might be withdrawn for sale under controlled conditions, "all arms for accurate firing, such as rifles, magazine guns or breech-loaders" were in general to be reserved for colonial forces. Complicated calculations of national interest by Leopold II and the German authorities in East Africa lay behind this formulation; in West Africa its effect, when eventually implemented, was to inhibit programmes of military modernization by African rulers, and to ensure the technological superiority of European armies during the decade of conquest. Despite the warm-hearted humanitarianism which had motivated many promoters of the Brussels Conference, the measures which it enacted were thus to prove "the Magna Carta of the colonial powers" rather than of the African peoples.[19]

THE CRISIS OF "LEGITIMATE COMMERCE"

While the rhetoric of Brussels was revealing new European expectations about Africa's political future, economic relationships were also changing. The 'legitimate commerce" which had gradually superseded the Atlantic slave trade rested on a narrow foundation of European demand for palm-products and groundnuts, and during the 1880s this had begun to shake in time with the market fluctuations which characterized the "Great Depression". Some reactions by those affected have been chronicled in the first volume of this study; while European merchants attempted to establish some form of monopoly over the purchase of export crops, African middlemen and producers responded by enforcing their own restrictive practices. Professor Hopkins has catalogued the causes of conflict – trading malpractices, demarcation disputes, produce "hold-ups", quarrels over credit or escaped slaves – which frequently lay behind European complaints about the breakdown of order, or "tribal war".[20] The more perceptive Europeans knew that more was needed than the short sharp shocks administered by Yonni expeditions, or naval patrols. "I am strongly of opinion that the administration of the Oil Rivers has got beyond the 'Consul and gunboat' stage", wrote a senior British naval officer in 1889.[21]

These conflicts reflected the collapse of the simple economic assumptions behind the optimistic development theory of Christianity, civilization and commerce. Enterprising traders might seek to surmount the depression by discovering new staples; they achieved striking though temporary local successes in promoting exports of wild rubber. Yet even in this case, where a marketable commodity could be extracted without great changes in land use or land tenure, the limits to expansion soon became apparent. African entrepreneurs were not always available (as they were in Asante)[22] to organize production; and it was difficult for Europeans to recruit their own free labour force, as the Niger Company had discovered (vol. I, pp. 105–6). West Coast merchants, whose existing business depended on the collaboration by African producers and traders, could not adopt the brutal forms of coercion used in the Congo basin. But if African rulers used their own methods to recruit labour for new productive enterprises, the result might be to increase that internal slave traffic which so oppressed European consciences.

Perhaps the most promising approach to the blockage of African commercial development was through technical innovation. In marine transport the substitution of steam for sail, which had proceeded slowly since mid-century, was completed in the 1890s through the ruthless entrepreneurial drive of Alfred Lewis Jones. After using the small Liverpool shipping agency of Elder, Dempster and Company to acquire control of both existing British steamship lines, Jones joined Woermann in establishing a "conference system" to regulate freight charges between West Africa and northern Europe; he thus gave the merchants access to an improved maritime transport service, at the cost of dependence on his own pricing policies. Later Jones turned his attention to the organization of credit and currency, helping found the Bank of British West Africa in 1894.[23] These measures lowered costs, but to the advantage of foreign capitalists, rather than local entrepreneurs, African or European.

To such men the construction of government railways had since the 1870s seemed the most promising method of opening new markets, encouraging new forms of production, and lowering costs. Sir George Goldie, whose own enterprise depended on a monopoly of river navigation, was prudently sceptical about the wilder projects for trans-continental lines; but he did admit in 1891 that "certain stretches of Central African railway are indicated by nature as possibly worth laying at once as a means to future development".[24] By this time the British Colonial Office, though still unwilling to become so directly involved as the French, was beginning to modify its doctrine that those who wished to build railways in Africa must raise their own capital and carry their own risks. While philanthropic arguments that railways would help combat the slave-trade may have counted for something, more important seems to have been the growing insistence of leading merchants that improved transport held the key to "the unlocking of the tropics",[25] and the concern of many Governors to prevent these keys being monopolized by foreign rivals. The Colonial Office gradually realized that improved transport and increased trade might provide routes to solvency; by sponsoring an experimental survey of the short Axim–Ancobra line in 1890, they moved tentatively towards the programme of government railway construction which Joseph Chamberlain would endorse five years later.[26]

As Goldie recognized, any dramatic economic transformation in Africa would take a long time: "although ivory and other existing products cannot make Central Africa worth holding, they form the temporary basis on which the subsequent creation of agricultural wealth must rest".[27] The railway projects which now came under serious study were relatively modest affairs, intended to increase exports by lowering costs of "existing products". Even these were however liable to encounter political opposition as well as technical difficulties, as French experience in Cayor had shown. Although commercial expansion would depend on the continued collaboration of African farmers, brokers, and political authorities, schemes of inland penetration were justified by attacks on charges and restrictions imposed by undifferentiated "middlemen" and by African rulers. Railway enthusiasts argued that the opposition of Africans with such vested interests could be mollified by financial compensation, or by euphoria at the prospect of cheaper imports; but it was surely naive not to foresee resistance from those whose dealings with European strangers had always assumed that they would remain in their natural location on the seaboard.

Still more serious complications were likely to arise from the grandiose schemes for railways across the continent or into the heart of the savanna, which found favour among some French apostles of *la colonisation moderne*. Since the capital costs would be heavy, all these plans assumed government support, preferably through some sort of charter conveying monopolistic powers similar to Goldie's.[28] After Binger's journey had shown that the *dyula* trade diaspora in the western Sudanic region was fully comparable to that of the Hausas in the east, his patron Arthur Verdier advanced vast monopolistic claims over the whole region between the Ivory Coast and the Niger; in particular he demanded a Charter for a *Compagnie du Kong,* which was to establish a *voie de communication* with that "*dyula* capital". These grandiose schemes were viewed sceptically by French officials[29] and Verdier eventually had to be content with a timber concession in the south-east of the colony; but his attempts to move inland showed that the Muslims who controlled inter-regional trade would oppose any such commercial revolution.[30]

The elaborate network of inter-regional trade into which European entrepreneurs now hoped to break was based largely upon consumption goods with little potential in European markets: on kola, salt, livestock and African textiles. Nor did the consumers whom the *dyulas* served offer promising markets for staple European exports. Good Muslims would not buy spirits or tobacco; imported textiles had few advantages over local products; and the Brussels Conference had just prohibited the one import for which there was a keen demand in some quarters: modern firearms. Moreover, African entrepreneurs were well content with human porterage. They had no religious or cultural inhibitions about using slaves, who could still be bought in Mende country for about £3 a head;[31] and *dyula* accountancy made small allowance for their own labour as caravan-leaders. Trade was an honourable and prestigious way of life rather than a means of securing rapid returns on capital; "Time is of so little object that a man will travel perhaps a couple of days to effect an apparent gain of six pence", commented a Creole who knew the *dyulas* well.[32] Established caravan routes were adequate to transport goods like gold and ivory, of high value in relation to bulk; railways, though necessary to develop exports of goods like raw cotton, would undercut the interests of those already involved in this commercial system.

Many experienced European merchants realized that seeking to accelerate *la colonisation moderne* might in the short run be counterproductive. In 1890, when the French in Dahomey seemed to be rashly forcing the pace of change, the London *Standard* summed up the case for letting commercial development proceed gradually:

> There is a general concurrence of opinion that in this part of Africa the influence of civilised Powers should be directly represented only on the coast. . . . Let the natives bring down their oil and other commodities to the trading stations at the river's mouth and barter them there for European goods. Let our missions into the interior be confined to purely business purposes, and let us keep free from all interference with the quarrels of the respective chiefs, unless and until their feuds stop traffic or menace our settlements. . . . What is needed . . . is simply an armed police. That is the system which has been adopted by the English authorities, and, on the whole, it has worked well. Civilisation filters through. . . . Slowly but surely the contact with the little communities of traders and officials which stud the littoral is accustoming the mind of the people to peaceful ideals . . . the tendency is towards better things. . . . Already the sons of the Sovereigns come to Oxford for their education. . . .[33]

Certainly this reflected Salisbury's view; "the pacific invason of England"[34] should be left to change Africa at its own pace, and dramatic initiatives by governments were likely to do more harm than good. But, as he later confessed, this ignored the possibility 'that if Britain left its hinterland alone, other nations might not do so'. (see, p. 123). From 1890 plans for the penetration of the west African interior were increasingly framed in a climate of fierce international competition, forced on by imperialist pressure-groups.

SOCIAL IMPERIALISM AND GERMAN *WELTPOLITIK*

It was of course not only in regard to Africa that the political and economic expectations of Europeans were changing dramatically. The 1890s were a period of fundamental shift in relationships between the capitalist nations of the North Atlantic seaboard and the rest of the human race; the new assumptions about Afro-European relations belong to the same global context as Jameson's raid on the Transvaal, growing foreign encroachments on Chinese sovereignty, the construction of the Trans-Siberian railway and the German battle-fleet, Italy's invasion of Ethiopia, the enactment of Jim Crow laws in the southern United States. As Europeans became more confident of their own military and technological power they abandoned their former hopes that commercial and missionary contacts would make African rulers willing and competent to collaborate in European schemes for improvement; instead they began to assume that Africans, probably because of racial incorrigibility, would actually resist civilization. Progressive Europeans argued that intervention was justified by their superior moral and scientific resources, which would enable colonial governments to control the environments which constrained African developments; less progressive ones, that white nations should not hesitate to exert their power wherever it would assist their struggle for survival in an increasingly competitive world.

Those who voiced the new doctrine of "Social Darwinism", most strongly rarely showed deep acquaintance with contemporary biological thought. In the international context this creed was based upon two sweepingly crude suppositions. The first was that social as well as biological evolution was achieved through a process of struggle among genetically distinct races: white-skinned being clearly superior (despite signs of a coming challenge from yellow Orientals), and Black peoples at the bottom of the pile. Such a belief could absolve European governments from moral inhibitions about exercising their military or economic strength against coloured peoples; but it need not have impelled them so urgently to exercise direct colonial control but for the second Darwinesque supposition – that a struggle for riches and power was simultaneously taking place within the White world, not as Marxist socialists believed between classes but amongst nation-states.

The political context of the later nineteenth century favoured the propagation and vulgarization of both suppositionstions. Since the leading capitalist states had all recently extended the political franchise to substantial numbers of adult males, the doctrine that the future wealth of nations would depend upon controlling men, land and resources on a continental scale was publicized far beyond those political and intellectual elites which had formerly decided policy. In 1895 the Deputy Henri Lavertujon, introducing one of many narratives of heroic deeds by the French colonial army, claimed that public support for expansion reflected recognition that *l'avenir est aux grands états*, and that a France confined to the historic hexagon would soon be overwhelmed by Britain, Russia, and the USA.[35] Similar themes recurred in much European literature of the 1890s – in high art as well as popular novels, academic treatises as well as political propaganda. "Imperialism", a word which originally entered the Victorian vocabulary as a disobliging description of the domestic regime of Napoleon III, now implied that control of overseas resources had become an imperative concern not only of the state but of society.[36]

Historians of this new "social imperialism" now see the partition of Africa as only one manifestation of this new force, and not that most significant for Europeans (though it was clearly so for Africans). Their attempts to interpret the new phenomenon raise broad theoretical problems, to which this study offers only a modest contribution. Some believe the new ideology to have been more or less deliberately manufactured from above, as a technique by which well-established landed, military, or administrative elites could delude or manipulate the new democratic electorate and preserve their own hegemony, Others emphasize the pressures coming upwards from society: though "society" may here mean different things. One major historiographical tradition stresses the influence exercised by commercial, industrial or financial capital, but others spread responsibility more widely. Max Weber, a particularly well-placed observer, commented on the role of intellectuals in promoting the expansion of a German nation within which they enjoyed prestigious and privileged status; Lenin himself noted how sections of the working-class had been misled, so that they might believe their own employment and prosperity to depend on the extension of their nation's markets in the developing world.[37]

This issue has been most explicitly debated with reference to Wilhelmine Germany, which in the wider context of international history seems to be the crucial case. Followers of Hans-Ulrich Wehler emphasize the role of imperialism as a "social safety-valve";[38] Bismarck in 1884, he argues, was responding to an emerging "ideological consensus" about the current economic crisis in order to win support from middle-class, possible working-class, voters who might otherwise be attracted to more radical solutions (cf. vol. I, pp. 23, 28, 34–5). But though Wehler shows that certain ideas about the economic crisis were widely expressed, especially by Chambers of Commerce, it is not clear how far this "ideological consensus" extended; nor does he conclusively show that Bismarck's manipulation of popular nationalism was indeed intended to retard "the rising tide of modernization".[39] Geoff Eley prefers to interpret colonial imperialism as a modest tributary current, part of a much broader movement of radical Pan-German nationalism, which did represent a challenge by diverse sections of the German middle class to the essentially conservative structures of the Bismarckian Reich.[40] Historians of Africa cannot settle this debate, but they may note that the protagonists began their researches at different starting points: Wehler was concerned to explain changes of policy by Bismarck at a time when his control of the imperial executive was still relatively secure, Eley to explain the growth of the Navy League in the later 1890s. Radical nationalists exercised growing influence after the fall of Bismarck; colonial expansion, though only a minority concern, benefited accordingly.

Bismarckian Germany is now fairly generally seen as an authoritarian regime, sustained politically through the "alliance of iron and rye" and utilizing the influence of notables (*Honoratiorenpolitik*) to combat those groups within the new electorate (represented by the "Radical Right" as well as by Progressives and Social Democrats) which demanded some genuine shift of power. The *Kolonialverein* of 1882 was a relatively minor stirring within the middle-class, largely led by intellectuals, or missionary statesmen like Friederich Fabri,[41] who believed that colonies could provide constructive outlets for restless elements at home, but its arguments attracted some sympathy from influential bankers and industrialists worried by the economic depression. In 1887 its union with the *Gesellschaft fur Deutsche Kolonisation* brought in small-scale investors, speculators and adventurers who may be thought to represent the potential populism of the *petite bourgeoisie*;[42] its journal, the *Deutsche Kolonialzeitung*, went over to weekly publication and assumed a more stridently nationalist tone.

All this seems more like a coalition of pressure-groups than any broad social movement. The *Deutsche Kolonialgesellschaft* formed by this uneasy union remained a relatively small body, rising to 18 250 members by 1892. It included groups with conflicting views on colonial policy; those anxious to establish monopolies of exploitation, for whom Karl Peters was a national hero, were opposed by merchants and missionaries with West African experience who admired British methods of commercial and cultural penetration. One influential figure was Ernst Vohsen, former President of the Sierra Leone Association (vol. I, pp. 172–3). Born in Mainz in 1853 (just too late to see active service in the Franco-Prussian war) Vohsen had begun his career as Verminck's agent in the Nunez, becoming Freetown manager of his companies from 1877 until 1887 (and from 1881 acting as German Consul). In 1888, after the *Deutsch-Ostafrikanische Gesellschaft* was reorganized at Bismarck's request, Vohsen succeeded Peters as its representative in East Africa; but his attempts to put the enterprise on a sounder commercial basis were cut short by the Abushiri rising. One returning to Berlin in 1889 Vohsen became an influential adviser on colonial policy, dividing his time between colonial literature (he became head of a Berlin publishing house in 1895) and sponsoring the inland expansion of Togo and Kamerun.[43] The liberal, pro-British, colonial policies which Vohsen favoured were advocated equally strongly by J. K. Vietor, the evangelical Bremen merchant whose grandfather had first established the German presence in Togo, and who resisted demands for monopolistic grants by strongly advocating policies based on collaboration with "free peasants, happily and peaceably cultivating their fields with their wives and children".[44]

More conspicuous in the work of the colonial societies than substantive debates about policy was the pressure which they exercised for further expansion, both by persistent propaganda and by organizing expeditions. As Peters in East Africa and Flegel on the Niger (vol. I, p. 99) had earlier demonstrated, such initiatives could complicate the conduct of German diplomacy. After 1890 the social and political climate of the Reich increasingly made it expedient for the government to respond to the patriotic arguments of colonialists. Bismarck, even after his initiatives of 1884–5, had hoped to leave financial responsibility and administrative control in the new dependencies to those directly interested; colonies were to serve, never control, his tactical objectives of European policy. But once colonies existed, the bureaucracy could not ignore calls for their consolidation and expansion. By 1890 the tiny section of the Foreign Ministry which looked after them had to be raised to full Departmental status, under the direction of Dr Paul Kayser. This ambitious and legalistic bureaucrat with East African interests, originally a *protégé* of Bismarck, was frequently able to influence the erratic "New Course" of foreign policy under Caprivi, and his forceful advocacy of African boundary claims began to affect German relations with France and Britain[45] (cf. vol. I, pp. 206–23, vol. II, pp. 191–5).

As regards policies within existing colonies also, specific interests within the colonial movement could often impose their objectives on officials innocent of preconceived doctrines or policies. In October 1890 Caprivi, anxious to appease colonialist critics of his recent territorial concessions to Great Britain, decided to constitute a *Kolonialrat,* an advisory council where colonial experts (who at this period were unavoidably also usually interested parties) could debate policy issues. This innovation doubtless helped rally colonialists to support Caprivi's *Sammlungspolitik*, but it also provided them with new means of leverage upon public resources.[46] And their enhanced status helped them to win increasing public support, not because ordinary Germans knew or cared much about Adamawa or Kete Krachi, but because colonial imperialism could fit in easily to popular attitudes towards the assertion of German power in a competitive world. The colonies became "a rich source of political images" which could be adopted to serve competing parties or interests.[47] During the 1890s membership of the *Kolonialgesellschaft* at last rose sharply, to 36 000 by 1900, though largely in the shadow of the much more popular (and populist) Navy League.[48]

Whether German imperialism is regarded as originating with the state or with society, the colonial movement thus came to exercise a growing influence upon the often rudderless *weltpolitik* of Wilhelm II. Besides making its own distinctive contribution to a political climate which exalted German national power and racial pride, it developed specific demands and interests to reinforce those powerful external pressures which were accelerating the penetration and partition of the African interior. In West Africa, however, its impact was not comparable to that of the small but increasingly effectively organized French colonial movement.

THE ROOTS OF THE FRENCH COLONIAL PARTY

By 1889 the structures necessary for a forward French policy in Africa seemed solidly established. The Colonial Department had been freed from control by the Ministry of Marine (with its tendency to regard colonies as outposts of metropolitan power, rather like warships) and was represented in the Cabinet by an able and ambitious politician. Diplomacy had secured a large, if still incompletely defined, area within which French agents need no longer be inhibited by fears of opposition by European rivals. The government of Senegal was facing the problems of organizing a protectorate within its historic sphere of influence, while on the upper Niger ambitious military commanders were preparing to confront the Muslim empires. The commercial outposts in Guinea, the Ivory Coast, the Popos, and Porto Novo had been grouped under a Lieutenant-Governor, Jean Bayol, who clearly intended to expand their influence; further south Savorgnan de Brazza, an established figurehead of France's *mission civilisatrice,* faced wide prospects within the Congo basin.

What remained in doubt was the political will to act decisively within these structures – to recognize African expansion as a genuinely national interest. Germans confident in their country's expanding power might look naturally towards underdeveloped continents; French patriots had priorities nearer home. Increasing the nation's domestic staff, Deroulède had suggested, was no compensation for the lost children of Alsace and Lorraine; such widely-shared attitudes had brought down Ferry in 1885 and inhibited colonial expansion throughout the decade (vol. I, pp. 51–7). Anti-colonial sentiment was based not only on arguments of financial extravagance and diversion of energy, but of diplomatic priority: African expansion meant increased friction or conflict with Britain, and might eventually entail reconciliation with Germany in some form of Continental League.[49] Only a Franco–German alliance would have enabled France to compete with England in the division of the world, writes Hannah Arendt; hence, she suggests, "France . . . never developed a full-fledged imperialist party."[50] But even if the Third Republic never became so committed to *weltpolitik* as the Germany of Bülow or the Britain of Chamberlain, groups of officials, soldiers and entrepreneurs who had hitherto pursued their own dreams and their own designs did combine during the 1890s, and persuaded Republican politicians that colonial imperialism could provide a safe and even rewarding platform from which to address their patriotic electors.

Their success is not easy to explain. Most objective assessments now agree that tropical Africa was a region of no more than marginal importance for French society. Unlike Germany, there was no pressure for emigration; even in Algeria more than half the settlers were Spaniards or Italians. Of course there were always individuals who turned to Africa in search of adventure or achievement, especially from peripheral areas like Corsica and Brittany, and their numbers much increased once organized colonies provided the structure of an alternative society. But even then, the tendency was most marked among young military officers seeking martial glory; for civilians "the prestige of overseas service was low".[51]

Nor was the business world eager to provide the capital or the expertise which an active policy of "modern colonization" would have required. Of course, certain industries (textiles and distilling, for example) and certain ports, were interested in African markets; the Chambers of Commerce of Marseille and Bordeaux had much experience in persuading the state to defend established interests in Africa (for example, *Prelude*, pp. 131–2, 180–91; vol. I, pp. 55–6, 244). But the great commercial firms which were now forming depended substantially on foreign capital and personnel; the foundations of the commercial empire of CFAO (founded in 1887) had been largely laid by Swiss and German agents, and when the *Société Commerciale de l'Ouest Africain* was constituted in 1906 it was in direct succession to the Swiss house of Ryff and Roth.[52] Such merchants tended to be cosmopolitan rather than imperialist in outlook, unless foreign governments directly threatened their trade; knowing that any territorial partition was likely to cut across their own interests they tended to cling to the old patterns of legitimate commerce and free trade as long as possible, and rarely feature prominently in early demands for colonial expansion.

If the interests of commerce and industry in African colonization were marginal, those of the French financial world were more so. The larger banks were indeed encouraging greater investment overseas, rather than in real estate at home – but in government loans and railway stocks in regions like Russia or the Ottoman empire, where capitalist development was more advanced than in the tropics. African railway projects did however hold some interest to small investors and company promoters, especially if there were possibilities of government subsidies. During the 1880s political followers of Gambetta who were connected with financial speculators and Algerian *colons* built some ten thousand kilometres of Algerian railways with the backing of government guarantees.[53] Although the technocratic dream of a trans-Saharan line had been fatally damaged by the Flatters disaster of 1881, some of these railway promoters were now turning their attention further south; and with Eugène Etienne's return to the colonial under-secretaryship in March 1889 they saw possibilities of attaching their own schemes to wider visions of French African policy.

Although historians, as well as contemporary critics,

sometimes claim that Etienne's colonial policy revolved around the distribution of state patronage among special interest groups,[54] he professed a much broader vision of how colonial expansion could help sustain French prosperity and power in a competitive world.[55] As Minister he was able to assist the re-emergence of a colonial myth which identified empire not merely with France's interests but with her national traditions. This was no sudden development. French "social imperialism" can be traced long before the Great Depression, in the notion of empire as a "safety-valve for the social order"; the overseas policies of Gambetta and Ferry have been seen as essentially manipulatory techniques, designed to satisfy that "alliance of capitalists and petty producers" which formed the basis of the Third Republic.[56]

Ardent Republicans were already writing histories which presented colonial expansion as a continuing national destiny, a civilizing mission which had sometimes required the spread of Catholic Christianity, sometimes of Liberty, Equality and Fraternity.[57] Even the sceptical eye of Professor Ageron sees "an astonishing historical continuity" across the centuries, and dates the new "imperialist conception of colonisation" to the last decade of the Second Empire.[58] But hitherto such doctrines had been advanced only by scattered groups and individuals; they had not protected Ferry against those who regarded colonial expansion as an inexcusable diversion from patriotic priorities. "France possessed colonialists, but no colonial party."[59] Neither of the two imperialist factions which would later conflict over the form and method of colonialism felt strong enough to take open initiatives during the later 1880s; the military clique of Desbordes and Archinard operated under serious political and financial constraints, while the civilian advocates of modern colonialism lacked leadership, as well as funds. In 1890 the formation by the Paris merchant Léon Tharel of a *Syndicat du Soudan* provided one of the first signs of interest by metropolitan capital in the West African interior. About the same time Tharel began to promote more vigorous expansion of the equatorial colony of Gabon-Congo.

Here Savorgnan de Brazza, an early hero of the colonial lobby,[60] had since 1886 faced less congenial challenges as

Commissaire-Général. Hampered from raising taxes (except in Gabon) by the international regime which the Berlin and Brussels treaties imposed on the "conventional basin" of the Congo, Brazza was under continuous pressure from Paris to make his little-developed colony self-supporting. By advocating the general principle of granting concessions with far-reaching privileges to private companies Brazza pleased most civilian colonialists; but many judged him excessively cautious in expanding French influence. Marius Daumas, a leading merchant closely linked with Leopold's Congo Free State, criticized Brazza's emphasis on developing independent routes to the ocean through the Ogoue and Kwilu valleys; ardent young members of his staff wanted to emulate his own earlier explorations by spectacular northward thrusts to forestall British or German occupation of the savannas around Lake Chad.

During the summer of 1890 Chad was adopted as the objective of a new *Syndicat du Haut-Benito* formed by Tharel and other businessmen – *des commercants et non des speculateurs*, they insisted – with financial backing from the Paris Rothschilds, and political sympathy from Etienne.[61] The *Syndicat* took up a proposal by an adventurous young Lorrainer called Paul Crampel "to traverse, and to conquer for France and for science, the whole unknown territory which stretches between the Ubanghi and Lake Chad". After signing treaties with Bagirmi and Bornu which would deny Britain and Germany access to the lake, Crampel planned to return triumphantly across the Sahara to Algiers. It was Hippolyte Percher, an ambitious journalist who wrote as Harry Alis, who perceived how such a scheme might provide a public focus for the colonialist cause, if presented as part of a grand design "to unite our possessions in Algeria-Tunisia, in the Senegal, and the Congo by way of the central Sudan, and so to found in Africa the greatest colonial empire in the world".

The supposedly rich resources of the interior would provide economic rewards; Alis identified Bagirmi as "an African Eden, rich in cotton". And besides advancing national prestige, the enterprise might serve as a social safety-valve for "the large number of young people who have suddenly found themselves *déclassés* through the spread of education" and could not find satisfying employment in France.[62] Beyond this, Alis realized that the glorification of Chad would justify the ambitions of soldiers in the western Sudan and railway projectors in Algeria, as well as the Congolese expansionists; it would bring backing from imperial visionaries to hard-headed men on the make. The romantic image of the lake could provide a dramatic back-cloth against which many special pleaders could appeal for national support.

But government support *would* eventually be necessary; and in 1890 it was still politically hazardous to take colonial schemes to Parliament. Etienne, whose support was early recruited, was anxious to follow British and German examples by granting charters to private companies willing to serve as agencies for expansion and development. Unfortunately this was contrary to French law, and such a proposal was almost as controversial as official expansion. In July 1890 the principle was approved by a Commission under the chairmanship of the Commerce Minister, Jules Roche; but widespread suspicion of financial intrigue and political jobbery prevented approval of its suggestion that the grant of such monopolies might be approved by decree on the recommendation of the recently established *Conseil Supérieur des Colonies*. Even Ferry attacked such a procedure for by-passing Parliament, and it was not possible to change the law until 1897.[63]

This setback to private enterprise did not deter the political advocates of colonial expansion. Etienne supplied Crampel's party with arms and scientific instruments, and tried to persuade a sceptical Brazza to be more co-operative.[64] And although it seemed inexpedient to publicize the mission itself, a parliamentary interpellation on the conflict with Dahomey on 10 May 1890 gave Etienne an opportunity to associate himself with the covering myth. To the perturbed astonishment of Alexandre Ribot, recently appointed Foreign Minister, in a new Freycinet government, Etienne concluded a rhetorical statement of determination to defend French interests at Porto Novo by a remarkable claim, which the Chamber applauded:

If you drop a perpendicular from the [eastern] border of

> Tunis, through Lake Chad and ending on the Congo, you may say that the greater part of the territories embraced between this line and the sea – excepting of course Morocco and the coastal possessions of Britain, Germany and Portugal . . . are French, or destined to be included in France's sphere of influence. We have there a vast, immense domain which it is for us to colonize and make fruitful. At the present time, given the movement of expansion which is taking place throughout the world, when foreign markets are being closed to us and when we intend to resume control over our domestic market, I believe . . . it is prudent to provide for the future by reserving for French commerce and industry the outlets which have been opened in and through our colonies.[65]

By implication, this speech extended the scope of the Chad design even more widely. Porto Novo, and presumably Assinie and Conakry also, were it seemed to become bases for a policy of empire-building which was likely to cause conflicts with Germany, and above all with Great Britain.

A further opportunity for the new colonial movement to "come out" was provided by the Anglo-German Agreement of 1 July 1890, the principal effect of which was greatly to enlarge Britain's sphere of imperial influence in eastern Africa in return for the cession of Heligoland.[66] Although this agreement had already been in preparation under Bismarck (cf vol. I, pp. 219–23) the circumstances of its conclusion increased international uncertainty about the direction of the "New Course" proclaimed by his successors. At this point, with the young Wilhelm II in a mood of Anglophil euphoria induced by his appointment as an Admiral of the British Fleet,[67] the agreement (seen in conjunction with the lapse of Germany's Reinsurance Treaty with Russia) seemed to mark a more definite move towards alliance with Britain than Bismarck had ever contemplated.

In view of what is now known about the lack of clear direction among the new policy-makers, as well as the more profound pressures of German imperialism, this interpretation was clearly exaggerated; but the effects on France's international policy were profound. Ribot and Freycinet could now move cautiously towards an alliance with Russia, which Alexander III became less reluctant to contemplate. This would eventually afford military guarantees against a German attack (though no real prospect of recovering Alsace-Lorraine), and so remove some of the patriotic prejudices against colonial expansion. Shrewd diplomatists like Paul Cambon, who regarded Britain and Italy as France's natural allies, saw the writing on the wall with grave misgivings; the Russian alliance would encourage friction with Britain over secondary overseas issues, and particularly over Egypt, now essentially a matter of aggrieved national sentiment rather than true national interest. "*Quand le vin est tiré, il faut le boire*", Cambon grumbled; "there are people and even nations who prefer to die of thirst".[68] During the 1890s Cambon came to fear that the nation might turn to the stronger liquor of colonialism, and in its cups accept a Continental League against the British Empire.

French newspapers of all tendencies denounced the Anglo-German agreement as an unfavourable development in the international situation, with serious Egyptian implications: and also as jeopardizing specific French interests, notably her rights in Zanzibar under an Anglo-French Declaration of 1862.[69] Somewhat vaguer fears were expressed about the effects on the Chad Plan of new provisions for Anglo-German commercial co-operation and mutual notification of treaties in the still undefined frontier area to the north of the Benue (cf vol. I, p. 104). The Niger Company at this time appeared to be moving into a new phase of expansion. Early in 1890 Goldie (prompted by Anderson and the Foreign Office) had sent his Sierra Leonean agent D. A. King back to Sokoto and Gwandu, whence he returned with extremely dubious "treaties" purporting to grant the Company full jurisdiction over all foreigners within these states. Goldie claimed that these documents, together with an equally questionable Treaty relating to Borgu, "complete[d] the protection of the Middle Niger from the possibility of French interference either overland from the upper Niger or from Dahomey".[70] For future expansion he now looked towards the Nile (a river which always fascinated Goldie), asking government help to secure "a free hand eastwards through Bornu, Wadai and

Darfur to the Egyptian Sudan".[71] But Anglo-German co-operation in such a design might preclude the grandiose programme of expansion to which Etienne, Tharel and Alis had just given their support.

Although Freycinet and Ribot did not share Etienne's desire to confront the British Empire, nor even the Niger Company, diplomatic convention required them to seek the compensation which public opinion demanded for interests and susceptibilities ignored by the Anglo-German Agreement. Besides recognition of the French Protectorate over Madagascar, they sought guarantees of access to Lake Chad from the north, so as to secure continuous links between the military empire of the upper Niger and the Saharan hinterland of the North African territories.[72] Salisbury was willing to comply; by the Anglo-French Declaration of 5 August 1890 France obtained recognition of a sphere of influence extending from the Mediterranean as far south as an imaginary line from Say on the Niger to Barruwa on Lake Chad, though subject to leaving to the Niger Company "all that fairly belongs to the Kingdom of Sokoto".[73] This has become a classic example of how diplomatists drove imaginary lines through African territories about which they had no precise information, and which they would be unable physically to occupy for many years; but at the time it seemed satisfactory to both sides. Although the French would have liked to see the Say–Barruwa line marked out by the early appointment of Boundary Commissioners like those provided for the 1889 Agreement,[74] they believed they had set limits to Goldie's megalomania, and most of the active colonialists not committed to opposing the Freycinet ministry for other reasons welcomed the Anglo-French Declaration as a step towards realizing the Chad design.[75]

Yet it clearly was only a first step. The Anglo-French Declaration did nothing to secure the southern approach to Chad; Crampel's mission might still be cut off from Bornu and Bagirmi by Anglo-German co-operation. Ribot first sought a diplomatic solution by inviting Germany, as her own "compensation" to France for the Anglo-German agreement, to accept a demarcation of spheres of influence along the River Chari, leaving Bornu to Germany and Bagirmi to France.[76]

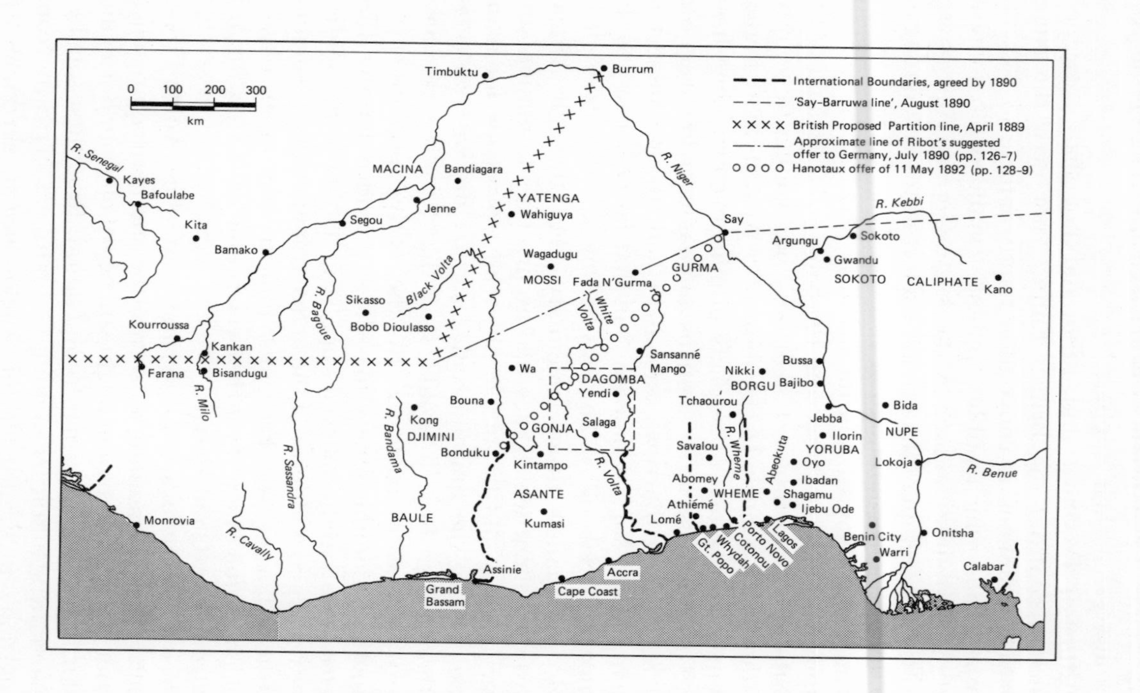

Map 1 *Partition proposals of the 1890s*

Bismarck might have seen this as a useful step towards a colonial entente; but his successors took a narrower view of compensation and were not yet willing to make "gratuitous" commitments which might prejudice future expansion in Kamerun.[77]

In the absence of diplomatic safeguards for the southern approach to Chad, Etienne agreed to sponsor a second expedition inspired by the Haut–Benito syndicate. Lieutenant Mizon proposed to utilize France's right to free navigation on the Niger and Benue to lead a "scientific and commercial" expedition through the Company's sphere, whose real objective would be to link up with Crampel and secure political treaties from the rulers of Bagirmi and Bornu. Although Etienne's stated objectives were still limited to the former country he agreed to facilitate Mizon's release from the army and to contribute 60 000 francs towards this hazardous scheme; and although the details are unclear the *Conseil de Ministres* gave some form of endorsement to an expedition which was certain to cause trouble with the Royal Niger Company.[78]

Meanwhile Etienne was re-appraising the Chad plan's third line of advance, that from the Sudan. He was already following up Gallieni's call for peaceful penetration towards the Gulf of Guinea (vol. I, p. 92) by authorizing expeditions intended to advance French boundary claims in Guinea and the Ivory Coast, and had begun to yield to pressure from Borgnis-Desbordes and Archinard for an outright offensive against the Tokolor empire. In August Commandant P. L. Monteil, an ambitious and able patriot long interested in Sudanese exploration, who was about to leave for the Ivory Coast *en route* for Kong and Mossi, was at Alis's suggestion diverted to a more ambitious project: to explore the westward route towards Lake Chad (which one day the colonial army might hope to follow). After Monteil had persuaded Etienne's adviser J. L. Deloncle that he would require only a subsidy of 70 000 francs and an escort of ten soldiers his plan was formally approved by the Council of Ministers; in September he left Bordeaux on a two-year journey which would eventually provide interesting information about the boundary which France had just accepted.[79]

As these expeditions set out, the various groups interested in African expansion drew together to present a more coherent case for colonialism, and to combat the reservations and suspicions which still inhibited government support for military campaigns, or the granting of chartered privileges. Although expansionist arguments were already being voiced in newspapers like *Le Siècle* (edited by François Deloncle, Deputy for Basses-Alpes and cousin of Etienne's official) and the weighty *Journal des Débats* (with which Alis was associated), supporters of the Benito Syndicate saw a need for "a nucleus of people capable of supporting the efforts being made in Africa within public opinion, and of giving moral and material support to the travellers".[80] It was they who in October 1890 took the initiative in bringing together "a certain number of persons inspired by patriotic zeal" to form the *Comité de l'Afrique française*.[81] One of its aims was to raise funds for expeditions to peg out claims which the government was not ready to underwrite; during 1891 the *Comité* not only despatched a mission under Dybowski to follow up Crampel's thrust towards Lake Chad, but supported several attempts by young officers to establish French claims on the western Ivory Coast (see below, pp. 53–7). During its first eight years the *Comité* was to spend 384 000 francs out of a total income of 562 000 francs (£22 500) on such expeditions.[82] These schemes were not intended to force the hand of the Colonial Department, but to mobilize financial and political support for sympathizers within the administration. As its President soon ruled, "the Committee would exceed its proper role if it claimed to dictate a line of conduct to the government, whose efforts it ought rather to be supporting".[83]

The formation of the *Comité de l'Afrique française* heralded the emergence of a broader *parti colonial*, whose membership has been closely scrutinized by scholars seeking to identify the true source of French colonial imperialism.[84] The original sponsors of the *Comité* included representatives of provincial cities like Lyon, Nantes, Le Havre, and Marseille (though the long-established African merchants of Bordeaux were notably absent); one careful analysis of the whole colonial party over the period 1890–1914 reveals members who can be held to represent "the principal interests in each major sector of the

French economy".[85] But while this demonstrates the unsurprising fact that some business men regarded colonial activity as worth supporting during this period of economic difficulty it hardly proves that the new thrust towards expansion in Africa was economically determined. Rather does the *Comité* appear as a coalition of individuals and small groups whose interest in Africa might arise through business, public service, political ambition or intellectual interest: economists like Leroy-Beaulieu sat alongside military heroes like Caron the navigator of the middle Niger, Binger, and Borgnis-Desbordes. "Patriotic zeal" had temporarily cemented an alliance between civilians, concerned to secure state patronage for peaceful schemes of "modern colonization", and military officers who regarded the Sudan as their private exercise-ground.[86]

Military participation was perhaps essential if colonial expansion was to be accepted by reluctant tax-payers conditioned to fear the subterranean influence of *les affaires*; the brave officer performing heroic deeds in the name of France was to become a central figure in colonialist propaganda. As Alis had suggested, the surplus energies of the adventurous young, recently often directed into Boulangism, might find safer and more satisfactory outlets in the "alternative society" of the colonies.[87] The "Sudanese" officers showed real talent for the new technique of public relations; their heroic exploits, fed back to readers of the popular press or the popular novel, could provide fertile sources for popular myths and images – for the *idées-force*, in Professor Girardet's phrase, of an emerging colonial ideology.[88]

But French national pride had so long been focussed on Europe that something more was needed. Certainly the improvement in relations with Russia lifted some of the constraints which had prevented many French patriots from risking conflict with Britain so long as they felt threatened by Germany. But patriotic zeal carried furthest when reinforced by moral fervour; this had been well understood by those who in 1883 had used Brazza's attractive personality as the focus of their publicity campaign.[89] The impact within France of Lavigerie's anti-slavery crusade provided the colonial party with welcome moral reinforcements.

Ever since 1868, when as recently appointed Archbishop of Algiers he had founded the new missionary order of White Fathers, Lavigerie had urged French Catholics to accept special responsibilities in Africa. In 1871 he had appealed to Catholic refugees from Alsace and Lorraine to settle in Algeria and identify themselves with a new *France africaine*: "by contributing to the establishment of a hard-working, moral, Christian population on this still infidel soil you will become its true apostles, before God and the fatherland".[90] But it was the White Fathers' experience of the "Arab" slave trade in the Great Lakes region which made Lavigerie seek the relief of African suffering through the anti-slavery crusade. Hitherto the French anti-slavery movement, though as old as the British, had been much more a fragmented, minority, concern; French Catholics, Father Renault suggests, "saw in slavery individual miseries to be relieved, Protestants an institution to be fought".[91] Old hostilities still inhibited co-operation among French philanthropists; even now Lavigerie refused to appear under the chairmanship of the veteran Republican abolitionist Victor Schoelcher;[92] but the moral fervour which he had generated produced closer co-operation between Catholics, Protestants and secularists, not only within the torpidly respectable *Société Antiesclavagiste* but in the new colonial movement.

Indeed, colonial expansion was already providing a stage for rehearsing the *ralliement* of French Catholics to the Republic; it was no coincidence that it was Lavigerie whom Leo XIII chose to lead the appeal to Catholics to recognize and participate in the political institutions of their country. In his famous speech of November 1890 Lavigerie described himself as "an old Archbishop who like [the representatives of the Algerian administration] has made Africa his second country in order the better to save France".[93] Already the presidency of the *Comité de l'Afrique française* had been accepted by Prince Auguste d'Arenberg, monarchist Deputy and head of an ancient Catholic family; already new foundations had been laid in Africa for practical collaboration between representatives of Church and State. Whereas in France the parish priests' daily experience of conflict with anti-clerical schoolmasters and sub-prefects reinforced their hostility towards the Republic, missionaries in Africa were compelled to work closely alongside even Godless administrators – who might in turn learn to appreciate that some holy Fathers could be the most effective emissaries of French civilization (cf, for example below, pp. 159–60). As Etienne himself later put it:

> Even if the necessities of internal politics have led us to consider [the French religious orders] with a certain mistrust, it would be a fatal mistake to seem to disavow them in these distant lands where they faithfully serve their country, and where moreover we could not replace them.[94]

During the 1890s the *Société Antiesclavagiste* discovered in the foundation of *villages de liberté* another method by which Catholics could support the civilizing mission of the Republic.[95] Gradually Catholics, and other humanitarians, were led to believe that the worst oppressors of Africans might be their own rulers, and that liberation from their bondage would come only through the armed force of a colonial state. New images of Africa gained currency which ignored some of the insights achieved by earlier generations, and "the colonial enterprise as a whole came to be regarded as the legitimate continuation of the struggle against the slave-trade".[96]

Secular theorists too were increasingly justifying France's imperial mission by claims of superiority. Whereas earlier colonialists had written much about *assimilation* – and even, in the four *communes* of Senegal, taken tentative steps in that direction – by the later 1880s influential voices argued that French civilization was too far beyond the mental grasp of Africans for its extension to be a serious object of policy.[97] In 1889 the French government convened an International Colonial Congress in Paris, not to excite support for further extension but to encourage the exchange of experience and opinions among dignitaries who passed as specialists or experts. (The occasion does not seem to have been regarded seriously by France's principal competitors; although Spain, Portugal and the Netherlands sent official delegations Germany was not represented, and Britain only by itinerant New Zealanders.) Sonorous orations claimed that colonizers now had "a more elevated and humane understanding of what their overseas possessions ought to be", that their duty to their subjects was "not only to treat them with humanity, but to make them participate as brothers in the benefits of civilisation".[98] But it seemed that this would be a long process. Gustave Le Bon, an army doctor who had travelled in India, claimed that modern theory confirmed the lessons of experience: the most difficult things to change were the *sentiments héréditaires* of half-civilized or barbarian peoples. Though Le Bon and his followers did not argue that these "inferior races" could never reach the level of European civilization, this would be a matter of gradual evolution over many centuries; meanwhile the exercise of imperial power was justified, both morally and scientifically.[99]

This Congress signalled a new period when, in France as elsewhere, social theory was increasingly cited in support of colonial rule. Anthropological generalizations, based on limited observation and shallow understanding, became commonplace; popular journalists converted these into grotesque misrepresentations, such as that "the family does not exist in Africa".[100] Cultural differences were increasingly held to indicate not merely cultural but racial inferiority – which was presumably immutable. A battery of "social-imperialist" arguments and stereotypes entered the received wisdom of the French public which colonial pressure groups soon learned they could exploit to their advantage; thus from the start of the Franco-Dahoman conflict of 1890 several illustrated journals and Catholic newspapers began to emphasize the sheer horror of human sacrifice in Dahomey.[101] Two years later, when this particular press campaign had gathered force, an organized colonial party in the Chamber of Deputies was prepared to draw political conclusions. Meanwhile it was the military wing of the colonial movement which was best placed to demonstrate France's civilizing mission.

THE ADVANCE OF THE COLONIAL ARMY

Tension between civilian and military versions of colonial policy had long been familiar within the four *Communes* of Senegal. Controversy centred in the first place on the need to use military force within the colony's traditional sphere of influence, as provisionally defined in the 1889 Agreement with Britain. Groundnuts produced in these territories accounted for half the colony's domestic exports, and during the 1880s production fluctuated violently, in response to unstable market prices, variable weather, and political unrest.[102] Merchants had often differed as to whether military intervention against Wolof and Serer rulers who defaulted on their political or financial obligations did more harm than good; but now the soldiers began to argue that the colony's future required action against the Tokolor empire also. Attempts to expand groundnut cultivation were impeded by emigration of the rural labour force to "Nioro", as Ahmadu's empire was now known; between 1882 and 1888 the Fula-speaking population of the directly administered environs of St Louis fell from about 30 000 to under 10 000. The call of religious solidarity was reinforced by demands which the French themselves imposed – for labour, taxes, even for the weakening of servile bonds. Family heads whose domestics were seeking emancipation on French soil in the *communes* were anxious to move their households eastwards, away from such temptation.[103]

Faced with such evidence of the unity of Senegambian Islam, military leaders within the colony updated old phobias about a Muslim coalition to justify attacks upon such limited independence as their neighbours still enjoyed. In May 1890 Al-Bouri Ndiaye, chased from Jolof in a brief campaign, chose to join Ahmadu in his *hijra* towards Sokoto; next year Abdul Bokar Kan was driven from Futa Toro to die in Mauritania. Their rule was replaced by a protectorate system which left no real autonomy to those whom it recognized as chiefs, but confined the privilege of citizenship, the application of French law, and the sphere of the elected *conseil-général* to the four communes.[104]

Despite the growing authoritarianism, Senegal remained a commercial colony, dedicated to promoting agricultural production for export. In 1889 the 10 000 electors, by returning a former Governor, Admiral Vallon, as Deputy, emphasized the essential unity of mercantile interest and official policy. Even the military campaigns against Abdul Bokar and Al-Bouri were led by Colonel Alfred Dodds, a *métis* from Saint Louis with connections in the commercial community and a certain sensitivity for the intricacies of African politics. But French merchants showed little eagerness to exploit the wider markets supposedly awaiting exploitation in the far interior, at least until Tharel formed his *Syndicat du Soudan* in 1890. About a dozen agents of Saint Louis merchants maintained stocks of gunpower, *guinées*, and other trade goods at Kayes, to exchange for gum and gold brought down by the *dyulas*;[105] these *enfants du pays* had already shown, by attempts to exclude Sierra Leonean and Gambian competitors from Bakel and Medine, that they expected highly preferential treatment in return for their modest contribution to the expansion of French influence.[106] But beyond this there was no serious *élément civil* to balance the power of the Military Commandant;[107] any restraint would have to be applied through Paris.

In formulating policy for the Sudan, Etienne had to choose between the advice of "economists", whose preference for gradual commercial penetration his experience and his political connections disposed him to share, and that of the soldiers, whose exploits, if successful, might capture the imagination of the nationalist public for the colonial cause. In Professor Person's opinion, Etienne never quite made up his mind.[108] Although during 1889 Archinard, bound by restrictive instructions from Etienne's predecessor,[109] was obliged to confine his military ambitions to the capture of Koundian (vol. I, pp. 192–4), there is some evidence that during a visit to Paris Etienne encouraged him to plan a more aggressive campaign for 1890, in accordance with his new interest in Lake Chad. Nevertheless in January 1890 Etienne sought formal advice from a Departmental Committee heavily biassed towards the "economists". The majority consisted of officials; there were four commercial representatives and two deputies, Vallon and François Deloncle; the key figure was Gallieni, the soldier least committed to military solutions, most ready to develop commercial links with the Gulf of Guinea. Etienne's own opening speech insisted that France's primary economic interests indicated a reduction of expenses, even a move towards civilian administration; but Gallieni easily convinced the committee that this would be premature.

Although European rivals might be excluded from the French sphere by international treaties, these alone would not ensure French control: "so long as commerce has not mastered the Soudan we shall have to keep military forces there". The French sphere traversed a "desert" which, if the troops were withdrawn, would be dominated by Ahmadu and Samori; the Committee agreed that "diplomatic penetration can be followed up by regular and serious commerce only so far as the country is known and pacified, as usable roads are marked out, and as commercial agents and their merchandise are secured against aggression".[110] In a supplementary Note Gallieni indicated how the power of France's Muslim adversaries might be subverted, and eventually, "in a distant future", eliminated; France should discreetly intervene in the succession disputes which would surely divide the Tokolor empire when Ahmadu died, utilize the opportunities for discord provided by the "bizarre constitution" of Futa Jalon, encourage further revolts among Samori's subjects.[111] This somewhat devious recipe for imperialism on the cheap doubtless appealed to Etienne as a convenient compromise, but he had no means of ensuring that the Commandant in the Sudan did not add his own ingredients.

From his first appointment in 1888 Archinard had contemplated the forcible destruction of Ahmadu's empire, interpreting the tide of migration as evidence of deep-seated Muslim hostility rather than of spontaneous reaction against the new realities of French rule. Yet even while depicting Ahmadu as a menace Archinard emphasized the fragility of his rule; from the sparse and contradictory intelligence reports which reached his headquarters[112] he selected reports of friction between Ahmadu and the Tokolor zealots who surrounded him in Kaarta, and argued that military pressure from without would complete the disintegration. Then – a clinching argument addressed towards the Chambers – it would be possible to reduce France's financial commitment. In a specious Report written to justify his offensive Archinard would claim that:

> It was finally necessary to organize our new colony, to render it productive, to draw a revenue from the collection

of taxes; it was necessary that it should come to the aid of the metropole, which has been making heavy sacrifices for its sake for ten years. Now, such an organisation was impossible given the proximity, and the hostility of Ahmadu.[113]

Although it was Nioro, where Ahmadu had based himself since 1884, that was the goal of the Senegambian migration and so the centre of any direct threat to French interests, Archinard's plan for 1890 was to attack his former capital of Segou. Capturing this famous city, Archinard claimed, would irreparably damage Ahmadu's prestige (what he did not add was that it would greatly advance his own – Segou was a well-known name in France, which Nioro was not). The fall of Segou would thwart the supposed intention of the Commander of the Faithful to re-unite his provinces and constitute a 'vast coalition'' of Muslim states against the French; it would so transform Ahmadu's attitude that he would accept innocuous exile.[114]

Archinard's updating of the doctrine of Tokolor hostility, the staple argument of French expansionists since Faidherbe,[115] took little account of Ahmadu's actual situation. Although the major challenges to his authority from rebellious subjects and insubordinate kinsmen seem temporarily to have been held in check, his empire was in no condition to adopt offensive policies. While some of his counsellors wanted to resort to military *jihad,* Ahmadu, still guided by Seydou Djeylia, clung hopefully to the Treaty of Gouri. "We do not wish to revenge ourselves for what you have just done," he assured Archinard after Koundian, "we shall not lose patience nor silence, and we turn our back on a declaration of war."[116] The French received evidence of this conciliatory attitude in July 1889 when a postal employee visited Nioro and successfully negotiated the return of a woman who had deserted the French headquarters at Kayes.[117]

Certainly Ahmadu knew that he might merely be gaining time, and after Koundian he took diplomatic precautions. His *talibes* continued to influence the Muslims of Futa Toro and the Wolof states; overtures were made in the direction of Futa Jalon, and in December 1889 an agreement for joint defence was apparently reached with Samori.[118] But these measures do not indicate preparation for a military *jihad*; in view of recent French behaviour, they were no more than prudent precautions. The famous Muslim coalition was largely invented by Archinard and Thomas to justify their planned aggression; the much more limited regroupings which actually took place were examples of history imitating art. (cf vol. I, p. 84).

Meanwhile Archinard's aggressive designs proceeded. In the Sudan, his officers tried to turn long-standing Bambara hostility to Tokolor rule into active collaboration with France; in August 1889 Lieutenant Marchand obtained the secret agreement of Mari-Diara, the Bambara claimant to Segou, to assist the French attack.[119] Archinard himself was in Paris, seeking the still more vital collaboration of French politicians. According to his eulogist Méniaud, Archinard received oral assurances of Etienne's full support, which effectively neutralized much more cautious instructions recorded in anticipation of future criticism.[120] If this is so, Etienne's Commission on the Sudan must have been a purely diversionary tactic. In his official report, Archinard claimed only that Etienne had left him full latitude to respond to Ahmadu's hostility and ensure French primacy in the Sudan.[121] In either case some justificatory pretext was needed, and on his return to Kayes Archinard set out to provoke one.

Sabone, a village occupied by the Tokolors within the northern salient of the Baoule branch of the Senegal,[122] could on the most favourable interpretation of the boundary be regarded as French. On 16 January 1890 Archinard, feigning righteous indignation, demanded a clear statement of Ahmadu's territorial claims.[123] Ahmadu fell into the trap; his exasperated reply, reproaching Archinard for falsifying the recent history of Franco-Tokolor relations, and declaring his continuing intention to subdue his rebellious subjects, reached Kayes on 22 February. Archinard's column had already left to attack Segou, but this document, added to dossiers about the hostile Muslim coalition, induced Etienne to give the necessary authority on 27 February: "*Faites pour le mieux*".[124] A proclamation declaring war on Samori (apparently so drafted to mislead Tokolor spies within headquarters) was amended by substituting Ahmadu's name;[125] Mari-Diara provided the promised Bambara auxiliaries; and on 6 April Segou was bombarded and occupied without French casualties. The Tokolor garrison of Ousseboogou, attacked on 26 April, offered much fiercer resistance: although Archinard employed his Bambara auxiliaries as cannon-fodder, he lost two European sergeants and thirteen Africans were killed, four Europeans and sixty Africans seriously wounded, out of a force of under three hundred.[126]

After these victories Archinard believed the Tokolor empire would quickly collapse. He peremptorily offered Ahmadu honourable exile to a village near Dinguiraye, in the western province, but it seems unlikely that Ahmadu seriously considered this. As the French returned towards Kayes the railway and telegraph were repeatedly sabotaged; from 31 May Muslim forces, aided by deserters from the *tirailleurs* and informed by spies in the French headquarters, harassed a party escorting captive members of Ahmadu's family. Out of a strength of 124, forty-three were killed or wounded, including all the Frenchmen except two; intimidation was needed to prevent mass desertions.[127] But while this counter-attack placed the French army under strain, it also confirmed their commitment to the destruction of the Tokolor state.

Once the situation along the railway was under control Archinard decided to take the calculated risk of an offensive into Kaarta; on 16 June he occupied the fortress of Koniakari, in preparation for an attack on Nioro after the rains. Back in Kayes he drafted a report describing his triumph over the hazards which an enforced search for economy had imposed:

> I was afraid of offending the Department, which likes to think that everything can be obtained pacifically, and of seeming too fond of gunpowder, while on the contrary I wanted to find ways of striking blows which might have settled our dispute with Ahmadu finally and conclusively.

Archinard apologized for excessive leniency towards the Tokolors, inveterate enemies of France, and moreover,

> boastful, predatory, over-confident, shirking no perfidy.

> They are harder on their slaves than other Blacks, whom they consider their inferiors. The generous, almost egalitarian, manner in which we treat them convinces them that a Tokolor is as good as a white man.[128]

The 1890 campaign thus not only brought Archinard his desired promotion, but provided an ideological charter for further aggression.

So Ahmadu no longer had much choice; diplomacy gave way to *hegira* and resistance. On 1 January 1891 Nioro fell to Archinard's renewed offensive; after a last disastrous battle Ahmadu and Al-Bouri retreated westwards – and Muslims working on the railway came out on strike.[129] The French army still faced many obstacles in their long march towards Lake Chad; but by 1893 they occupied the last Tokolor province of Macina, and their opponents withdrew into the Sokoto caliphate. Here, after Ahmadu's death in 1897,[130] Al-Bouri and others would fall in battle against what they had come to see as the British wing of the European invasion.

But Archinard was not content to challenge the Tokolors; even before attacking Nioro he had also lost patience with the uneasy truce established in relations with Samori (vol. I, pp. 192–4). In May 1890 Archinard followed the capture of Segou by despatching Captain Quiquandon and a small military detachment to encourage Tieba, once he had subdued a threat to his rear in Fafadugu, to prepare for renewed operations against "Samori, our common enemy".[131] Samori, equally distrustful of the French, carefully avoided provoking them; but he continued to re-equip his enemy with modern firearms supplied through Freetown and to re-organise his army after the "great revolt" within his empire. When Archinard returned from leave in September 1890, having secured a still greater degree of autonomy for his command, he began to soften up Etienne by false and exaggerated reports of Samori's hostility. Paris and Saint Louis both tried to prevent Archinard from launching a dangerous and costly diversion from the eastwards advance towards Chad, but Archinard skilfully evaded their instructions by the unanswerable argument of military security. On 2 April 1891 he invaded Samori's territory in the Milo valley, quickly occupied

Kankan and raided Bisandugu, and so committed France to what would prove the most arduous military campaign of the whole European invasion.[132] It was also a campaign which would carry the colonial army into the hinterland between Sierra Leone and Guinea, between the Ivory and Gold Coasts, raising problems in Anglo-French relations which the 1889 Agreement had not dealt with.

NOTES

1. Mackay, 8 March 1887, J. W. H[arrison], *A. M. Mackay* (1890) pp. 347–9.
2. FO 84/1991, PQ by E. M. Marum, 26 March 1889; cf Hansard, 3rd series 334, 845.
3. FO 84/2008, RNC to CMS, 22 July 1889.
4. R. A. Adeleye, "Rabih Fadlallah 1879–1893: Exploits and Impact of Political Relations in Central Sudan", *JHSN*, v, 1970, pp. 223–42.
5. F. Renault, *Lavigerie, l'esclavage africain et l'Europe* (1971), esp. II, pp. 74–82. The text of the sermon is in C. Lavigerie, *Documents sur la fondation de l'oeuvre antiesclavigiste* (1889) pp. 45–73.
6. Renault, *Lavigerie,* II, p. 111.
7. FO 84/1996, Lavigerie to Salisbury, 28 May 1889, cf S. Miers, *Britain and the Ending of the Slave Trade* (1975) pp. 30–3; H. Temperley, *British Anti-Slavery* (1972) pp. 265–7.
8. FO 84/1927, Cameron to Kirk, 24 August 1888; Kirk to Hill, 27 August. Miers. *Ending of the Slave Trade,* pp. 203ff.
9. FO 84/1895, Minutes by Hill, Lister, Salisbury on Vivian, 30 Af., 16 August 1888; FO 84/1927, Minutes by Fergusson 27 August, Salisbury, 1 September 1888.
10. FO 84/1927, Memo by Hill, 4 September 1888; minutes by Lister, Salisbury.
11. Renault, *Lavigerie,* II, pp. 152–6.
12. For a full study of the Conference and its complex international background see Miers, *Ending of the Slave Trade,* pp. 229–35 for these "preliminaries".
13. AE, Afrique 117, Etienne to Spuller, 1 October 1889 (also 26 October 1889).
14. See, for example, FO 84/2010, Vivian to Currie, Pte. 24 November 1889.
15. The text of the General Act may be found in Miers, *Ending of the Slave Trade,* pp. 346–63.
16. FO 84/1995, CO to FO, 29 June 1889, encl. Report by Firminger 30 April 1889 of a visit to Salaga in May 1887.
17. Hansard, 3rd series, 334, 26 March 1889.
18. AE, Afrique 117, Etienne to Spuller, 16 November 1889.
19. Miers, *Ending of the Slave Trade* p. 318.

20. A. G. Hopkins, *An Economic History of West Africa* (1973) pp. 154–5.
21. FO 84/2004, Capt Stopford, 7 August, encl. in Admty to FO, 14 October 1889.
22. R. E. Dumett, "The rubber trade of the Gold Coast and Asante in the nineteenth century: African innovation and market responsiveness", *JAH*, XII, 1971, pp. 79–101.
23. See P. N. Davies, *The Trade Makers* (1973); *Sir Alfred Jones* (1978).
24. George Goldie, "France and England on the Niger", *Paternoster Review*, January 1891, reprinted in D. J. M. Muffett, *Empire Builder Extra-ordinary* (Douglas, 1978) p. 66.
25. In the words of West Africa's first economic historian: L. C. A. Knowles, *The Economic Development of the British Overseas Empire* (1924) pp. 138–52.
26. British projects are usefully catalogued in O. Omosini, "Railway Projects and British Attitude towards the Development of West Africa, 1872–1903", *JHSN*, v (1971) pp. 491–507. For the economic principles of the CO, sce R. E. Dumett, "Joseph Chamberlain, imperial finance and railway policy in British West Africa in the late nineteenth century", *EHR*, 90, 1975, pp. 289–94.
27. Goldie, "France and England" (1891) pp. 66–7.
28. H. Brunschwig, "Politique et economie dans l'empire français d'Afrique noire, 1870–1914", *JAH*, XI (1970) pp. 401–17; cf T. W. Roberts, "Railway Imperialism and French Advances towards Lake Chad, 1890–1900", PhD thesis, University of Cambridge, 1973.
29. ANSOM, Côte d'Ivoire XV/4/c, Verdier to Etienne, 8 June 1891 and note by Deloncle.
30. P. Atger, *La France en Côte d'Ivoire*, pp. 130, 172–3, 180–1, 187–8. See also A. Verdier, *Trente-cinq ans de Lutte aux Colonies* (1897) and the documentary appendix.
31. CO 267/372, Parkes to Hay, Aborigines 345, encl. in Hay Conf. 36, 30 May 1890.
32. SLA, NALB (Conf) Parkes to Hay, Aborigines Conf. 13, 2 June 1890.
33. *Standard*, 6 October 1890, filed, interestingly, in ANSOM, Dahomey V/4/c.
34. Salisbury to Temple, 2 September 1878, quoted by G. N. Uzoigwe, *Britain and the Conquest of Africa* (Ann Arbor, 1974) p. 16.
35. Introduction to J. Poirier, *Campagne du Dahomey, 1892–94* (1895).
36. R. Koebner and H. D. Schmidt, *Imperialism: The Story and Significance of a Political Word* (Cambridge, 1964).
37. For example, Max Weber, *Economy and Society* in G. Roth and C. Wittich (eds), vol. II (NY, 1968) pp. 921–6; V. I. Lenin, *Imperialism: the Highest Stage of Capitalism* (1916; London ed., 1933) p. 99.
38. H. U. Wehler, "Industrial Growth and early German Imperialism", in R. Owen and B. Sutcliffe (eds), *Studies in the Theory of Imperialism* (1972) p. 83; also *Bismarck und der Imperialismus* (Köln, 1969) *passim*.
39. W. J. Mommsen, *Theories of Imperialism* (1980) pp. 97–9.
40. G. Eley, *Reshaping the German Right* (New Haven, Conn, 1980); also "Defining Social Imperialism; Use and Abuse of an Idea", *Social*

History, I, 1976, pp. 265–90, and "Some Thought on the Nationalist Pressure Groups in Imperial Germany", in P. Kennedy and A. Nicholls (eds), *Nationalist and Racialist Movements in Britain and Germany before 1914* (London, 1981).

41. K. J. Bade, *Friederich Fabri und der Imperialismus in der Bismarckzeit* (Freiburg, 1975).
42. F. F. Muller, *Deutschland – Zanzibar – Ostafrika* (E. Berlin, 1959) chs I, IV; cf Eley, *Reshaping*, p. 46.
43. Obituary in *Sierra Leone Weekly News*, 16 October 1920: F. F. Müller, *Deutschland – Zanzibar – Ostafrika* (E. Berlin, 1959) pp. 358–61.
44. J. K. Vietor, *Geschichtliche und Kulturelle Entwicklung unserer Schutzbebiete* (Berlin, 1913) pp. 143–4; cf. Bade, *Fabri, pp. 480–1.*
45. E. Eyck, *Das Persönnliche Regiment Wilhelms II* (Zurich, 1948); H. Labouret, *Monteil* (1937) pp. 176–7; F. F. Müller, *Deutschland – Zanzibar – Ostafrika*, p. 296.
46. H. Pogge von Strandmann, "The Kolonialrat: its Significance and Influence on German Politics from 1890 to 1906", DPhil, University of Oxford, 1970.
47. W. D. Smith, *The German Colonial Empire* (Chapel Hill, 1978) pp. 120–5.
48. Eley, *Reshaping*, pp. 101n, 120–1, 141. Eley's references to colonial societies are not numerous, and they seem to lie somewhat uneasily within his powerful general argument.
49. For example, Deroulède's article in *Le Drapeau*, 10 January 1885, in C. R. Ageron, *L anticolonialisme en France de 1871 à 1914* (Paris, 1973) pp. 67–8.
50. H. Arendt, *The Origins of Totalitarianism* (2nd edn., 1958) p. 50.
51. W. B. Cohen, *Rulers of Empire* (Stanford, 1971) studies early recruitment to colonial service. For the personnel of the colonial army, see A. S. Kanya-Forstner, *The Conquest of the Western Sudan* (Cambridge, 1969) pp. 8–15.
52. Catherine Coquery-Vidrovitch, "L'impact des interêts coloniaux: SCOA and CFAO dans l'Ouest africain, 1910–1965", *JAH*, XVI, 1975, pp. 595–621; cf. A. Macmillan, *The Red Book of West Africa* (1920) p. 257.
53. T. W. Roberts, "Railway Imperialism and French Advances towards Lake Chad, 1890–1900", PhD thesis, University of Cambridge, 1973, chs 1 and 2.
54. T. W. Roberts, "Railway Imperialism"; cf. the Introduction to E. Etienne, *Son Oeuvre: Coloniale, Algérienne et Politique*, vol. I, (1907) p. 19.
55. For Etienne's early career as a colonialist, see H. Sieberg, *Eugene Etienne und die französiche Kolonialpolitik* (Köln, 1968) pp. 1–16; for his economic views, pp. 77f; for text of his speech to the Conseil Supérieur des Colonies, 21 January 1891, pp. 198–9.
56. S. Elwitt, *The Making of the Third Republic: Class and Politics in France, 1868–84* (Baton Rouge, 1975) esp. ch. VII; C. R. Ageron, *France Coloniale ou parti colonial?* (1978) pp. 44 ff; R. Girardet, *L'Idée coloniale en France de 1871 à 1962* (1972).

57. For example P. Gaffarel, *Les Colonies françaises* (4th ed., 1888; originally published 1879): "Depuis 1815, et surtout depuis 1871, nous assistons donc à une veritable renaissance coloniale." cf. M Dubois and A Terrier, *Les Colonies françaises: une siècle d'expansion coloniale* (1902): those behind colonial policy "ont le droit de se déclarer solidaires, à bien des égards, de quelques traditions constantes qui révèlent . . . notre caractère nationale en ce qu'il à d'original et de fixe".
58. Ageron, *France coloniale*, pp. 14, 27.
59. C. M. Andrew and A. S. Kanya-Forstner, *France Overseas* (1981) p. 23.
60. Rosaline E. Nwoye, *The Public Image of Savorgnan de Brazza and the Establishment of French Imperialism in the Congo* (Aberdeen, 1981).
61. For the foundation of the *Syndicat*, see "Histoire sommaire des incidents qui ont précedé la constitution du Comité de l'Afrique française", BCAF, I, ii, 1891. For an analysis of the interests involved, Roberts, "Railway Imperialism", pp. 82–9. For Brazza's priorities, ANSOM, Gabon-Congo I/36/a. Brazza to Chavannes (draft), January 1889.
62. H. Alis, *A la Conquête du Tchad* (1891) pp. 69–72, 104, 280.
63. Etienne gave his views on this controversy in a series of articles for *Le Temps* in 1897, reprinted in *Son Oeuvre*, vol. II, pp. 17–54. See also C. Coquery-Vidrovitch, *Le Congo aux temps des grandes Compagnies Concessionaires* (1972) pp. 27 ff; Sieberg, *Etienne*, pp. 80 ff.
64. Alis, pp. 85 ff.
65. E. Etienne, *Son Oeuvre*, I, pp. 86–93; for Ribot's reaction cf. p. 34. On the Dahoman campaign, see below, pp. 145 ff.
66. E. Hertslet, *The Map of Africa by Treaty* (3rd edn., 1909, reprinted 1967) III, pp. 899–906.
67. See Wilhelm II to Sir E. Malet, 14 June 1889; *Queen Victoria's Letters*, 3rd series, vol. I (1930) p. 504.
68. P. Cambon, *Correspondence*, I (1940). Cambon to Spuller, 11 March 1889, pp. 331–3; to d'Estournelles, 19 June 1891, p. 343.
69. A. S. Kanya-Forstner, "French African Policy and the Anglo-French Agreement of 5 August 1890", *HJ* XII (1969) pp. 630–2.
70. FO 84/2086, RNC to FO, 22 July 1890; Speech by Aberdare to RNC, 29 July 1890. On King's "treaties", J. E. Flint, *Sir George Goldie and the Making of Nigeria* (1960), pp. 159–63; R. A. Adeleye, *Power and Diplomacy in Northern Nigeria, 1804–1906* (1971).
71. FO 84/2087, RNC "Precis on Niger Basin", 24 July 1890.
72. Kanya-Forstner, "French African Policy", pp. 636–43.
73. Hertslet, *Map of Africa*, II, pp. 738–9.
74. DDF, VIII,132, Waddington to Ribot, Pte., 26 July; 133, Ribot to Waddington Tel., 28 July. ("Je vous prie d'insister pour que Lord Salisbury désigne sans aucun retard des délégués . . .".)
75. Kanya-Forstner, "French African Policy", pp. 641–50; cf Roberts, "Railway Imperialism", pp. 95 ff.
76. ANSOM Afrique VI/84, Ribot to Etienne, 24 July 1890; DDF VIII, 156, Ribot to Herbette, Tel., 21 August 1890.

77. *Die Grosse Politik*, VIII, 1693, 1694; Minutes by Holstein, Kayser, 18 July 1890; DDF, VIII, 146, 164, Herbette to Ribot, 13, 27 August 1890.
78. A. S. Kanya-Forstner, *The Conquest of the Western Sudan* (Cambridge 1969) pp. 169–70 (citing Alis to Etienne, 19 July 1890). Alis, *A la Conquête*, pp. 122–6. ANSOM, Missions 6, Rapports au SSEC, Conf. 13, 25 August 1890. cf. Flint, *Goldie*, pp. 169–72.
79. ANSOM, Missions 4, Rapport au SSEC 21 August 1890; Monteil to Etienne, 1 September, Etienne to Monteil 15 September; P. L. Monteil, *Souvenirs Vécus* (1924) pp. 54–7 gives Monteil's retrospectively dramatized account of his appointment; cf his earlier presentation in *De Saint Louis à Tripoli par le lac Tchad* (1894) pp. 1–12; cf Yves de Tessières, "Un episode du partage de l'Afrique: La mission Monteil de 1890–1892", RFHOM, LIX, 1972, pp. 345–410.
80. Alis to Monteil, 14 November 1892, see H. Labouret, *Monteil, Explorateur et Soldat* (1937) pp. 131–3; cf Alis to Etienne, 10 July 1890, Alis, *A la Conquête*, p. 120.
81. BCAF, no. 1, January 1891.
82. C. M. Andrew and A. S. Kanya-Forstner, "The French 'Colonial Party': Its Composition, Aims and Influence, 1885–1914", *HJ*, XIV, 1971 p. 105; cf. H. Brunschwig, *Mythes et Réalités de l'impérialisme colonial français* (1960) pp. 116–21. Roberts, p. 115n says the sum spent on missions was 420 000 francs, not counting earlier grants to Crampel and Mizon.
83. D'Arenberg, 9 June 1892; *BCAF*, II, vii, July 1892.
84. See works by Andrew and Kanya- Forstner and by Brunschwig in the Bibliography. Further detail on the wide range of groups eventually associated with the colonial party may be found in P. Grupp, *Deutschland, Frankreich und die Kolonien* (Tübingen, 1980) Part I and Apps.
85. L. Abrams and D. J. Miller, "Who were the French colonialists? A Reassessment of the *parti colonial*, 1890–1914", *HJ*, 19, 1976, p. 695.
86. Cf Y. Person, *Samori: une revolution dyula*, vol. III (Dakar, 1972), Oxford, pp. 1275–6.
87. T. Zeldin, *France, 1848–1945*, vol. II (1977) p. 934; Alis, *A la Conquête . . ., p. 280.*
88. R. Girardet, *L'idée coloniale en France* (1972) p. 81.
89. R. Nwoye, *The Public Image.*
90. C. Lavigerie, *Aux Alsaciens et aux Lorrains exiles* (1871); Girardet, pp. 36–7.
91. Renault, *Lavigerie*, I, p. 150.
92. Ibid., II, pp. 84–5.
93. J. de Arteche, *The Cardinal of Africa* (1964) pp. 182–4. For broader background, see A. Sedgwick, *The Ralliement in French Politics, 1890–98* (Cambridge Mass, 1965).
94. Etienne in *Bulletin du Comité de l'Asie française*, 3 October 1901; Sieberg, *Etienne*, p. 153.
95. D. Bouche, *Les villages de liberté en Afrique noire française* (1968) pp. 168–72.

96. R. Girardet, *L'idée coloniale en France,* p. 88.
97. Cf R. R. Betts, *Assimilation and Association in French Colonial Theory* (NY, 1961).
98. *Congrès Colonial International de Paris* (1889) p. 14 (Admiral Barbey) p. 27 (C. Faure).
99. Ibid., pp. 70–2 (Le Bon), p. 83 (Dr Poitou-Duplassy). For Le Bon, see Betts, *Assimilation,* pp. 64–9.
100. Girardet, *L'idée coloniale,* p. 91, quoting *Revue Hebdomadaire.*
101. V. Campion-Vincent, "L'image du Dahomey dans la press française, 1870–95", *CEA,* VII, 1967, pp. 27–58; cf. below, p. 171.
102. Senegal's exports in 1891 were valued at 12 948 358 francs, including 2 285 769 for re-exports. Groundnuts accounted for 5 472 029 francs, gum for 4 182 792 francs. Ministère du Commerce, de l'Industrie et des Colonies (Sous-Secretariat des Colonies) *Statistiques Coloniales pour l'année 1891* (1894).
103. F. Renault, "L'abolition de l'esclavage au Sénégal: L'attitude de l'administration française, 1848–1905", RFHOM, LVII, 1971, p. 38.
104. Eunice A. Charles, *Precolonial Senegal: The Jolof Kingdom, 1800 to 1890* (Boston, 1977) ch. 8; David Robinson, *Chiefs and Clerics* (Oxford, 1975) ch. 8; H. O. Idowu, "The Establishment of Protectorate Administration in Senegal, 1890–1904", *JHSN,* IV, 1968.
105. ANS, I D 100, Archinard 32, 13 December 1888 encloses a petition with thirteen signatures; six names are Africans, seven appear to be French (probably mulattos).
106. ANS, I D 100, Archinard to Governor, 20 January, 8 February 1889; cf John D. Hargreaves, "Another Creole frontier: the Upper Senegal, 1889", *Journal of the Historical Society of Sierra Leone,* I, 2, 1977, p. 65.
107. ANSOM, Soudan VII/I/I, Report by Picanon, 20 January 1890.
108. Person, *Samori,* III, pp. 1275–6.
109. ANS, I D 94, de la Porte to Archinard, 19 October 1888.
110. ANSOM, Soudan VII/I/I, Rapport de la Sous-commission, p. 10.
111. Ibid. Note by Gallieni, 29 January 1890.
112. Some of these are collected in ANS, I B 76 and I D 103.
113. ANS, I D 105. Archinard, *Rapport Militaire, Campagne 1889–90,* 12 July 1890, f. 2. cf. Kanya-Forstner, *Conquest,* p. 179, Méniaud, *Pionniers du Soudan,* I, p. 430.
114. ANS, I D 105, *Rapport,* 1889–90, ff. 1–7.
115. Y. Saint-Martin. "La volonté de paix d'El Hadj Omar et d'Ahmadou dans leurs relations avec la France". *Bulletin de l'IFAN,* XXX(B) 1968, pp. 785–802.
116. Letter c. March 1889, quoted by Y. Saint Martin, *L'empire toucouleur et la France* (Dakar, 1967) p. 384. This paragraph owes much to M. Saint-Martin's study.
117. ANS, I G 76. Report of Demba Samba.
118. Y. Person, *Samori,* III, pp. 1295, 1352–3.
119. Saint-Martin, *L'empire toucouleur et la France,* pp. 392–7: cf. B. O. Oloruntimehin, *The Segu Tukolor Empire* (1972) pp. 278–9, 287–90.

120. Méniaud, *Pionniers*, I, p. 433; cf Kanya-Forstner, *Conquest*, pp. 178–9 see note 108.
121. ANS, I D 105, Archinard, *Rapport Militaire 1889–90*, 12 July 1890, f. 1.
122. Not on the Niger as stated by Oloruntimehin, *Segu Tukolor Empire*, p. 292.
123. Saint-Martin, pp. 404–9: ANS, I G 76 Archinard to Ahmadu, 6 December, 29 December 1889; 18 January 1890; cf Méniaud, p. 443, Archinard to his brother, n.d.
124. Ahmadu's reply is partially quoted in Saint-Martin, p. 410; cf. Kanya-Forstner, *Conquest*, pp. 180–1.
125. Saint-Martin, pp. 412–15; the original is in ANS I G 76.
126. ANS, I D 105. Archinard, *Rapport Militaire*. A somewhat garbled version of the purely military sections of this report is printed in Méniaud, *Pionniers*, I, pp. 446–514.
127. ANS, I D 105. *Rapport Militaire*, ff. 47–55. The version printed in Méniaud, I, 492 ff is heavily garbled, omitting Archinard's fiercest strictures.
128. Ibid., ff. 52–3, 62.
129. Saint-Martin, *L'empire toucouleur et la France*, 426.
130. R. A. Adeleye, *Power and Diplomacy in Northern Nigeria* (1971) pp. 169–70, 194 (cf p. 299).
131. Méniaud, *Pionniers*, I, p. 533, quoting Quiquandon's report.
132. Person, *Samori*, III, pp. 1292–1300; Kanya-Forstner, *Conquest*, pp. 183–6.

8 Confrontation in the South-West

Diplomats at the Berlin Conference had been primarily concerned to regulate the scramble to control the coast and navigable rivers which gave access to such resources as the African interior might prove to contain. By 1889 only the littoral between Grand Bassam and the Moa river, hitherto that least receptive to foreign traders, remained unappropriated by a European power. Much of it was indeed claimed by Liberia, but the future of that weak Afro-American republic seemed increasingly problematic.

Hitherto, the Africans who controlled the internal trade of this region had used Freetown as the principal port through which to convey their gold, ivory and hides to international markets; its Creole population perceived that Samori's "*dyula* revolution" had created a political structure with which fruitful collaboration might be possible (vol. 1, pp. 176–84). But the Anglo–French demarcation of 1889, followed as it was by France's military offensive against Samori, excluded this possiblity. It seemed that the upper Niger valley, together with Futa Jalon and Guinea rivers, would become dependent on France's established base in Senegambia.

Binger's exploration had however revealed another possibility, as Verdier quickly appreciated. If the cartographers' "Kong" represented not a mountain barrier but a commercial metropolis, the river valleys which pierced the forests to its south might offer alternative access to the trade of the western Sudan, including the newly revealed kingdoms of the Upper Volta. As these prospects unfolded, the hitherto unclaimed littoral acquired new importance. Since British officials were slow to appreciate this, the French were able to establish an early predominance; but after 1892 they faced stiffer resistance, from British diplomacy and also from British expeditions towards the interior. They also found that Samori's

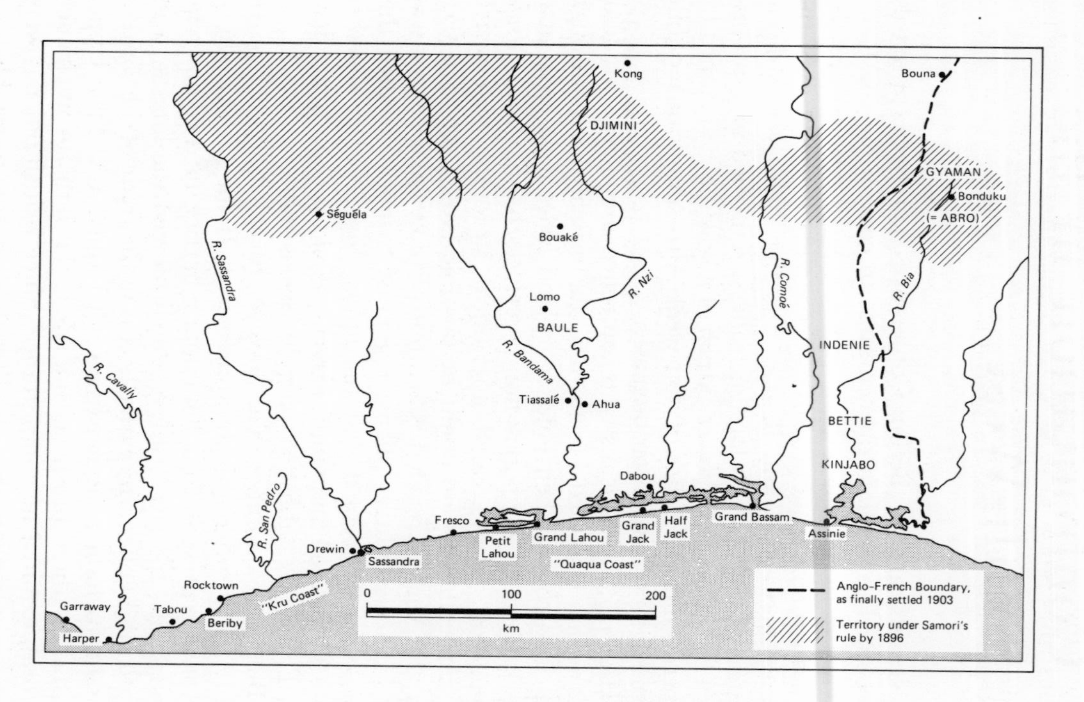

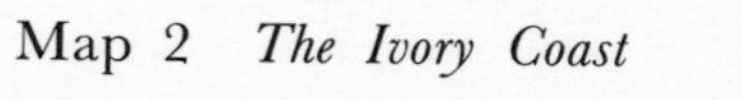

Map 2 *The Ivory Coast*

military power, removed with difficulty from the upper Niger, had rematerialized on another front. Nevertheless, the French state did eventually secure rewards for its efforts in Guinea and the Ivory Coast. Sierra Leonean dreams of inland penetration were reduced to very modest size, and the Republic of Liberia was placed in a most vulnerable position.

THE IVORY COAST: UNCERTAIN START TO A NEW ERA

Once Binger had joined hands with Treich-Lapleine at Kong in January 1889, that dedicated expansionist Etienne quickly appreciated the opportunity to outflank the British West African empire. On 23 July he proposed to send an emissary from Grand Bassam to establish contact with the French establishments on the upper Niger and in Guinea, and thus "to isolate the colony of Sierra Leone, which would shortly be reduced, like the colony of Bathurst, to a veritable enclave in the middle of our possessions".[1] But among his colleagues the urge to economize was still stronger than patriotic euphoria. The Foreign Ministry declined to meet the modest costs of such an expedition, insisting that colonies should finance their own expansion. Etienne therefore proceeded to constitute the Ivory Coast settlements as an autonomous administration, under the supervision of Lieutenant-Governor Bayol from Conakry; Treich–Lapleine was appointed as salaried Resident. Although his instructions referred to French protectorates extending as far inland as Kong, the prior necessity of raising revenue meant that the Resident's first duty was to formalize French control over the rulers of the coastline, and to impose customs duties on their trade.[2] His attempts to do so led to conflicts with both African and European merchants.

These conflicts, no doubt inevitable, were exacerbated by the aggressive and neurotic patriotism of the first Resident. Treich–Lapleine, still under thirty, was determined to assert his authority, and also his independence from Arthur Verdier, his former employer and uncle by marriage. Verdier expected to be rewarded for past services to the French Republic by far-reaching privileges; his agents took liberties and made demands whose presumption infuriated harassed local administrators. In Paris however Verdier still enjoyed influence with Etienne; in an unguarded moment the Minister accepted his proposal to impose high rates of import duty on foreign goods only, forgetting that such discrimination was contrary to the Anglo-French Agreement he had recently signed. When this was pointed out, the *arrêté* was amended to apply the same heavy duties to French imports also;[3] this meant that Verdier's trade in liquor and firearms at Grand Bassam and Assinie was subject to the same burdens as that of his British rival Swanzy, and that both lost the advantage previously enjoyed over British ports on the Gold Coast.

Verdier's anguished complaints could however be overridden more easily than those of the African trading population known as the Alladians, or Jack-Jacks. Although the French held treaties on the so-called "Quaqua coast" which dated from the 1850s, and in the 1868–70 had actually installed customs posts as far west as Grand Lahou, the Alladians remained linked with British merchants in a long-established trading system.[4] Contracts were completed aboard Bristol sailing-ships by which the Alladians received goods on credit against stipulated quantities of palm-oil from coastal districts, or of gold, ivory and cloth to be procured through trading networks which extended far northwards through the forest. France's attempt to impose heavy taxes on this commerce predictably provoked strong opposition from all who shared in it.[5]

On 22 October 1889 Treich-Lapleine announced that discriminatory duties on non-French imports, together with heavy anchorage dues, would be imposed at Half-Jack, chief centre of the Alladian trade. But the building which he had purchased for a custom-house from a wealthy trader with French connections was quickly occupied by the Alladians, encouraged by British captains. Only after the warship *Brandon* had bombarded the town in 29 November could customs officers be landed. They soon found difficulty in buying food in the local market, and in January 1890 they were physically attacked; these humiliations raised the blood-pressure of Treich-Lapleine, and no doubt contributed to his early death in March. Meanwhile the British captains had transferred their trade to Grand Lahou, where they believed their rights to be protected by an old treaty of 1842. When another custom-house was established here in February 1890 there was more resistance, while the traders found yet another landing-place for their goods, at Petit Lahou. Not until late 1891 did the French succeed in enforcing fiscal control over the whole Quaqua coast, through seven custom-houses, requiring twenty-two European staff, and a garrison of sixty *tirailleurs*.[6]

Even more seriously, the French had roused the hostility of the Baule, the dominant people of the Bandama valley. Historically, their principal commerce had been with the Asante, their fellow-Akan; but as European goods became available on the Quaqua coast in the nineteenth century they established transit markets where these could be exchanged with Alladians for gold, ivory, slaves and woven cloth. These southern markets in turn were linked by alliance and inter-marriage with villages throughout Baule country; the town of Tiassalé was the centre of a flexible "trading chain" which extended from Grand Lahou to Lomo in the north, while a rival chain from Half-Jack ran through Ahua. French attempts to appropriate revenues on the coast thus sounded alarm bells which resounded along the Bandama valley as far as the savanna zone.[7]

Early in 1891 Etienne, anxious to penetrate the Ivoirian interior but still lacking funds, encouraged the recently formed *Comité de l'Afrique française* to sponsor three missions to the western Ivory Coast, led by young officers seconded from the army in search of adventure. Towards the end of February Vicomte Armand (son of a monarchist Deputy) and Lieutenant Tavernost reached Tiassalé. Chief Etien Komenan, no doubt warned by his Alladian associates, refused their high-handed demand for interpreters for their journey northwards, and first Armand, then Tavernost, returned to the coast. Shortly afterwards there arrived Voituret and Papillon, two equally imperious agents of a commercial company which was hoping for a concession covering the western Ivory Coast;[8] as they disembarked from their canoes they were attacked and killed. Although some reports suggested that these traders had provoked this attack by *mauvais procédés et exactions contre les indigènes,* it seems that the ambush had been prepared for the return of Armand and Tavernost, and may have been instigated by the chief of Grand Lahou. The dismembered bodies were distributed among Etien Komenan's allies; the heads were said to have reached the Kru chief Mané of Beriby. A column of fifty-four *tirailleurs* was despatched through the forest to punish Tiassalé, where there were said to be few firearms; but French traders had recently responded to market opportunities by supplying some, and on 11 May the French force was ambushed by several hundred well-armed men. Having lost two dead and thirteen wounded it retired to the coast, and attempts to penetrate the forest by the Bandama valley were abandoned for two years.[9]

Meanwhile the French turned further westward, in search of revenue and routes to the interior. Between Lahou and Monrovia the coastline was largely occupied by strongly independent village communities of traders and fishermen, grouped in local alliances or federations with distinctive ethnic identities, and collectively known as the Kru. To nineteenth-century Europeans the Kru were remarkable for their skills of seamanship, and their willingness to apply them by entering into genuinely free contracts to work aboard European vessels, or in coastal settlements; as steamship trade expanded during the latter nineteenth century, access to Kru labour became an increasingly valuable resource.[10] In addition the Kru coast provided the off-shore trade of the Bristol sailing-ships with a thousand tons a year of palm-oil and a similar amount of kernels, together with gold, ivory and timber; the annual value of British imports and exports was roughly estimated at £100 000, and relatively recently the steamship lines had begun to call and trade with European or Sierra Leonean brokers resident onshore.[11]

In 1889 the extent of foreign rights over this coast remained obscure. Bristol merchants believed the whole coast to be under some form of British protection under the treaty with Grand Lahou of 1842; but neither Foreign nor Colonial Office could substantiate this.[12] The Liberian government claimed sovereignty along the coast as far as the San Pedro river, although they exercised virtually no control over the fiercely independent Kru (who resented their attempts to collect customs-duties) and had no settlements beyond Harper, near Cape Palmas; nevertheless until 1889 this claim was usually tacitly accepted by both British and French governments. French archives contained two treaties purporting to cede territory on the Kru coast – one of 1838 with Garraway, west of Cape Palmas, the other, signed in 1868 with Mané of Beriby, a ruler who now claimed that his rights extended along the coast between the San Pedro and Cavally rivers. As recently as 1887 Etienne had decided not to try to enforce these rights, so long as France experienced no difficulty in recruiting Kru seamen.[13] But the new prospects which Binger had opened for the Ivory Coast changed this; in April 1889 Etienne advised the Foreign Ministry that his mission, which had

> traversed important territories bordering the region disputed with Liberia, spreading French influence among the natives, has led me to re-open my study of this question and to wonder whether, by conceding so completely the claims of the Republic of Liberia, we have not compromised our position in these regions.[14]

In November Treich-Lapleine was instructed to try to secure treaties which would protect France's "primordial interest" in preventing foreigners from encroaching on the coast between Lahou and Cape Palmas "and the corresponding regions of the interior".[15] The new colony was thus committed to expanding on the one sector of the West African coast still unclaimed under the procedure laid down in 1885; this threatened not only the interests of British traders but political claims of Liberia.

* * *

The French, still unfamiliar figures on the Kru coast, began their expansion with sparse resources. Etienne, having failed to secure additional funds for expansion, could offer Treich-Lapleine only 10 000 francs for the purpose of "establishing our preponderance in the vicinity of Liberia and completing the political blockade of Sierra Leone".[16] In October 1890 Bidaud, another former Verdier agent, made a highly discouraging political reconnaissance. Mané recalled that he had signed a treaty in 1868 but also that France had withdrawn two years later; he claimed that he was now bound to Britain by a treaty of friendship. Nor could Bidaud take advantage of discontent among village chiefs whom Mané claimed to control, which had been stimulated by falling palm-oil prices and the establishment of onshore trading agencies. The dominant political and commercial influence was exercised by the syndicate of W. D. Woodin, a former Liverpool purser, working through a resident agent at Rocktown, Frank Williamson, and a mailboat captain, C. Harvey;[17] under their influence a group of chiefs and traders reacted to news of French proceedings at Lahou by inviting a naval officer to take the coast between the Cavally and San Pedro rivers under British protection.[18] And the syndicate's influence extended eastwards to the Sassandra; Governor Griffith, returning to Gold Coast on Harvey's ship, had recently been presented with a similar petition from chiefs of that region, headed by the playfully named George Buggery.[19]

Unable to assert French influence directly, Etienne tried to work through the *Comité de l'Afrique française*. On 13 March 1891 he was formally told of the departure of three exploring missions under officers of the regular army; his department had in fact already asked the War Ministry to grant these men paid leave, provided letters authorizing them to conclude treaties, and assured them that colonial officials would support their *missions gratuites*.[20] This was to be imperialism financed by private patriotism; three days before departure Lieutenants Quiquerez and Segonzac learned that the *Comité* could afford only 5000 francs towards expenses estimated at 15 000 and that they were each expected to contribute a similar sum.[21] None of these missions was truly successful. The failure of Armand and Tavernost to penetrate Baule country has already been noted; Lieutenant Arago made only a short journey up the Sassandra river; but Quiquerez and Segonzac, at tragic cost, did lay foundations for French claims on the Kru coast.

Quiquerez, an arrogant and quarrelsome young dragoon,

had clearly come to Africa in search of patriotic glory.[22] When his companion suggested prudence in face of African hostility, he treated this as cowardice; suggestions that the advice of British traders might be helpful drew the comment that it was not for French officers to make advances to an Englishman. According to Quiquerez, Segonzac wanted to abandon the journey after learning of Voituret's fate; late in April he fell ill with dysentery and Quiquerez left him for days at San Pedro, commenting "the poor chap is completely demoralized". To his father-in-law he complained that Segonzac had become a mere incumbrance.[23] Despite these heroics, Quiquerez's attempt to ascend the Cavally was frustrated by the hostility of a chief and an Afro-American missionary; rejoining Segonzac, he tried to explore an alternative route to the Sudan by the San Pedro river. But here the Frenchmen again obtained no co-operation from riverain Africans; about 22 May they were attacked, and their canoe over-turned. Segonzac returned to report that his companion had died of fever; in fact he seems to have shot himself in a frenzy of patriotic frustration.[24]

These exploits were not entirely fruitless; by one means or another the expedition had secured a dozen assorted treaties with coastal rulers, some of which were eventually used to sustain French territorial claims. More decisive perhaps was the simultaneous appearance on the coast of Lieutenant-Governor Ballay in the *Brandon*; having been authorized to negotiate a frontier agreement with Liberia, Ballay was seeking to strengthen his hand by collecting treaties on his own account. The most important of these was with Mané who, after prolonged consultation with his chiefs, agreed to accept renewed French protection in return for a stipend of 25 000 francs, an assurance of support against Liberia, and recognition of his own claim to the whole coast between the Cavally and the San Pedro.[25]

This did not in itself ensure the actual implantation of French rule. Mané's dubious claims to paramountcy were rejected by many local rulers, and Williamson's influence was still very strong. In December 1892 a naval officer sent to distribute stipends reported fierce resistance from "bellicose tribes"; as late as August 1894 the French were still struggling vainly to get Kru chiefs to acknowledge Mané's claims, now inflated to cover the coast eastwards to Grand Lahou.[26] Indeed, French political intervention complicated their vital practical task of recruiting seamen and labourers. Early in 1891 twenty-four Kru recruited by an African agent at Sassandra had found their way to the Congo Free State; by October it was known that six of them were dead, and the French were being held responsible.[27] In February 1893 the *Mésange* found Mané virtually powerless to provide workers, in face of the dominant position of British recruiting agents in most villages; a prolonged voyage, extending to Cape Palmas, produced only forty-seven men.[28]

Diplomatically, however, Ballay and Quiquerez had secured sufficient fig-leaves to cover an assertion of French claims under the Berlin rules. The Foreign Office had in fact already decided that Britain had no valid political titles to the western Ivory Coast and that it would not be in her interest to create such. Provided that France would agree that the guarantees against differential customs-duties contained in the frontier Convention of 1889 extended as far as the Quaqua and Kru coasts, they assumed (correctly, in the short term) that British traders would be able to hold their own. Their only doubts concerned possible future French encroachments on Liberian independence; but official attitudes to that Republic remained highly ambivalent, and on 12 March 1890 Salisbury decided "not . . . to recommend that this strip of coast should be annexed".[29]

The Colonial Office was only slightly more hesitant. Hemming noted an international dimension to the problem:

> If there is any probability of the Slave Trade Conference agreeing to an international prohibition of arms into W. Africa it will be necessary that this bit of coast, which is at present a "No-man's land", should be taken over by some civilized power – whether ourselves or France does not, I think, very much matter.[30]

Herbert went a little further:

> I think the territory is morally within the French "sphere of

> influence" and we should be rather poaching if we absorbed it . . . On the whole I do not covet this territory.[31]

Governors and naval officers on the coast were more inclined to secure treaties of protection (which would not have been difficult at any time in 1890); but the Colonial Office had no desire to assume responsibility for territories physically detached from existing colonies, nor to take up Moloney's suggestion of a new Chartered Company. For a time Hemming characteristically wondered whether "it would be as well to preserve authority over the territory, as it might come in well for exchange purposes in the future"; but the Office did not dissent from Salisbury's ruling of 12 March, that this territory should be allowed to go by default.[32] They did become a little disturbed when they later received estimates of the commercial value of the Kru coast, provoking the Foreign Office to cynical comments on the relativity of their moral principles; in fact all they were suggesting was early negotiation with France about fiscal guarantees, and they never seriously contemplated a political challenge.[33] When on 26 October 1891 the French eventually produced a selection of treaties Salisbury accepted these as a valid notification under the Berlin Act, reserving his position only with regard to Liberian claims between the San Pedro and Cavally rivers.[34]

British merchants now accepted the necessity of coming to terms with their French overlords. By March 1891 the Bristol merchants were said to be working fairly well with the French on the Quaqua coast, though Messrs King (who could exercise a certain amount of political influence through their MP, Sir Michael Hicks-Beach) continued to complain about the loss of the Kru coast, and to press the Foreign Office for permanent guarantees against differential duties.[35] The Liverpool syndicate, after failing to secure British recognition of a purported land concession in the San Pedro area, drawn up in Freetown by Samuel Lewis, took a more direct approach. During the autumn of 1892 Woodin was in Paris, offering to transfer his concession to the French, in return for the grant of a trading monopoly, or a period of complete exemption from duties.[36] But he received little encouragement from Jamais and by 1893 was reconciled to paying customs duties in return for the prospect of increased security under French rule. By July his associates Harvey and Williamson were backing an appeal from an educated Kru, Horatio Johns, that France should actually extend her control to his uncle's country on the right bank of the Cavally, recently recognized as Liberian.[37]

The Liberian government, though more persistent than the British in asserting its territorial claims, had already proved incapable of enforcing them beyond the Cavally. After securing the treaty with Mané in April 1891 Ballay proceeded to Monrovia in the *Brandon*, and produced his diplomatic credentials; his arrival, on election day, clearly worried Liberians who recalled Havelock's method of settling their northern boundary in 1882.[38] Pleading, no doubt truthfully, that they had not prepared the necessary documentation, they persuaded Ballay to go away until September. When he returned President Johnson stoutly refused to concede Liberia's claim to the San Pedro (which he pointed out had been recognized on official maps of the 1880s); after demanding arbitration he agreed to transfer negotiations to Paris, and named as his plenipotentiary Baron de Stein, a German aristocrat of cosmopolitan interests.[39] But Stein could make no headway against French intransigence: on 8 December 1892 he gave way and signed a treaty which, besides recognizing the Cavally frontier, contained certain ominous provisions. One granted France the right to carry out engineering operations on either bank of the Cavally; another gave her conditional rights to enter Liberian territory in pursuit of "her own rebellious chiefs"; most important, Article V gave France the right to abrogate the treaty should Liberian independence be impaired, or any part of her territory alienated.[40] The expansion of the Ivory Coast had not only over-ridden Liberian territorial claims which were no more tenuous than many similar claims by Europeans; it was now bringing the very survival of Liberian independence into serious question.

* * *

Difficulties even more formidable than those of controlling the coastline had been created by Verdier's schemes to exploit the resources of the Comoe and Bia valleys and to monopolize the trade with Kong. As in the Bandama valley, the inhabitants of the forest resisted French penetration; even in France's supposed protectorates of Kinjabo, Bettié and Indénié the Akan rulers had close links of kinship and commerce with the Gold Coast, and when the new French tariff suddenly raised the cost of imports through Grand Bassam and Assinie they naturally tried to intensify these. In the northern savannas the conflicts of interest and loyalty among France's prospective collaborators proved even stronger.

In September 1890 the French Cabinet at last agreed to finance Etienne's proposed mission towards the upper Niger. The original plan was for Captain P. L. Monteil to approach Kong through Tiassalé and the Bandama valley; but he was diverted to the more ambitious expedition to Chad and his replacement, Lieutenant Marie Ménard, was persuaded by Binger and Verdier to take the Comoe route in order to combat British influence.[41] Ménard seems to have encountered more difficulties than he expected, not only in the three southern protectorates[42] but also in the former Asante dependency of Gyaman, whose capital, Bonduku, had been correctly identified by Binger as an important transit market. Local power-brokers were still pursuing their complex schemes of alliances, internally and externally, oblivious of the agreed intention of French and British diplomatists to partition their country.[43]

It took Ménard seven months to pass through these countries; and when he eventually reached Kong in June 1891 he discovered still graver problems. The "*dyula* capital" proved to be merely the centre of a loosely organized confederacy, many of whose members were strongly opposed to developing the French connection. Still more seriously, Samori's influence was in the ascendent among the *dyula* of Kong, and even more so in the countries to the west, through which Ménard's return route would have to pass. Archinard's offensive of April 1891 had in fact sealed Ménard's fate. Having allied with Vakuru Bamba, one of the opponents of Samori's movement to the east, Ménard and his ten *tirailleurs* were killed on 4 February 1892 when the *sofas* captured the town of Seguéla.[44]

Meanwhile officials on the Gold Coast were showing increasing interest in the transit markets of Asante's former northern dependencies, which could offer commercial access to the Niger through the upper Volta basin. At first their efforts centred on Salaga; when German expeditions began to arrive the British government tried to secure continued access by establishing the Neutral Zone of 1888 (vol. 1, pp. 86–7, 215–17). But as the danger of rival European intervention increased, the Gold Coasters began to seek greater control, to the north-west as well as the north-east of Asante; Lethbridge's mission to Bonduku in 1889 had been one sign of this. Captain Lang of the Gold Coast Constabulary, British representative on an Anglo-French Boundary Commission which met in January 1892 to implement the arrangement of 1889, shared this assertive attitude. Binger, his French colleague, was outraged to discover that Lang refused to accept the simple line of territorial partition which seemed already agreed in principle for the southern section of the frontier, but tried to push British territory westwards by claiming jurisdiction over "Appollonian" migrants from British territory who had settled within Kinjabo.[45] After stormy disagreements the two Commissioners proceeded separately northwards, each seeking to advance his claims by enlisting African allies; by April all pretence at a joint survey was abandoned. Salisbury, belatedly persuaded to adopt a more vigorous African policy (see below, pp. 81–3), applauded Lang's truculence and approved new treaty-making initiatives;[46] Binger visited Bonduku and Kong, but found both centres less amenable to French influence than his earlier visits had led him to expect.[47]

In August 1893 Binger returned to the Ivory Coast as first Governor of an autonomous colony, and a period of more consistent administration began. Although Binger had made his military reputation by exploring the savannas, as civilian Governor his first priority was to foster the coastal commerce of palm-oil, rubber, coffee and mahogany, on which short-term financial solvency depended. Nevertheless he did attempt to renew the northward thrust. His former companion

Captain Braulot returned to Kong in June 1893, only to find that news of the French destruction of Jenné – the major *dyula* market of the middle Niger – had further increased Muslim hostility. Unable to proceed to Bouna, he had to withdraw southwards to strengthen French influence in Gyaman.[48] Meanwhile Binger persuaded the ebullient Captain Marchand, who while serving at Sikasso had occupied himself by devising routes for a *trans-nigérien* railway connecting one or other of the Ivory Coast rivers with the navigable waters of the Niger and its Bagoue tributary,[49] to make another attempt to penetrate the Bandama route. Delcassé, the new Colonial Under-Secretary, though still constrained by political pressure to economize, found 60 000 francs from metropolitan and colonial funds, and with small supplements from the Foreign and Education ministries Marchand left France in March 1893.[50]

Marchand soon discovered that reports of diminished Baule opposition were over-optimistic; but he succeeded in finding collaborators among the trading rivals of Etien Komenan at Ahua, and on 25 May an improvised column captured Tiassalé, where it installed a new chief and a small French garrison.[51] After the rains Marchand resumed his advance, and by 11 November had reached Bouaké. But the results were disillusioning; Marchand soon realized that his *trans-nigérien* project rested on false assumptions, both topographical and political. By January 1894 the upper Bandama valley was dominated by Samori's forces continuing their eastern *hegira*; the *dyulas* whose support Binger hoped to win had been outraged by Archinard's conquest, and the surrounding populations, weakened by famine, regarded the *sofas* as more effective protectors than the French. When Marchand reached Kong in April 1894 he was received even more apprehensively than Braulot. Swallowing his military pride, Marchand promoted the French cause by opening a market-stall where he personally sold French imports; but as Samori's armies drew nearer he returned to the coast to seek military reinforcements.[52] During the dry season these materialized in the form of an ill-fated column under P. L. Monteil (see below, p. 220).

* * *

Binger by this time was fully occupied in asserting French control of the coast. Despite – or because of – the installation of customs-houses during 1893 the Kru refused to acknowledge French authority, and created new difficulties over recruitment of seamen and labourers. In January 1894 an Ordinance required recruiters to obtain official authorisation and to pay a tax of twenty-five francs a head; but since the government lacked the power to compel the Kru to sign on with French ships or to exclude foreigners this did not help much. After British complaints Delcassé abolished the tax, leaving Binger to negotiate informal arrangements locally.[53]

These difficulties made him covet those Kru ports which had been recognized as Liberian. After an official visit to Monrovia, Binger concluded that within two years Liberian independence would be undermined by insolvency, and suggested appointing a resident Consul to ensure French predominance.[54] On his way home Binger visited the coast west of the Cavally, where Horatio Johns and his British advisers were now ready to accept French protection in order to escape Liberian misrule. Disregarding the frontier Convention of December 1892 (which Liberia had not yet ratified) Binger signed treaties annexing this coastline to France, blandly adding that it should be possible to advance a further fifty kilometres each year.[55] When ordered by Delcassé to relinquish these claims Binger complied, grumbling about the risk that Britain or Germany would take France's place.[56] In November 1894 he proposed to blockade part of the Liberian coast, professedly to prevent arms reaching Samori during Monteil's campaign, but also with ulterior motives: France might reclaim the cost of the blockade from the Liberian government, and use her inability to pay as a pretext for territorial occupations.[57] Liberian independence now seemed more precarious than ever.

TOWARDS THE SIERRA LEONE PROTECTORATE

While the French on the Ivory Coast were with difficulty laying foundations for what would eventually become their most prosperous African colony the British belatedly struggled to organize their residual sphere of influence behind Freetown, once their prospective gateway to the Sudanese commercial networks. Early in 1890 the creation of a Frontier Police force with an initial establishment of four British officers, four Creole sub-inspectors and 280 men, with the appointment of two travelling commissioners, marked a reluctant recognition by the Colonial Office of the need to assume additional authority, at least within the immediately neighbouring districts from which the Colony drew most of its trade and revenue (vol. 4, pp. 198–9; Map 3).

These innovations represented reactions to changes in the African political environment, rather than any deliberate imperial thrust; the very progress of commerce generated conflicts which threatened its peaceful continuance. Neighbouring rulers quarrelled over borderlands which had suddenly gained economic value; subordinate chiefs well placed to profit rejected the authority of their overlords. The amount of indebtedness increased vastly as produce prices fluctuated, and the long-established custom which allowed Creole creditors to distrain upon the property of the debtor's countrymen created conflicts which seemed to require more consistent British intervention.[58] The Frontier Police, which would eventually provide the basis for a quasi-military form of administration, initially had the limited role of settling such difficulties and plugging gaps in the *pax africana,* within an area bounded by a new road running from Kambia to Sulima through the heads of navigation on the various trading rivers. Their instructions were "to maintain peace and persuade the natives to develop the resources of their country" – to provide a reserve of force behind the policies of moral suasion favoured by Rowe and his successor, Sir John Hay. As far as civil government was concerned, J. C. E. Parkes, their Creole adviser on "Native Affairs" envisaged British and Creole officers, appointed as magistrates, exercising "paternal, advisory" jurisdiction in association with the chiefs and in accordance with "the laws that prevail in the district".[59]

In 1890, British problems in the regions south and east of Freetown did not seem to be complicated by any imminent danger of foreign intrusion. After Crawford's short and successful campaign of January 1889 against the Mende

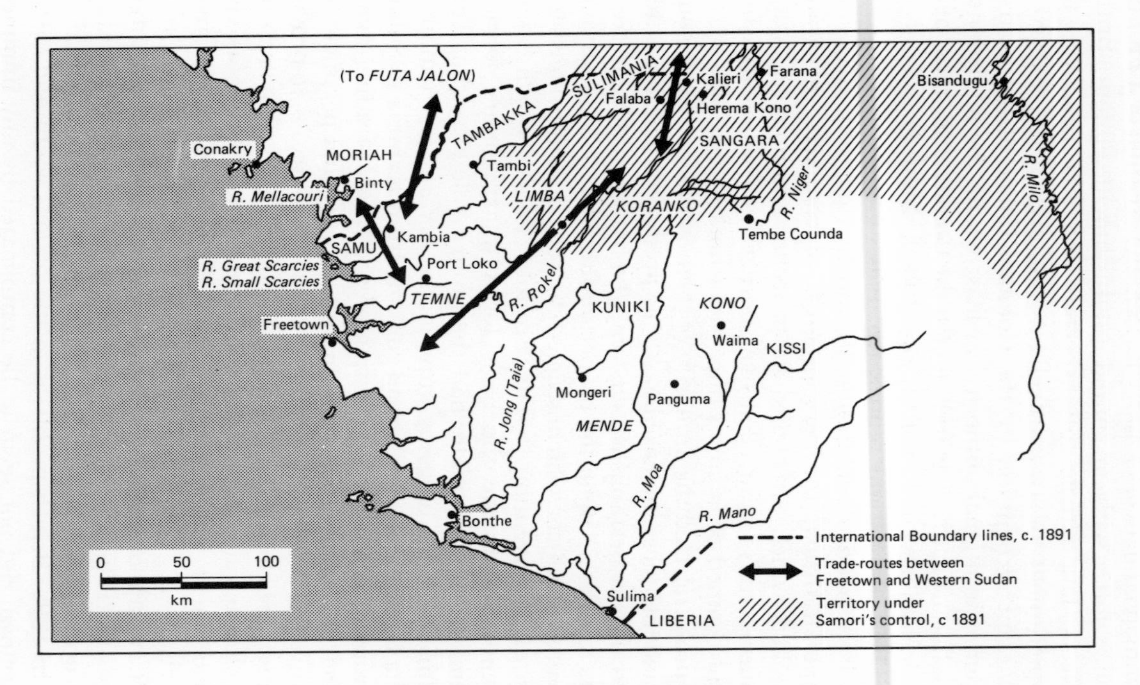

Map 3 *Sierra Leone c. 1891*

war-chief Makaia it seemed possible to hope that British authority might gradually come to be accepted as it had been in the Gold Coast Colony. "Complete peace reigns for the first time", wrote Meade, a little optimistically, on All Fools' day, 1890.[60] The frontier which Havelock had imposed on Liberia would serve for the time being, and the French were a long way off. However, they might not remain so. Hemming had noted a claim by Gallieni that French possessions extended to Liberia's inland frontier; since that seemed an extremely uncertain limit, Travelling Commissioner Alldridge's first mission was to explore the upper Mende country, and secure as many pre-emptive treaties as possible.[61] But it could still be hoped that this productive region would respond favourably to the civilizing force of commerce, backed up by fatherly advice from Alldridge and occasional demonstrations of fire-power.

In the north however the consolidation of French control over what was to become the colony of Guinea greatly increased British difficulties. The boundary agreed in 1889 was to divide the basin of the Mellacourie from the lower Scarcies, and then to follow an imprecisely defined route north-eastwards towards the tenth parallel; attempts at a more comprehensive partition having failed, it was to terminate at 13° West of Paris (10°40 of Greenwich). This curious construction cut through what has been called the "Sierra Leone–Guinea system",[62] a region united by long-established commercial relationships, though divided politically by complex patterns of conflict and alliance between Africans which bore no relation to this new partition. The new boundary was certain to complicate the fiscal and political problems already created by the relations with Samori's empire.

The fiscal problem was the oldest. Ever since Hennessy's tariff of 1872 had raised the duties on liquor and tobacco, imports of these goods had tended to enter through the Guinea rivers; thence they could be moved overland and exchanged for African produce in Kambia, Port Loko, or even Freetown itself. French fiscal policy naturally encouraged such trade, and the British would continue losing revenue until their custom-men could control the still notional boundary. The concession to France of Futa Jalon, key to one of the two trading corridors which linked Freetown with the *dyula* network, meant that more revenue was lost, as French administrators worked strenuously to divert its caravans to Conakry. They never succeeded completely, and cattle from Futa Jalon continue to supply the Freetown market today; but the colony's links with the Sudan now depended increasingly on alternative routes through Falaba.

But the basins of the Scarcies and Rokel rivers, which these routes traversed, had been thrown into turmoil during the 1880s, and the moral influence which Freetown had formerly possessed among the Temne, Limba and Loko peoples was greatly weakened. The vacuum created by Samori's withdrawal to deal with the revolt of 1888 had been partly filled by the "Muritey", a mercenary force under the Susu warrior Karimu, based on a stockaded camp at Tambi, in the upper valley of the Little Scarcies. With tacit encouragement from French officials, Karimu raided British clients within "the Queen's Garden"; Temne forces under Sattan Lahai and Bai Bureh responded by intervening in Moriah, where the French had installed Karimu's father-in-law Dauda as Bokkari's successor (vol. 1, pp. 197–8).[63] The countries of the region, the Alikali of Port Loko complained in July 1891, "all are nothing but smokes".[64] The Frontier Police still lacked the numbers, and the training, to control this disorder; in April 1891 they failed humiliatingly to capture Tambi, which remained a challenge to British ascendency until an expedition by the West India Regiment was authorized a year later.

It was difficult for either Power to stabilize its sphere of influence until the notional boundary of 1889 had been marked on the ground. But the French were in no hurry to do this until they had acquired more information, and stronger political cards. In December 1890 Etienne quietly sent Captain Brosselard-Faidherbe (grandson of the General) to survey a route for a railway from Benty to the Niger through the Scarcies valley; besides gathering topographical information he was also expected to secure treaties which might justify improvements in the boundary, though in fact his political methods proved counter-productive.[65] When administrator Lamadon and Captain Kenney, the French and British

Boundary Commissioners, eventually met in December 1891, it soon became clear that they were pursuing incompatible political aims. After failing to agree in Samu, where the 1882 and 1889 Agreements seemed relatively explicit, they discovered that the states of the Scarcies valley mentioned in the text had no easily ascertainable borders. Each Commissioner stoutly championed the aims of his African allies (and may have been manipulated by them). Lamadon maintained close relations with Karimu, and played on fears of the *sofas* to persuade Britain's Limba clients that their interests lay with France; Kenney, relying on the advice of Sattan Lahai, was accused of condoning continued Temne intervention in the French sphere. By the end of January 1892 the Commission had broken up without agreement.[66] But even the most conciliatory Commissioners would have found it hard to complete the delimitation in 1892; the "Sierra Leone–Guinea system" was still over-shadowed by the power of Samori, with whom, though he was now at war with France, the British still retained a special relationship.

* * *

By the beginning of 1890 Samori had largely succeeded in re-establishing his power over his rebellious subjects, and could give more attention to the menace of Archinard's army. A primary objective was to secure continuing supplies of modern firearms. His empire's resources of gold and ivory were ruthlessly exploited (by requisitioning, or by exchange for slaves) and directed towards the Freetown trade-routes. But the manner in which Bilali exercised military supervision of these western provinces introduced new complications into relations with Freetown. Despite Samori's promise to respect the "Queen's garden", the Limbas of Biriwa and Warra Warra went in terror of reprisals for their attacks on *sofas* during the great revolt; and other peoples in the highlands to the east of the Rokel were now subject to Bilali's pressure. Although the British had little knowledge of the Koranko, Kissi or Kono countries they now became anxious to prevent them falling under Samori's control, if only because this might ultimately mean reversion to France.

On 20 February Hay briefed his two new Travelling Commissioners for journeys intended to secure diplomatic counters against the French. G. H. Garrett was instructed to make treaties with Sulimania, Koranko, Sangara, "and other districts . . . not bound by Treaty obligations to any Foreign Power"; T. J. Alldridge, while mainly concerned with upper Mende country, received similar instructions for Kono and Kissi.[67] Sulimania and Koranko were believed to lie south of 10°N and west of 13°W, and so to form part of the British "sphere" defined in 1889; Sangara, lying east of 13°W, was regarded as "open". But Garrett soon discovered much to disturb him. Sulimania and Koranko were already dominated by Bilali; Sangara, which straddled the headwaters of the Niger, had been devastated by smallpox as well as by *sofas*; many of the wretched inhabitants regarded the French as potential liberators. Garrett had to contend with widespread suspicions that he and his Arabic interpreter, Momodu Wakka, were accomplices of Samori, from whom they kept receiving friendly messages. He nevertheless secured treaties from leading Jalunka and Koranko chiefs; but suspicions were revived on 24 April by his friendly reception in Kalieri, a town whose *sofa* garrison was commanded by Momodu Wakka's cousin, and by the visit of Bilali with an army of 2500 men. Hoping to turn the entente with Samori into some form of guarantee for those whom his cruelties threatened to throw into French arms, Garrett decided to proceed to the capital of Bisandugu.[68]

He arrived on 21 May, after an exhausting and harrowing journey. Samori received him cordially, re-affirming his over-riding interest in a secure trade-route to Freetown; he would willingly spare the inhabitants of the "Queen's garden", if the British could guarantee his arms dealers free passage. Samori complained bitterly of French duplicity, emphasizing that he had returned their treaty of 1889; he suggested that the British should protect the trade-route against them by stationing troops at Falaba, and at Farana, on the right bank of the Niger. On 24 May he signed a treaty, drafted in Arabic, promising peace and protection to trade, and undertaking not to "cede any of my territory to any other power, or enter into any agreement, treaty or arrangement with any Foreign Government, except through and with the consent of the Government of Her Majesty". Garrett then returned slowly to Freetown, hoisting the Union Jack at Falaba and Farana (there were no Frontier Police to spare as garrisons): and followed by Samori's old emissary Nalifa Modu.[69]

Hitherto, Hay had been trying to combine friendly relations with Samori with the attempts to maintain influence over "stipendiary chiefs" who were deeply fearful off Samori but beyond the protection of the Frontier Police.[70] Garrett's report suggested that a closer alliance with Samori might secure a more extensive hinterland; Hay telegraphed to Knutsford: "Earnestly desire opportunity to confer with you in person on future policy of greatest importance to Empire and Colony."[71] The Imperial Government now had to decide how far they had prejudiced this possibility by recognizing the French protectorate over Samori.[72] Hemming – the official most sympathetic to Freetown's ambitions – argued that any French protectorate had been modified by the Anglo-French Arrangement of 1889, so that Britain was at least entitled to negotiate directly with Samori about Sulimania and Koranko. Over the rest of the empire, Hemming favoured temporization. Samori might be found to have renounced the French protectorate; but in any case seemed headed towards an armed conflict whose outcome was unpredictable. Should the French Chamber tire of the expense, Samori might well recover a degree of independence; his lands east of 13°W would then remain open to British influence and Freetown might yet fulfil its once manifest destiny in the Western Sudan.

Imperial priorities however firmly excluded any commitment which might entail conflict with France. Despite belated doubts about the validity of France's treaty of 1887, the Foreign Office felt bound to recognize that of 1889; if African rulers were permitted to renounce their obligations at will there would be no end to disputes among rival European powers. After hesitation, the War Office agreed that Garrett's treaty must be abandoned – even if, as its maker feared, "Sierra Leone was ruined. . . . We must pay the penalty of our past hesitation, of our unwillingness to spend money, and of our fear of fighting."[73] The Colonial Office, grumbling about the diplomatists' indifference towards West African colonies, reluctantly acquiesced; they regretted, not the fate of Samori – "a slave-hunting ruffian"[74] – but the certain prospect of increased French discrimination against British trade.[75]

Hay now had the delicate problem of telling Samori that Garrett's treaty was rejected. Disappointed in his hope of practical assistance against France the Alimami might no longer respect the Queen's garden, or might allow Bilali to extend his predatory raids into the Kono, Kissi and Kuniki countries. The Freetown authorities managed to keep Nailifa Modu waiting until November 1891, meanwhile trying to make the flesh of the home government creep by envisaging future French threats to the coaling-station.[76] But the Foreign Office saw nothing to be gained by procrastination, and considerable danger that the French military might anticipate negotiation by physical occupation. When a new Commission was constituted in Paris to implement the Anglo-French Declaration of 1890 concerning the Say-Barruwa line (see above, p. 27), the British members persuaded their French colleagues to give prior attention to clarifying and extending the 1889 agreement. The uncertainties of that document, which Hemming believed compatible with British expansion into Samori's empire, might equally have been used to justify French penetration of Mendeland; to avoid conflict it was necessary to remove ambiguity. On 26 June 1891 the Commissioners therefore agreed that in the north-east Sierra Leone's frontier should be based on the 13th meridian and the western watershed of the Niger, as far as a place called Tembe Counda.[77]

But while the boundary was being drawn, trade with Samori continued. Merchants of all nationalities, not least the *Compagnie française*, continued to supply modern precision firearms. During 1890, 207 breach-loading rifles passed through the Freetown customs, but in 1891 the figure reached 2543 before the end of December.[78] This trade was contrary to the Brussels agreement of July 1890, but this had not yet been ratified; the Colonial Office, perceiving that "this prohibition of the importation of arms of precision is much more in the interests of the French and Germans, who want to fight with and conquer the natives, than in those of the repression of the slave trade", saw no need to "anticipate the evil moment", injure business and antagonize Samori by enforcing a ban until the requisite diplomatic procedures had been complied with.[79]

Commercial interest was reinforced by the sympathy for Samori which had been generated during the 1880s, not only in Freetown's Muslim community but among Creole Christians influenced by Blyden.[80] Within the Secretariat these attitudes were temperately expressed by J. C. E. Parkes. Unless Samori were restrained by British advice, Parkes argued, he would resume his attacks upon Freetown's clients in the "low country", so giving the French an excuse to intervene and squeeze the Colony's hinterland still further. Pan-African sentiment apart, it seemed essential to maintain good relations with Samori.[81]

To British officers of the Frontier Police, and particularly to Captain Lendy its brave and headstrong Inspector-General, such a policy seemed both immoral and unwise. Knowing that the gold, ivory, hides and cattle with which Samori's *dyula* purchased firearms had often been obtained in exchange for human beings ruthlessly enslaved, they feared the effects on British prestige in the region if the credit for the inevitable defeat of this tyrant were left to the French army. The Frontier Police became champions, not only of old British *protégés* like Suluku (who still distrusted the *sofas* and interfered with their arms supplies),[82] but of selected participants in an extremely complicated struggle for power in the highlands east of the Rokel, where Bilali was seeking new routes to the waterside. During 1892 Lendy urged military action to support the Mende war-chief Vonjo of Mongeri and his allies the Kuniki Temnes against Kono and Mende antagonists who were beginning to look to Bilali for support. Parkes, tactlessly pointing out that the prestige of the Frontiers had been weakened by their failure at Tambi, argued in favour of diplomacy and moral suasion, criticizing those "who consider force is the only remedy for these native squabbles".[83] Under Governors Quayle-Jones and Fleming, Parkes's views tended to prevail; but Lendy remained determined to restore the honour of the Frontiers by military action against the *sofas*.

Once the French had launched their offensive against Samori in April 1891, supporters of the Anglo-Samorian connection were living on borrowed time. Archinard's capture of Kankan failed to subdue Samori, who continued to harass French forces in the Milo valley through the rainy season of 1891; but British visitors to Heremakono sensed his increasing disappointment with the Freetown connection.[84] A private initiative by the Liverpool shipping tycoon Alfred L. Jones, who sent Captain G. A. Williams to negotiate with Samori on behalf of his Sierra Leone Coaling Company, only increased France's determination to stop the arms supply. In June 1892 Williams produced a treaty which, in return for payments of £5 a year and a present of four hundred rifles, granted Jones extensive rights to cut timber, develop minerals, build railways and other public works, issue coinage, and exercise full economic and political control of Samori's territories between Kankan and Kouroussa. Since these were precisely the territories now occupied by France, these terms were less generous than they seemed; Samori was grasping at a hope he had expressed to Kenney, that the Boundary Commission might interpose British territory between himself and the French.[85]

There was of course no possibility of the British government endorsing this curious document; although Jones may have been aware of Hemming's lingering sympathy for his ambitions, he was probably too realistic to expect his hints of a Charter to be taken seriously. Williams's expedition complicated British relations not only with the French but with the Africans of the "low country"; many who mistrusted this new gesture towards Samori became more responsive to French blandishments. In April 1892 the "evil moment" arrived when the Sierra Leone government was finally obliged to undermine its relationship with Samori by passing an Ordinance to restrict the import and sale of modern precision weapons in accordance with the Brussels Act. Supplies did however get through until the end of 1892; the colonial authorities agreed that Freetown merchants should be allowed to dispose of stocks imported before the passing of the Ordinance, despite protests from the Paris Embassy, supported by Salisbury himself.[86] In October Samori sent Nalifa

Modu on one last mission to Freetown to ask his friends of the Coaling Company for a passage to England to beg the Queen to mediate with the French. The Colonial Office wondered whether the French might possibly welcome this opportunity to escape a heavy military commitment, but the Foreign Office would take only half-hearted soundings, and Nalifa was not allowed to leave Africa.[87]

> It is a most unfortunate thing that we cannot help Samadoo in any way [wrote Hemming]. He has always been very loyal in keeping his promises to us, and has shown a great desire to be friendly . . . the situation is a bad one and the outlook gloomy . . . We are now reaping the fruits of years of inaction and of our "laissez-faire" policy in W. Africa.[88]

Already, about February 1892, Samori had apparently despaired of effective British help and decided on an armed *hegira,* transferring the centre of his empire towards the northern Ivory Coast. During their withdrawal his *sofas* not only harassed the French by well-directed attacks but carried out a scorched-earth policy; the effects of their depredations, added to those of epidemic cattle disease, not only denied provisions to the French army but intensified the sufferings of the settled populations. Once the Freetown arms supply was closed Bilali and his army left Heremakono (which the French promptly occupied, to British fury); but the western provinces were not wholly abandoned. Flintlocks and powder could still be legally bought in Sierra Leone, and new markets might be found on the Liberian coast. Remnants of the *sofas,* under a warrior called Porekere, continued to move into Kuniki and Kono, ravaging an upland area which the British had hardly penetrated, where the Anglo French boundary remained an arbitrary line drawn on unreliable maps.

Lendy and the Frontier Police now saw an unanswerable case for military action – to attack the slaving *sofas,* assure their victims of British benevolence, and forestall any French claim to occupy territories ravaged by Samori. After bitter and prolonged argument in Freetown the Colonial Office, encouraged by the apparently salutary effects of military action in Ijebu (see below, pp. 120–2), overruled Governor

Fleming's continued preference for moral suasion and authorized a joint expedition by West Indian troops and Frontier Police to drive the *sofas* out of the British sphere. On 13 December 1893 a force of four hundred left its advanced base at Panguma in upper Mende to pursue Porekere into Kono. The main French army was now following Samori eastwards; but a detachment under the ambitious Lieutenant Maritz was also collecting treaties and pursuing Porekere in Kono. Early on 23 December Maritz attacked the British camp at Waima, which his Kono ally Kuria Wuria had told him was occupied by *sofas*. In a fierce and confused exchange of fire about a dozen of each force were killed, including Maritz, Lendy, and two other British officers.[89]

Apart from infuriating ultra-colonialists in Britain and France, and provoking prolonged wrangles over compensation, the Waima tragedy did not seriously affect the partition of West Africa. Five days later Porekere was killed by a Frontier Police detachment under a Creole sub-inspector, and the remaining *sofas* were quickly driven out of the British sphere. In March 1894 the pacific Governor Fleming was replaced by the vigorous Colonel Frederic Cardew, who began to organize the administration of a diminished Sierra Leone Protectorate, relying on the military discipline of the Frontier Police rather than on the Creole tradition of African diplomacy. Waima indeed hastened the final demarcation of the boundary. The conflicts between Kenney and Lamadon had confirmed the difficulty of locating frontiers on the basis of political geography, and strengthened the diplomatists' resolve to draw clear dividing lines regardless of African realities. Once recognition of the French protectorate over Samori had foreclosed any substantive British interest in the region, only hot-headed colonial patriots – or conceivably, Africans – would worry about details. "Far away from an African sun and its notoriously irritating influences, unexposed to the narrowing advice of narrowly jealous local authorities", diplomatists were seeking workable compromises;[90] Waima gave them added urgency. When in May 1894 Cardew suggested a revised boundary line which would pay greater attention to African political alignments and trade-routes and respect the integrity of Samu and Luawa chiefdoms, London recoiled from the prospect of further protracting argument and uncertainty.

> I sympathize strongly with Col. Cardew's desire not to divide the territory of Native Chiefs [wrote Lord Ripon, the Liberal Secretary of State]. It is a wretched system, unjust to the chiefs and their people, and a fruitful source of disputes and trouble to the dividing Powers. But of course we cannot deal with these matters as if the negotiations were to be entred upon for the first time.[91]

After unsuccessful attempts to incorporate the question in a wider Anglo-French settlement, a boundary was finally defined on 21 January 1895, and demarcated by new commissioners in April 1896.[92] Despite these rearguard actions by local officials, the British government had already lost its opportunity to make Freetown the great commercial port of the Western Sudan.

MERCHANTS PROTEST

Recalling how factious opposition in the French Chamber had prevented ratification of the Convention of 1882 (*Prelude*, pp. 289–94), the French and British governments had agreed to be discreet in publicizing their "arrangement" of 10 August 1889. After early requests for information by Liverpool merchants were turned aside by the Foreign Office,[93] it was brought into force by an exchange of notes in November; in France ratification was quietly completed by a Presidential Decree dated 12 March 1890. Meanwhile the text had been published as a British Parliamentary Paper on 13 February; it clearly attracted little attention, for two weeks later Sir George Baden-Powell asked in Parliament when the terms would become available. Since the principal Sierra Leone article simply confirmed the provisions of 1882, which had never been published in Britain,[94] and since no map was attached, its effect was not easy to understand. More spectacular events – the Anglo-Portuguese dispute in Nyasaland, the launching of Rhodes's British South Africa Company, Stanley's "relief" of Emin Pasha – were engaging the attention of the small section of the public interested in the partition of Africa; even the Chambers of Commerce were pre-occupied in ensuring that no Charter for the government of the Oil Rivers would be granted to the Niger Company or the African Association. Whereas the Declaration of 5 August 1890, allocating vast areas of little-known territory by the sweeping fiction of the Say-Barruwa line, required public defence by Salisbury in a notably ironical parliamentary statement, it seems that even the merchants concerned did not examine the turgid topographical detail of the Sierra Leone border until the Boundary Commission was preparing to mark it out.

On 15 October 1891 the Manchester Chamber of Commerce, apparently prompted by Parkes, wrote to the Colonial Office urging that the Commission should secure British control of the Niger crossing at Farana (and received a somewhat disingenuous reply); but it seems to have been Alfred Jones who first realized what British interests were at stake.[95] His initial alarm may have been raised by the threat which French protectorates on the Kru coast, and their possible further encroachments on Liberia, posed to the recruitment of seamen. Elder Dempster, which now controlled the agencies for both British steamship lines to West Africa, had already established an alliance with Woermann's which would in 1895 develop into a full-scale Shipping Conference; but French ship-owners remained outside this ring.[96] Jones's interest in the region also extended into the mainland. Working with influential associates he had recently taken over a far-reaching rubber concession in Liberia, and also the Sierra Leone Coaling Company. Besides providing fuelling facilities (supplied from Jones's Welsh collieries) that company was conducting a varied retail business in imported goods, and supplying Samori with firearms; it had recently made proposals to construct the dock which Freetown's excellent harbour still lacked, while Jones was actively interested in plans for a railway. At the same time as he was despatching Captain Williams from Liverpool on his quixotic mission to re-establish the alliance with Samori, Jones, with greater political realism, began to organize a united mercantile protest against the government's feeble responses to French expansion.[97]

Students of political activity by British Chambers of Commerce interested in African trade have recently been evaluating their response to the shorter and longer term problems revealed by the "Great Depression". Although individual Chambers frequently solicited the Foreign and Colonial Offices for modifications of tariff, diplomatic representations to foreign powers, military action to improve access to inland markets, and other interventions in the name of free trade, there had been few examples of a concrete mercantile front since the campaign against the Gambia exchange in 1876 (*Prelude*, pp. 186–9). Manchester pursued a particularly independent line, until 1890 usually that of J. F. Hutton; only in 1892 did it follow the example of the Liverpool and London Chambers by establishing a distinct West African section, and it did not join the Association of British Chambers of Commerce until 1898. In general it seems more realistic to regard the political initiatives of the Chambers as *ad hoc* responses to the latest difficulties reported by correspondents in Lagos or Freetown – interpreted, no doubt, in relation to prevailing interpretations of market trends or developing structural crises in the cotton industry – rather than as symptoms of some deep Wehlerian consensus over the danger of over-production.[98] The growing protectionist movement from agriculture and industry in metropolitan France, which in 1892 would culminate in the Méline tariff, was not primarily concerned to protect colonial interests, and sometimes worked against them.[99] But when seen in conjunction with French commercial policies in Guinea and the Ivory Coast, and with the attack on Samori, it can only have increased anxiety over British interests in the region.

On 18 November 1891 the Liverpool Chamber of Commerce addressed a printed Memorial to Lord Salisbury, urging that Samori's desire for British protection should be "taken into acount" by the forthcoming Sierra Leone Boundary Commission and praying that "no arrangement will be made with the French which may allow them, as at the Gambia, to limit those areas of trade that have been opened by British enterprise". Salisbury passed the responsibility for receiving a deputation to an unenthusiastic Colonial Office; a meeting was fixed for 8 December with Percy Anderson to represent the Foreign Office. Meanwhile the Manchester and Glasgow Chambers of Commerce added their own protests, and delegates from London and Birmingham also arranged to attend.[100]

It was therefore a formidable deputation of about sixty which on 8 December was ushered into Knutsford's office by W. H. Cross, a Liverpool MP and son of the Secretary of State for India. Twenty-eight of the members represented the Liverpool Chamber, and four others Jones's Sierra Leone Dock Company. Nine MPs were present – five Conservatives, three Liberals and one Liberal Unionist – and two peers.[101] African representatives – Archdeacon Henry Johnson of the Upper Niger, Cornelius May, editor of the *Sierra Leone Weekly News,* and Herbert Macaulay, a young engineering student from Lagos – attended to express their Empire Loyalism "as representatives of the native population". Spokesmen for Liverpool and Manchester opened the meeting by emphasizing the threat to Sierra Leone's commercial future from French expansion and French protectionism (and by reviving long-running grievances concerning property rights in Matacong). But Sierra Leone was set in a wider West African context. Although Goldie, who accompanied the deputation as a London representative, left early, and the Liverpool delegates assured Anderson privately that they were not worried about the Niger,[102] Frederick Swanzy (who had sold his Freetown interests in 1889) feared the effects on the Gold Coast of official French support for Verdier's claims to monopoly, and of German penetration towards Salaga. Others complained about the possible effects on the recruitment of Kru labour, as well as on trade and property rights, of French advances along the coast towards Liberia. Jones thus seems to have created a broad-based consciousness of British interests in danger.

Knutsford, replying from Hemming's brief, could offer little for the deputation's comfort, except documented assurances that the concessions recently accepted might have been worse. The partition of the Northern Rivers dated back to 1882 (and a Liberal government); the possibilities of inland penetration were unavoidably limited by France's treaties with Samori, which it would be imprudent to suggest could be abrogated by the African signatory: "if we once admitted the possibility of native chiefs setting aside agreements which have been solemnly entered into I think we should find ourselves, not only in West Africa but in territories south of the Zambezi, in a very awkward position". On the Ivory Coast likewise, British interests did not rest on formal treaties which could be opposed to French claims. But further east, where the British had always seen the brightest prospects, Knutsford could be more reassuring; Salaga had been neutralized, and in Borgu and Gurma it was the Niger Company which could produce treaties against possible European rivals.

These assurances did not mollify the Liverpudlians. Their Chamber continued to bombard the government with complaints of inadequate information, expressions of "astonishment and regret", and demands that areas where British trade predominated should be confirmed as British spheres of influence. Articles and letters in Liverpool newspapers warned the government that even loyal Conservatives could not tolerate such surrenders.[103] Clearly it was too late to improve matters at Sierra Leone; Jones's mission to Samori remained a spectacular piece of theatre. But the merchants' hackles were up. The Manchester Chamber belatedly set up an African section;[104] and on 25 February the Council of the Liverpool Chamber received the report of the deputation with forthright condemnations of government neglect which distressed loyal Conservative supporters. Liverpool now demanded the appointment of an Under-Secretary for Africa, to be assisted by a Consultative Council with mercantile members, and more energetic action to exclude foreigners from the Gold Coast and Lagos hinterlands.[105]

With an election pending, Salisbury felt obliged to respond. Liverpool was a government stronghold; in 1886 it had returned seven Conservative MPs out of nine, four of them unopposed. One of these, de Worms, was Colonial Under-Secretary; Sir George Baden-Powell was a diligent questioner on African topics; two other Members, Cross and W. F. Lawrence, had been on the deputation of 8 December, together with R. Neville, who held the Liberals' only Liverpool seat by a majority of seven votes. It is likely that the despatch of Imperial troops to Tambi in March was intended to satisfy these critics. Even more satisfactory to them was the military expedition which occupied Ijebu Ode in May, thus opening the way for Lagos to expand northwards while the French were still embroiled in Dahomey (see below, pp. 115–22). Government policy also began to change in the Gold Coast; Binger attributed his difficulties with Captain Lang to the arrival of new instructions inspired by the merchants. Certainly the despatch of G. E. Ferguson in April 1892 to seek treaties with the rulers of Dagomba, Gonja, Gurunsi and Mossi was a direct response to the fears of the Chambers.[106] There was of course no intention of seeking conflict with France – in July 1893 the Commissioners in Paris agreed on a clearer definition of the boundary up to the 9th parallel; but London was now prepared to allow the Gold Coast government to tighten its control of Asante with a view to further northward expansion (see below, p. 210). In the election of July 1892 these measures, though they did not prevent a narrow Liberal victory nationally, may have helped safeguard the Unionist base in Liverpool. Though the Liberal Neville raised his majority in Exchange from seven to sixty-six, Baden-Powell and Lawrence also improved their polls, and the five safe Unionist seats were held with majorities ranging from 16.8 per cent to 29.2 per cent.[107]

Salisbury had not changed his policy of conceding documented French claims in the extreme south-west; but he did now feel the need to explain it. On 21 December a long article justifying the concessions which had been made appeared in *The Times*; this bears much resemblance to a long despatch to the Paris Embassy which Percy Anderson began to draft shortly afterwards, and which was eventually laid before Parliament in June, just before its dissolution. Supposedly for the information of Constantine Phipps, a new Counsellor of Embassy who was about to take over responsibility for African negotiations, this despatch was really addressed to the interested public; backdated to 30 March, it was supplemented by copies of the Anglo-French agreements of 1882, 1889, 1890 and 1891, of correspondence concerning French annexations and tariff provisions on the Quaqua and Kru coasts, and of French treaties with Samori.[108] After comparing French preponderance in the western part of the region with British ascendency around the Niger delta and "the thriving Colonies of the Gold Coast and Lagos", Salisbury launched into a celebrated comparison between France's costly military expansion and Britain's "policy of advance by commercial enterprise".[109] Despite restraints imposed by the parliamentary Committee of 1865, he argued, British diplomacy had secured reasonable frontiers, and adequate safeguards for commercial interests; there was no evidence that British trade had yet suffered through interference with routes. Nevertheless the Embassy was publicly enjoined to ensure that safeguards against differential tariffs were secured in subsequent negotiations.

It was an eloquent despatch; but it was no longer quite good enough. Salisbury now recognized that British merchants might require stronger guarantees for the future than treaty clauses prohibiting formal discrimination by French authorities. *The Times* article of 21 December had identified Liberia as a country where "a very profitable field for English trade may yet be found"; and before leaving office in August Salisbury moved tentatively towards a more active policy in that Republic.

THE PRESSURE ON LIBERIAN INDEPENDENCE

After 1847 the Republic of Liberia was tolerated by both Britain and France, more out of diplomatic inertia than from any deep sympathy for the ideal of Negro independence; since the Monrovia authorities exercised little control outside the coastal settlements designated as "ports of entry", their territorial pretentions seemed an innocuous fiction. But as Britain and France consolidated their territories to north and south, an independent Liberia was liable to become a nuisance, offering routes for the evasion of colonial tariffs, and sanctuary for their African opponents. Other potential problems emerged when it became clear that the Brussels Conference might attempt to enforce a high minimum level of spirit duties, and a general embargo on imports of modern firearms. British officials quickly realized that an "impecunious and feeble Republic", however anxious to co-operate, would be incapable of enforcing such measures;[110] and the

French, with their highly specific interest in preventing Samori's arms-buyers from establishing new supply routes, were liable to take direct action to stop any leaks. The expanding claims to the Kru coast which Ballay and Binger advanced during the early 1890s represented a growing threat to Liberian independence – and so, indirectly, to Britain's future commercial prospects.

Economic constraints on Liberian independence seemed equally serious. Already heavily in debt from the usurious British loan of 1871, the Liberian oligarchy could see little hope of progress or even solvency unless it could attract foreign investment. Unlike colonial governments they could not appeal to a metropolitan Treasury to accept ultimate responsibility; they could only look to the United States, and more particularly to the meagre resources of Black Americans. This message was increasingly emphasized by Hilary R. W. Johnson, Liberia's first native-born president (1884–92). "At the present time", he declared in his message to the legislature of December 1889, "it is evident that the people of Liberia are more liberally disposed towards foreign enterprise and foreign capital than at any previous period in our history."[111] But the same address expressed concern about the terms on which foreign capital might be offered. A year later Johnson's message laid more emphasis on the dangers which would attend the expected "rush for concessions". Recalling his experiences as Secretary of State at the time of the 1871 loan, he warned that small states might find their funds "squandered or consumed by . . . so-called foreign friends . . . under the pretence of developing their alleged untold and inexhaustible resources", and that foreigners might seek power to control "the labour of free citizens".

Johnson himself still hoped that these dangers might be lessened if Liberia could rely on American supporters. For Negroes in the United States the 1890s held grim prospects of racial discrimination and conflict; lynchings and Jim Crow laws would reflect the delayed reaction of Southern racialists against defeat in the Civil War, and new tensions were being created by Negro immigration into Northern cities. Johnson was not alone in suggesting that release could only be found by a large-scale return to Africa.

> Whatever may be the individual opinions of the millions of our race abroad, the time appears to be approaching for the repatriation of them. Willingly or unwillingly, the most of them will have to return to the Fatherland. It is not necessary to speak of any special dispensation of Providence wrought to accomplish this object. The result will be reached through the operation of the ordinary laws of Nature.[112]

Black leaders like Bishop H. M. Turner (who was to visit Liberia and other parts of West Africa in 1891) were beginning to find support for the idea of mass emigration in certain Negro communities;[113] Black businessmen began to consider schemes for investment in Liberia, though they rarely possessed enough capital to carry them through. Earlier in 1890 Johnson had granted a railway concession to F. F. Whittekin of Tionesta, Pennsylvania on condition that he should "use his influence in promoting immigration of persons of Negro Race", whom he was to convey to settle the new lands which his railway would open up.[114]

The capitalists most likely to invest in Liberia, however, were whites, without sentimental attachment to the ideal of Negro independence. Several European trading and shipping firms were now represented at Monrovia; but most of them, like the important Hamburg house of Woermann,[115] were still content to operate under existing conditions, despite – or possibly because of – Liberia's administrative deficiencies. British bondholders of the 1871 loan however were beginning to despair of actually receiving the generous returns to which that sharp bargain seemed to entitle them, and to associate with businessmen interested in rapid exploitation of Liberia's resources of wild rubber. During 1889 the Liberian legislature granted a rubber concession to Benjamin L. Thomson and others, of London; but there was a dispute over the extent of the area involved.[116] In January 1890 this was replaced by a grant of exclusive rights to gather rubber on Liberian public lands, and to export all rubber wherever gathered, to a syndicate formed by Ellis Parr, L. A. Withall and Richard Pearson of London "and others who shall join them".[117] In March 1890 President Johnson travelled to London to sign this agreement; and he was shortly followed by Liberia's best-known citizen, Dr E. W. Blyden.

Though Johnson and Blyden were men of very different temperaments, who had long been political and academic rivals,[118] their views on Liberian policy at this time had much in common. While Johnson saw the encroachment of European political and economic influence, and the pressure to repatriate Afro-Americans, as inevitable, Blyden interpreted both developments as Providential confirmation of his own vision of Negro Africa regenerated. "Europe is rising", he had recently told a Washington congregation, "and her leading minds are contending for an international reparation to that continent for the wrongs inflicted upon her."[119] Like Johnson, Blyden knew that European capital and technology would be needed; but since he believed that the climate would always restrict European settlement, he believed it would have to be mediated through the agency of westernized Negroes in the coastal colonies. This spearhead of racial renewal would find a great broadening of opportunities as they carried modern civilization towards the established Muslim civilizations of the interior. Blyden therefore welcomed the focussing of European energies upon Liberia represented by the rubber concession; during his weeks in England he saw much of its promoters, encouraging their interest, (and also their idea of extending their activities to Sierra Leone in cooperation with Blyden's friend Samuel Lewis). "The men who have taken up this company", Blyden wrote ebulliently to an American patron, "are among the strongest in England, financially and socially. Several Members of Parliament have just become large shareholders."[120]

This was a characteristic exaggeration; but the syndicate formed in January had indeed transferred their concession to a new group, whose sponsors included the third Lord Raglan (1857–1921) and his brother-in-law the Honourable Arthur Cornwallis Ponsonby (1856–1918), fourth son of the seventh Earl of Bessborough and cousin to the Queen's Secretary. Ponsonby, who held a prosaic post as Inspector of Coal Cargoes at Cardiff, was undoubtedly acting on behalf of Alfred L. Jones, whose interest in Liberia has been noted. Woermann's, who were later to join Jones's shipping ring, also held shares in the Liberian Concessions Company until 1898.[121] Raglan and R. M. Maclean, another partner, visited Beriby in January 1891, presumably in connection with Kru recruitment; they were much alarmed by news of French activities in that area, and in June urged Salisbury to consider establishing a British protectorate over Liberia. The Foreign Office, disliking the company's attempts to exclude Sierra Leoneans from the developing rubber trade and trusting that American influence would save Liberia from foreign control, promptly turned this suggestion down.[122] But the company, having delivered an advance payment of £20,000 in bullion to the Liberian government, persisted. In November 1891 Ponsonby suggested to the Foreign Office that the incoming government of President Cheeseman might indeed be prepared to welcome a British protectorate.[123]

By now British officials were somewhat more alarmed by the prospect of French encroachment on Liberian independence, as well as by the prospect of more political sniping from the Chambers of Commerce. The War Office Intelligence Department, still concerned for the Freetown coaling-station, agreed that "it was of the very greatest importance that Liberia should not be occupied by any foreign naval or military power".[124] And the Colonial Office, aware of the growing merchant criticism, was disposed to encourage Ponsonby to explore the possibilities of a protectorate by offering informal assurances of governmental approval. "Liberia", wrote Hemming, "is undoubtedly a very rich country, which only wants steady development to become a most lucrative and thriving possession"; (moreover, the thrifty Lord Knutsford noted, its public revenues were actually showing a surplus). A French protectorate would not only prejudice the interests of British traders and bondholders, but would constitute "a grave source of Imperial danger in the event of war". British interests, officials believed, could be safeguarded without the responsibility or expenditure involved in annexation; Herbert spoke of making the Republic a protected state on an Indian or Malayan model. These various comments, judiciously edited to make their maximum impact, were printed as a proposal for submission to the Cabinet, and followed by a plaintive plea from Knutsford that something should be done to restrain the French.[125]

The plan did not reach cabinet level. Despite the mounting apprehensions of the merchants, Salisbury remained reluctant to become more deeply involved in West African responsibilities, and specifically sceptical about this supposed Liberian offer. His temperamental caution was reinforced by the analysis of Percy Anderson, who described Liberia as "a vain, inert, little state, with an undefined internal frontier and vast imaginary claims . . . to a hinterland up to the Niger". The purpose of inviting British protection would be to enlist support for these claims: the result for Britain, to "begin an awkward West African quarrel with France". But there were genuine dangers for British interests. Frustrated by lost territorial claims, Liberia might turn to France in search of a "protector", and "it would certainly not suit England to let Liberia become practically a French possession". Anderson hoped that an answer might be found by encouraging the United States to take a more active role in protecting Liberia against French encroachments; the ultimate result might be "a declared United States protectorate, which would keep Liberia neutral and make French aggression impossible". Meanwhile Britain might discreetly fortify the doctrine of Liberian sovereignty by encouraging her to adhere to the Berlin and Brussels Acts, and – Salisbury added – by inviting her to promise publicly not to seek any foreign protectorate. Such a policy seemed sufficiently positive to convince Knutsford that nothing more vigorous needed to be done.[126]

As the British imperial system came under increasing pressure during the 1890s, similar schemes of invoking American help to protect interests which the British government could no longer protect easily and cheaply for itself would be devised for other parts of the world; most of them, like this, proved to be abortive and premature. Ever since the original initiative of the American Colonization Society, the United States government had periodically expressed a general concern to support Liberia, using such phrases as "peculiar interest" and "quasi-parental relationship", and "next friend"; but whenever there was any question of an entangling commitment the tradition of continental isolationism proved too strong. During the 1880s some Americans had come to believe that their country might acquire a vicarious stake in the pending partition of Africa through Afro-American emigrants, supposedly well-equipped genetically and culturally; independent Liberia might thus serve as a useful surrogate for government action. A writer in the *New York Tribune* of 6 July 1891, for example, suggested that moral support for Liberia (in the form of direct steamship communication with New York, and the gift of a superannuated wooden warship) might be rewarded with rich commercial prospects.[127] But, as the British government soon discovered, it was far too early to expect the American government to make any active commitment to the cause of Liberian independence or the open door.

When the question of Franco-Liberian relations first arose in the 1880s, the American government saw its role as that of "conciliatory medium". In February 1886 their Minister in Paris solemnly declared that they took a "peculiar interest . . . of a moral character" in the independence and prosperity of Liberia; next year he repeated similar sentiments at greater length.[128] In 1890 the American representative at the Brussels Conference made a tardy and ineffective attempt to secure formal international recognition of Liberian independence, but a Liberian envoy to Washington apparently failed to get any specific assurance of support against France. Early in 1892 the State Department drafted a despatch refusing to recognize France's treaties on the Kru coast, but Secretary Blaine complained that this had been vetoed by President Harrison, who believed "that the Liberian colony is a failure and that the negroes are incapable of self-government". Instead the American Ambassador registered a somewhat formal protest on 13 July; its only effect was to make the French more anxious to resist the vaguely implicit doctrine of an American moral protectorate. Indeed the Americans, far from wishing to become Liberia's protector themselves, seem to have been quite willing to see the British undertake that role.[129]

The Liberian Anglophils now made another effort in that direction. In April 1892 Blyden was formally accredited as Minister to the Court of St James (Foreign Office officials having resolved their disdainful doubts as to whether such a state was entitled to diplomatic status).[130] As Ponsonby had already hinted, Blyden came prepared to seek a special relationship which would effectively establish British control over Liberia's foreign relations; on 2 June he offered Salisbury "special assurances relative to Customs Tariff and to the transit of goods", and communicated a resolution of the Liberian Senate declaring that "whereas the nations of Europe are forming plans for the partition among themselves of the Continent of Africa", Liberia would be willing to make a Treaty giving Britain the right to intervene, if requested, to defend her independence against foreign aggression.[131]

Although the Foreign Office received this overture cautiously, it did offer some hope of barring future French advances without too serious a commitment, and Clement Hill drafted a careful reply:

> successful commercial and other negotiations would naturally establish more intimate relations between the two countries . . . this result would be welcome to Great Britain. H M Government are convinced that confidence in the territorial integrity of Liberia and the independence of her actions are essential to her prosperity and progress. They would be quite ready to insert in a Convention a formal record of the interest which they take in the maintenance of that integrity and independence, which might take the form of an undertaking on the part of Great Britain to consider these to be a matter of special interest to her.
>
> In return for such an undertaking, it would obviously be necessary that Liberia should, on her part, undertake that no part of her territory would be ceded to any foreign power without the assent of Great Britain.

This cautious move towards commitment was approved by Salisbury and Hill's draft was laid before the Cabinet on 24 June. Lister was just about to prepare the letter for despatch to Blyden when Salisbury noticed that the draft had been sent to Ministers without any supporting or explanatory documentation; the Prime Minister saw that this rendered "the consultation . . . almost illusory" and insisted on waiting for more explicit Cabinet approval.[132] But the election-writs were moved on 28 June and the next cabinet was held under Gladstone's chairmanship; the prospects of securing even so guarded a commitment disappeared. When Anderson drafted a comprehensive statement of problems pending in the African Department for the new Foreign Secretary, he included no reference to Liberia;[133] instead Rosebery returned to the unpromising idea of seeking American collaboration in a general declaration of support for Liberian independence.[134]

So neither Liberia nor Britain could find a ready-made answer to the increasing French pressure during 1892. The boundary imposed by the Franco-Liberian agreement of 8 December was bitterly resented by the Americo-Liberians of Maryland County; under the presidency of Mayor J. H. Tubman they composed a rhetorical appeal to world opinion specifically calling on all civilized Negroes, wherever they may dwell" to show "an interest in Africa as your fatherland".

> We are not foreigners," [they claimed] we are Africans and this is Africa. Such being the case we have certain natural rights – God-given rights – to this territory which no foreigner can have. We should have room enough, not only for our present population, but also to afford a home for our brethren in exile who may wish to return to their fatherland and help us to build up this Negro nationality.[135]

This appeal, though reprinted and diffused at the expense of Liverpool merchants, found no effective response. The United States government did not regard the Treaty as prejudicing Liberia's sovereign rights, and without American co-operation the Foreign Office was prepared to do no more than seek assurances for the continued recruitment of Kru seamen.

And yet, international interest in Liberian independence had been demonstrated clearly enough to ensure that French diplomatists would restrain Binger's expansionist ambitions. The Quai d'Orsay wanted responsibility for Liberia no more than the British Foreign Office; only in 1896 would they even appoint a resident consular agent. As Samori moved further east the interest of the military in preventing arms imports through Liberia lessened. Meanwhile the Waima incident showed the need to define international frontiers in the region; and recognized frontiers implied at least provisional acceptance of Liberian independence. Reciprocally, British officers of the Frontier Police ambitious to extend their operations beyond the boundary of 1885 were restrained by fear that France might be provoked into counter-measures under article V of her treaty of 8 December 1892.[136] A mild form of "Hobbesian fear" thus led France and Britain to exercise a tacit self-denying ordinance towards Liberia, which later in the 1890s would be strengthened by shared fears of German intrusion.

NOTES

1. AE, Afrique 121, Etienne to Spuller, 23 July 1889.
2. ANSOM, Côte d'Ivoire I/2/a, Etienne to Treich-Lapleine, 9 November 1889. For fuller discussion of the problems of the colony, see P. Atger, *La France en Côte d'Ivoire de 1843 à 1893* (Dakar, 1962) Pt III.
3. Atger, *La France*. pp. 137–9.
4. B. Schnapper, *La politique et le commerce français dans le Golfe de Guinée, de 1843 à 1871* (1961) pp. 131–2, 158–9, 221, 226.
5. For accounts of this trade, see ANSOM Sénégal III/13/c, Report by Lt Hiart, November 1887; CO 879/32, CP African 389. no. 1 Bristol C of C to FO, 27 November 1889; no. 3 Hodgson to Knutsford, 29 November 1889.
6. Ibid., no. 10, Bristol C of C to FO, 2 January 1890; ANSOM, Côte d'Ivoire V/1/a, Report by Trobriant, 23 December 1889; Treich to Etienne, 15, 23 January 1890, Atger, *La France*, pp. 139–50.
7. T. C. Weiskel, *French Colonial Rule and the Baule Peoples* (Oxford, 1980) ch. I; also "The Pre-Colonial Baule: A Reconstruction", *CEA*, XVIII, no. 72, 1978.
8. ANSOM, Côte d'Ivoire XV/5/e, Societé d'Etudes de l'Ouest africain, Paris to Etienne, 7 July 1891. According to Person (*Samori*, III, p. 1671) this was another project by Verdier.
9. AE, Aff.Div. Pol. Afrique 7. Ballay Tel. 14 April 1891 and press-cuttings (esp. *Le Siècle*, 18 June); ANSOM Côte d'Ivoire V/1/b, Report by Lt Staup, 20 May 1891; Weiskel, "*French Colonial Rule*", pp. 38–40.
10. For historical and ethnographic references to the Kru, see Christine Behrens, *Les Kroumen de la Côte Occidentale d'Afrique* (Paris, 1974); George E. Brooks Jr, *The Kru Mariner in the Nineteenth Century* (Newark, Delaware, 1972); and A. Schwartz, "Quelques repères dans l'histoire des Kroumen", RFHOM, LXVII, 1980, pp. 151–5. Here the word Kru is used generally to cover coastal populations between Monrovia and Grand Lahou, including such distinct sub-groups as the Grebo.

11. CO 267/398, R. and W. King to FO, 9 February, 11 March 1892, encl. in FO to CO 4, 26 March; CO 879/32 CP African 389 no. 70, Griffith to Knutsford, Conf., 329, May 1890.
12. CP African 389 No. 10, King to FO, 3 December 1889. FO 84/1986, Memo by R. W. Brant (misplaced), 9 January 1890. FO 84/2008, CO to FO, 9 December 1889.
13. AE Afrique 121, MMC to MAE, 18 April 1886, 22 November 1887. Joelle Lassissi-Pinto, "Les Relations de la France et du Libéria", *Relations Internationales,* 18, 1979, pp. 131–47; also her *Mémoire de Maitrise,* "La France et le Libéria de 1880 à 1918: La Bataille pour un Territoire" (Paris-I, November 1978); Behrens, *Les Kroumen,* p. 88. For a summary of the British position, FO 403/129, Memo by Streatfield, 6 March 1890.
14. AE, Afrique 121, Etienne to Spuller, 16 April 1889.
15. ANSOM, Côte d'Ivoire I/2/a Etienne to Treich, 9 November 1889.
16. ANSOM, Dahomey III/1, Bayol to Etienne, 15 August 1889.
17. ANSOM, Missions 22, Etienne to Bidaud 4 September 1890, Bidaud to Etienne, 13 January 1891. CP, African 389, No 112, Griffith to Knutsford, Conf., 16 March 1891; cf F. J. Pedler, *The Lion and the Unicorn in Africa* (1974) pp. 229–30.
18. FO 84/2078, Admty to FO, 2 April 1890, encl. Ferris to Hay, 22 February with reports from Lt H. B. Rooper, HMS *Alecto.*
19. FO 84/2079, CO to FO, 11 April 1890, encl. Griffith to Knutsford, Conf., 27 February 1890. FO84/2080, CO to FO, 19 April 1890, encl. Griffith Conf., 10 March.
20. ANSOM, Missions 22 D'Arenberg to Etienne, 13 March 1891 and Minute; Etienne to Quiquerez and Segnozac, 3 March 1891.
21. Ibid. Confidential Note by Lt-Col Fix, 1891.
22. This account is based on the voluminous materials in ANSOM, Missions 22, notably: (1) Segonzac's report to Ballay, Conakry, 3 June 1891 (edited version in *JO,* 20 July, also in *Revue des Deux Mondes,* 107 1 September 1891, pp. 44–82); (2) Quiquerez, *Journal de Route* – copy supplied by his uncle and father-in-law, Lt-Col Fix, and largely set up in proof (edited version in *JO,* 31 July 1891). Fix inspired another published version, "Exploration Quiquerez à la Côte d'Ivoire", *RFECE,* XIV, no. 123, 1 August 1891, pp. 126–36 – to the embarrassment of the Colonial Department, which was not ready to publicize these treaties (see n. 25 below).
23. ANSOM, Missions 22, Quiquerez to Fix, sd.
24. Quiquerez's family refused to accept Segonzac's story; eventually a bullet was found in the dead officer's skull. Segonzac was charged with murder before a Dakar court-martial in October 1893 and acquitted, pleading that he suppressed the truth of Quiquerez's suicide to save the family pain. *BCAF,* III, 1893, p. 3.
25. Ballay's report is in AE, M and D Afrique 127, ff. 95 ff, Etienne to Ribot, 21 July 1891. The treaties on which the French based their diplomatic claims are listed in d'Estournelles to Salisbury, 26 October 1891; these include five signed by Quiquerez, one by Bidaud, and two

by Ballay (with Buggery and Mané). Only on 30 December did they produce Quiquerez's treaties with Mané's supposed subordinates. Ian Brownlie (ed.), *African Boundaries: a Legal and Diplomatic Encyclopedia* (1979) pp. 360–2. Some texts may be found in F. J. Amon d'Aby, *La Côte d'Ivoire dans la Cité africaine* (1951).

26. ANSOM, Côte d'Ivoire III/2/c, report by Lt Utier, 31 December 1892; Côte d'Ivoire IV/2/d, Report by Voisin, 1 August 1894.
27. ANSOM, Côte d'Ivoire XIV/1, Desaille to Cousturier, 258, 30 October 1891.
28. AM, BB4 1992, Report by Lt Le Bric, 9 February 1893. For wider background to French recruitment problems, Behrens, *Les Kroumen*, pp. 75–80.
29. CO 879/32, CP, African 389, no. 42, FO to CO, 26 March 1890.
30. CO96/208, Hemming minuté, 4 February 1890, on Hodgson Tel., 3 February.
31. CO96/213, Herbert minute, 21 February 1890, on FO to CO, 14 February.
32. CP, African 389, no. 14, Moloney to Meade Pte, 19 January 1890; no. 19, Hodgson to Knutsford Tel., 3 February; No. 40 Hay to Knutsford Conf. 6, 24 February 1890; no. 44, CO to FO, 8 April. CO96/213, Hemming minute, 27 February on FO to CO, 14 February (cf CO267/391, Minute by Hemming on FO to CO, 7 November 1891).
33. FO84/2079, CO to FO, 11 April 1890, minutes by Anderson, 22 April, Sanderson. FO84/2081, CO to FO, 3 May 1890; Minute by Lister, 6 May, note by Sanderson.
34. Texts in I. Brownlie, *African Boundaries*, pp. 360–3.
35. CP, African 389, no. 112, Griffith to Knutsford, Conf., 16 March 1891; CO267/398, R. and W. King to FO 2, 11 March 1892, in FO to CO 4, 26 March.
36. FO 84/2295 Woodin to FO, 23 September 1892, encl. "Indenture" of 28 October 1891; ANSOM Côte d'Ivoire IC/6/d, Jamais to Woodin, 7 November 1892: compare the three drafts in XV/6/b; ANSOM, Missions 22, Fix to Jamais, 26 December 1892, encl. Fix to Woodin, 7 December, Woodin to Fix, 17 December.
37. ANSOM, Côte d'Ivoire IV/1/a, Binger to Delcassé, 320, 12 October 1893; Côte d'Ivoire VI/2, Beckmann to Delcassé, 282 Conf. 11 August 1893, encl. Harvey to Beckmann, 24 July, with PS by Williamson.
38. *Prelude*, p. 243.
39. AE, Afrique 121, Ballay to Etienne, Tels., 8 May, 21 September. Ribot to Etienne, Etienne to Ribot, 28 January 1892. Jamais to Ribot, 18 March 1892.
40. J. D. Hargreaves, "Liberia: the Price of Independence", *Odu* ns 6, 1971, pp. 13–14; for text of the treaty, I. Brownlie, *African Boundaries*, pp. 363–4.
41. ANSOM, Missions 5, Rapports au SSEC, conf. 3, 6 September 1890; Monteil to Etienne, 9 August; Etienne to Menard, 12 September, 3 October; Binger to Ménard, n.d.; Ménard to Etienne, 13 November 1890.

42. Ibid., Ménard to Etienne (Bettié) 18 December 1890. For an appreciation of the situation in the region two years later, see Braulot's report in ANSOM, Côte d'Ivoire III/3.
43. On the complexities of Gyaman, see Person, *Samori*, III, pp. 1691–4; I. Wilks, *Asante in the Ninteenth Century* (Cambridge, 1975) pp. 287–97; and for a revealing contemporary account, R. A. Freeman, *Travels and Life in Ashanti and Jaman* (1898).
44. Person, *Samori*, III, pp. 1546–8, 1642–3; ANSOM, Missions 5, Ménard to Etienne (Sakhala), 7 December 1891.
45. ANSOM, Côte d'Ivoire III/3, Binger report, f. 8.
46. FO84/2208, Minute by Salisbury on Phipps to Anderson, Pte 22 April 1892.
47. ANSOM, Côte d'Ivoire III/3, Binger to Jamais, 20 October 1892; Person, *Samori*, III, pp. 1644–5.
48. ANSOM, Côte d'Ivoire III/3, Braulot report, undated.
49. ANSOM, Côte d'Ivoire VI/2, Lennoy de Bissy to Jamais, 17 May 1892, encl. Marchand (copy), 7 February 1892.
50. AE, ADP, Afrique 7, Delcassé to Develle, 1 March 1893, encl. Marchand *projet*.
51. Marchand's report of 20 December 1894, and other papers, are in ANSOM, Missions 8. See also Weiskel, *French Colonial Rule*, pp. 41–8; Person, *Samori*, III, pp. 1646–52.
52. Marchand report of 20 December 1894; Weiskel, *French Colonial Rule*, pp. 48–56. Person, *Samori*, III, p. 1565.
53. See ANSOM, Côte d'Ivoire XIV/1 and AE, ADP Afrique 7, *Recrutement de Kroumen*.
54. ANSOM, Côte d'Ivoire VI/2, Binger to Delcassé, 5i, 6 January 1894.
55. *Ibid.*, Binger to Delcassé, 5 January 1894.
56. *Ibid.*, Binger to Delcassé, Tel., 12 February; 14, 27 February: Delcassé to Binger, 24 February 1894.
57. *Ibid.*, Binger to Delcassé, Conf., 26 November 1894.
58. SLA. Aborigines Letter Book, Parkes to Col. Sec., Ab 249, 13 July 1889; CO 267/377, Foster to Knutsford, 299, 19 July 1889.
59. Memo by Hay, "Protection to Producing Areas", 8 April 1890 (SL *Royal Gazette*, 1890, pp. 71–2); SLA, Native Affairs Confidential Letter Book (NALB), Parkes to Hay, Ab. Conf. 11, 28 May 1890; cf J. D. Hargreaves, "The Evolution of the Native Affairs Department", SLS n. s. 3 (1954) pp. 177–9; "The Creoles and the Expansion of Sierra Leone: a sub-imperialism manqué", in *Etudes offertes à Henri Brunschwig* (Paris, 1982).
60. CO 267/381, minute by Meade, 1 April 1890, on Hay 75, 28 February, encl. Alldridge report; cf CO 267/383, minute by Hemming on Hay 249, 6 June 1890.
61. CO 267/379, Minute by Hemming, 3 December 1889 on WO 29 November; CO 879/32, CP African 387, no. 2c, Knutsford to Maltby, 1 January 1890; no. 35a, Hay to Knutsford, Conf. 7, 25 February 1890. See also A. Abraham, *Mende Government and Politics under Colonial Rule* (Freetown, 1978) pp. 90 ff.

62. A. M. Howard, "The Relevance of Spatial Analysis for African Economic History: the Sierra Leone–Guinea System", *JAH,* XVII, 1976, pp. 365–85; B. Harrell-Bond, A. M. Howard, D. E. Skinner, *Community Leadership and the Transformation of Freetown* (The Hague, 1978) pp. 20–6.
63. The best summary of this complex situation is in Person, *Samori,* II, pp. 630–5, 1183 ff. cf D. Skinner, *Thomas George Lawson* (Stanford, 1980) pp. 77–8.
64. CO 879/34, CP African 408, encl. 1 in no. 78, Arabic letter from Alikali and others.
65. AE, Afrique 129, Etienne to Ribot, 23 October, 14 November 1890; Person, *Samori,* II, pp. 1187–91.
66. AE, Afrique 130, Lamadon, 1 March 1892: also his final report. Kenney's reports are in CP African 422, esp. nos 81, 32. For a judicious summary, Person, *Samori,* II, pp. 1203–6.
67. CO 879/32, CP African 387, No 35a, Hay to Knutsford Conf. 7, 24 February 1890, encl. instructions to Garrett and Alldridge, 20 February; Memo by Parkes. For fuller discussion of Garrett's mission, Person, *Samori,* II, 1174–8.
68. Ibid. nos 77, 80, Garrett reports, 25 March, 1 April, 11 April encl. in Hay, 135, 12 April; Conf. 23, 24 April 1890. See also the extracts from Garrett's diary in T. J. Alldridge, *A Transformed Colony* (London, 1910); references to Momodu Wakka on pp. 301, 305, 310, cf NALB, Hay to Garrett, Ab. Conf. 7, 12 April 1890: Person, *Samori,* II, p. 1186. See also C. M. Fyle, *The Solima Yalunka Kingdom* (Freetown, 1979).
69. Alldridge, *Transformed Colony*, 312–27; CP African, 387, nos 115, 125, Garrett reports 8 June, 8 July 1890.
70. CP African 387, no. 80, Hay to Knutsford, Conf. 23, 24 April 1890.
71. Ibid., no. 114, Hay to Knutsford Tel., no. 124, Hay to Knutsford, Secret, 10 July 1890.
72. The following policy arguments may be followed in CP African 387, no. 99, Memo by Brackenbury, 6 June, encl. in CO to FO 18 June (based on Hemming's minute on Hay. Conf. 24, 28 April, in CO 267/382); no. 118, CO to FO, 24 July; no. 127, FO to CO, 2 August; no. 136, WO to CO, 22 August; no. 140, CO to FO, 4 September 1890.
73. Ibid., no. 136, Brackenbury to CO, 22 August 1890; cf CO 267/384, Minute by Antrobus of conversation with Garrett, 23 August on Hay Tel. 23 August 1890.
74. CO 267/382, Minute by Meade on Hay, Conf. 136, 30 May 1890.
75. CO 267/387, Minutes by Hemming, 10 August 1890, on FO 2 August by Meade, 28 August on WO 22 August.
76. CO 879/34 CP African 408, Nos 29, 47, 48, Hay to Knutsford Conf. 7, 15, 16; 31 January, 10 April, 11 April, 1891.
77. FO 84/2028, Lytton to Salisbury, 156 Af, 14 November 1890, encl. Egerton 13 November, and minute by Anderson; CP African 408, No. 56, FO to CO, 15 May 1891; Hertslet, *Map of Africa,* II, pp. 743–4, Agreement, signed at Paris, 26 June 1891.

78. CO 879/35, CP African 422, no. 11, Crooks to Knutsford, Conf. 40, 21 December 1891.
79. CO 267/388, Minute by Hemming, 19 February 1891 on Hay Conf. 4, 23 January; CO 267/391, Minute by Hemming on FO, 16 November 1891. CP African 408, No. 134, CO to FO, 25 November, 1891.
80. Cf above, vol. I, pp. 182–3. For Freetown Muslims, see B. Harrell-Bond *et al., Community Leadership*, pp. 88–94.
81. Parkes' views may be followed in the Confidential NALB; cf his memos of 28 April, 10 July 1890 in CP African 387, nos 82, 126.
82. NALB, Parkes to Quayle-Jones, NA Conf. 1, 27 January 1892; see also C. M. Fyle, *Almamy Suluku of Sierra Leone* (1979).
83. CO 267/394, Quayle-Jones to Knutsford, 147, 16 April 1892, encl. Parkes, NA Conf. 2 and 3, 11, 16 April. For Vonjo's war, Person, *Samori*, II, pp. 1212–15.
84. CO 879/35, CP African 422, no. 81, Report by Kenney, 24 May 1892; no. 112, Quayle-Jones to Knutsford, 208, 16 May 1892, encl. letter from Samori and report by Momodu Wakka.
85. Ibid. nos 91, 92, Elder Dempster to CO 14, 15 June 1892. See also Person, *Samori*. II, pp. 1215–20, and III pp. 2104–6 for the text of the concession.
86. CO 267/398, FO to CO, 29 June 1892. Salisbury Papers, A 59, Nos 49, 56, 57, 108. Dufferin to Salisbury, 8, 30 June, 1 July 1892; Salisbury to Phipps, Tel. 2 July. D 32, Salisbury to Knutsford 2 July; E. Knutsford to Salisbury, 4 July 1892.
87. CO 267/397, African SS Co to CO 3 December 1892, CO 267/399, FO to CO, 22 November.
88. Minutes by Hemming, 22 November 1892 (on CO 267/399, FO 22 November), 23 November (on CO 267/396, Fleming Conf. 31, 22 October).
89. The definitive account is Y. Person, "L'aventure de Porèkèrè et le drame de Waima", CEA, V, 1965, 248–316, 472–89. A lively but often inaccurate account from British sources is B. Freestone, *The Horsemen from Beyond* (1981).
90. CP African 422, no. 88, Phipps to Dufferin, 30 May 1892.
91. CO 267/409, Cardew to Ripon Conf. 38, 23 May 1892; Minute by Ripon, 27 June.
92. Hertslet, *Map of Africa*, II, pp. 757–9, Agreement of 21 January 1895; Procès-Verbal 9, 30 April 1896.
93. FO 84/2003, Minute by Anderson on CO, 23 September 1889; FO 84/2008, Minute by Anderson on CO, 4 December 1889.
94. FO 84/2179, Lp C of C to FO, 20 November 1891 and Minutes.
95. McC of C to CO, 15 October 1891, CO to Mc C of C, 27 October; Elder Dempster to CO 6 November 1891.
96. P. N. Davies, *The Trade-Makers: Elder Dempster in West Africa 1852–1972* (London, 1973) ch. 3.
97. For the Sierra Leone Coaling Company, CO 267/392, Ponsonby to CO, 29 May 1891, and Minute by Hemming 11 June. Davies, *Trade-Makers* p. 433 prints an advertisement, not publicizing their

arms business. For Jones's other activities, P. N. Davies, *Sir Alfred Jones: Shipping Entrepreneur par Excellence,* esp. ch. III; above, p. 74; below, pp. 86–7.

98. This account follows B. M. Ratcliffe, "Commerce and Empire: Manchester Merchants and West Africa, 1873–1895", *JICH*, VII, 1979, rather than W. G. Hynes, *Economics and Empire* (1979) and "British Mercantile Attitudes towards Imperial Expansion", *HJ* 19, 1976. See also A. Redford and B. W. Clapp, *Manchester Merchants and Foreign Trade* (Manchester 1956) p. 104.
99. For the relationship between French protectionism and the colonial movement, see H. Brunschwig, *Mythes et Réalités,* ch. 6 and C. W. Newbury, "The Tariff Factor in Anglo-French West African Partition", in P. Gifford and Louis, *France and Britain in Africa* (New Haven, 1971), pp. 238–40.
100. CO 267/392, Lp C of C to CO 18 November, 2 December 1891, McC of C to FO, 24 November 1891, minutes by Hemming, Herbert. FO 84/2179, Glasgow C of C to FO 26 November 1891.
101. The official record of the deputation is in CO 879/35, CP African 421. The names of those attending are taken from the reprint of the *Memorial to Lord Salisbury* by the Liverpool Chamber (copy in Rhodes House Library.) The MPs were W. H. Cross, Sir James Bain, C. W. Mills, H. Kimber, W. F. Lawrence (Cons); A. Provand, P. McLagan, R. Neville (Liberal); A. C. Corbett (L. U.). Two other MPs are mentioned as intending to attend in Lp C C to CO, 5 December 1891 (CO 267/392) – Sir Alfred Rollitt and Sir Edward J. Harland (two Conservatives with shipping interests): also Lord Brassey, secretary to the Admiralty under Gladstone, 1884–5.
102. FO 84/2180, Note by Anderson, 9 December 1891.
103. See the collection of cuttings in CO 267/392.
104. Ratcliffe, "Commerce and Empire", p. 296.
105. CO 267/397, L/p C of C to CO, 25 February, 9 April 1892, enclosing *Affairs of the West African Colonies. Report of the Committee of the African Trade Section*. These are only two of their many letters in this volume; cf Hynes, *Economics*, pp. 119–21.
106. ANSOM, Côte d'Ivoire, III/3, Binger report, f. 28; CO 267/397, Minute by Knutsford on L/p C of C 9 Ap. 1892: "We are dealing with the hinterland of the Gold Coast", cf R. E. Dumett, "British Official Attitudes", p. 170.
107. W. S. Craig, *British Parliamentary Election Results, 1885–1918* (1974).
108. PP 1892, LVI, C 6701, Papers relative to Arrangements between Great Britain and France respecting West Africa, June 1892. Drafts are in FO 84/2205; also CO 267/395, FO to CO, 17 March 1892.
109. See the independent comments on this passage by C. W. Newbury (pp. 222–3), J. D. Hargreaves (pp. 261–3), and A. S. Kanya-Forstner (pp. 409–10) in P. Gifford and W. R. Louis (ed.), *France and Britain in Africa* (New Haven, Coun., 1971).
110. FO 84/2007, Copy, Minute by Hemming, 5 November 1889; FO 84/2072, ff. 157 ff. Note of Meeting at CO, 8 January 1890.

111. Copy in FO 84/2076, ff. 198–201.
112. FO 84/2132, Johnson's message to the Legislature, 15 December 1890. The following pages incorporate a revised version of parts of John D. Hargreaves, "Liberia: the Price of Independence", *Odu*, n s 6, October 1971, pp. 3–20.
113. Cf E. S. Redkey, *Black Exodus: Black Nationalist and Back-to-Africa Movements, 1890–1910* (New Haven, Conn., 1969).
114. Proclamation by Johnson, 18 June 1890, in FO 84/2039.
115. The growth of Woermann's interests is traced in P. E. Schramm, *Deutschland und Übersee* (Braunschweig, 1950) pp. 236–43.
116. FO 84/2076, Johnson's message to the Legislature, 30 December 1889.
117. Act of 21 January 1890; copy in FO 84/2039.
118. According to M. B. Akpan, "The African Policy of the Liberian Settlers, 1841–1932" (PhD thesis, University of Ibadan, 1968), Blyden's section of the Whig Party emphasized racial exclusiveness, while Johnson's, though opposing the old mulatto oligarchy, worked for unity within the Americo-Liberian community. See also H. R. Lynch, *Edward Wilmot Blyden* (London, 1967); and, for Blyden's attitude to the comming partition, Ian Duffield, "Imperialism . . . as viewed by some early Pan-Africanists", in *The Theory of Imperialism and the European Partition of Africa* (University of Edinburgh, 1967); John D. Hargreaves, "Blyden of Liberia", *History Today*, August 1969.
119. E. W. Blyden, *The Elements of Permanent Influence*. Discourse delivered in the Fifteenth Street Presbyterian Church, Washington DC, Sunday 16 February 1890 (Washington, 1890) p. 14.
120. Blyden to Coppinger, 9 April 1890, quoted Edith Holden, *Blyden of Liberia* (NY, 1968) pp. 626–8.
121. See above, p. 78; D. M. Foley, "British Policy in Liberia, 1862–1912" (PhD thesis, University of London, 1965) ch. 2.
122. CO 879/35, CP African 418, no. 2, FO to CO, 16 July 1891, encl. Raglan, Ponsonby and Maclean to FO, 16 June; FO to Ponsonby, 14 July 1891; CO 267/387, FO to CO, 17 July 1890, encl. Hay 6 and 7, 10 June 1890.
123. FO 84/2041, Ponsonby and Raglan to FO, 14 May 1890; CO 537/11, Ponsonby to Hemming, 10, 11 November 1891.
124. CO 537/11, E. F. Chapman (WO) to Hemming, 20 November 1891.
125. CO 537/11, Memoranda by Hemming, Herbert, De Worms and Knutsford, 19 November 1891; an edited version is Conf. Print African (West) 421a, CO 879/35, FO 84/2270, Knutsford to Sanderson, 5 February 1892.
126. CO 537/11, Anderson to Sanderson, 8 February; Sanderson to Knutsford, 13 February; Knutsford to Hemming, 14 February 1892.
127. ANSOM, Afrique VI/95, article enclosed in MAE to SSEC, 22 July 1891. For compilations of anodine statements by the US Government, see FO 403/129, Memo by Streatfield, 12 March 1890 and R. W. Bixler, *The Foreign Policy of the United States in Liberia* (NY, 1957) chs 1 and 2.

128. Bixler, *Foreign Policy* . . . pp. 18–20; Lassissi-Pinto, "La France et le Liberia", pp. 27 ff; AE, Afrique 121, McLane to Freycinet, 3 February 1886, McLane to Flourens, 16 April 1887.
129. CO 879/35 African 418. nos 2, 11. FO to CO, 16 July, 3 September 1891: CO 267/398, FO to CO May 1892, encl. Pauncefote, 28 April; 9 August encl. Phipps 204, Conf. 1 August 1892. AE Afrique 121, Bohn to Jamais, 2 June 1892; Coolidge to Ribot, 13 July 1892; Note pour le Ministre, 30 July 1892.
130. FO 84/2270, Minutes by Bergne, Lister, on Blyden to FO, 25, 29 April 1892.
131. FO 84/2270, Ponsonby to Lister, 3 April 1892; Blyden to Salisbury, 25 April; Salisbury to Blyden, 28 May, Blyden to Salisbury, 2 June 1892 (printed in Holden, op. cit. pp. 639–41).
132. FO 84/2270, Draft to Blyden, June 1892; minutes by Salisbury and Lister. Blyden's overture was not even communicated to the Colonial Office until September; see CO 267/398, FO to CO, 16 September 1892.
133. FO 84/2256, "Notes for the African Department"; draft by Rosebery, annotations by Hill.
134. CO 267/398, FO to CO, 8 September 1892.
135. *France versus Liberia.* Statement and Appeal by the Citizens of Maryland County (Liverpool, 1893). Copy in CO 267/405, FO to CO, 25 August 1893, with enclosure from Liverpool C of C.
136. Foley, "British Policy", cf M. McCall, "Kai Lundu's Luawa and British Rule" (DPhil thesis, Univ. of York, 1974); above p. 60.

9 Towards British Nigeria

The British policy of "advance by commercial enterprise", which Salisbury's public despatch of 30 March 1892 was written to justify, had been the natural response of liberal statesmanship towards an undeveloped region of moderate importance. Since 1884 adequate diplomatic cover had been created to protect the dominant position which British capital and enterprise had secured around the lower Niger, long assumed to be the region's richest sector; elsewhere British governments had not judged the national interest great enough to justify much exertion or sacrifice. Towards the one strategic asset of Freetown harbour they had pursued a policy of "defence by partition", and the agreements of 1889 and 1895 seemed to secure an adequate landward perimeter;[1] they preferred to meet the threat of French protectionism by negotiating continuing rights of access for British trade in French colonies rather than by territorial claims which would carry heavy financial and military commitments.

But although the belated mercantile pressure of 1891 did not shake Salisbury's confidence in what had been done for the Gambia and Sierra Leone, it did have an effect on British policy in areas of more substantial interest further east. Gradually more active measures were adopted here, stimulated by irritation at French provocations, and by new perceptions of domestic political expediency. Attitudes towards the exercise of imperial power in Africa were also changing in Great Britain.

"SOCIAL IMPERIALISM": BRITISH STYLE

Earlier chapters of this work have suggested that mid-Victorian interventions in West Africa did not represent any consistent imperial policy, but improvised responses to perceived needs. Until the 1890s the British public could assume that commerce and civilization would continue to advance – erratically no doubt, but without major conflict – because Afro-European relations were governed by certain "stabilizing factors". "The imperialism of free trade" worked well while the world continued to demand African agricultural and mineral products in exchange for imported consumer goods; while political authorities in Africa were willing and able to encourage such exchanges; and while other Europeans remained content to operate under a regional *pax* based on British naval hegemony.[2] As these conditions weakened, moral suasion backed by occasional limited interjections of military force seemed a less satisfactory way to secure British interests. Hitherto, provided that the reasonable local requirements of merchants and missionaries could be satisfied, the public at large had complacently assumed that British power served the edifying purposes of advancing civilization and combatting the slave trade. But as confidence in the natural progress of civilization declined, Victorians began to expect less from their African collaborators and to demand more positive action from their own governments.

By 1890, hopes that the modernization of Africa might be successfully achieved through indigenous responses to Christianity, civilization and commerce were largely extinct; too many African societies had either rejected these challenges or responded to them in unacceptable ways (cf. vol. I, pp. 1–15). Those anxious to induce change were therefore re-examining their intellectual and ideological assumptions. Some effects of this process on the work of the Church Missionary Society were particularly evident to African Christians. British evangelicals now invested fewer hopes in the possibilities of "native agency"; the missionaries of the later 1880s, with their uncompromising standards of spirituality and morality formed at Keswick or at Cambridge, regarded an extended period of foreign tutelage as essential for the regeneration of an impure Church and a heathen continent.[3] This new perspective was shared by many secular rationalists, convinced that improvement would only come to Africa through the coercive power of superior races, sanctioned by the authority of science. As well-to-do Victorians became more aware of the gulf between their perceptions of African "savagery" and of their own urbane society they began to draw conclusions about racial difference which in the 1890s would be elaborated by "Social Darwinians".[4]

It is doubtful however whether racial theory counted for as much as simple moralism, whether Christian or secular. Nobody displayed the case for the forcible reformation of Africa more powerfully than free-thinking soldiers and travellers like A. B. Ellis, Richard Burton and Winwood Reade. As early as 1872 Reade had predicted that the unhappy history of Africa would be redeemed, not by any supernatural intervention, but by the triumph of Science and Reason; though even religion, this militant atheist argued, might "yet render service to civilization in assisting to Europeanize the barbarous nations whom events will in time bring under our control".[5] Successive editions of *The Martyrdom of Man* appear to have had more influence on men actually engaged in African expansion (like Harry Johnston) than the amorphous social theorising of Benjamin Kidd.[6]

Increasingly, then, those who sought development and improvement in Africa, whether out of secular or Christian concern, came to favour more vigorous use of British power. Patriotic pride had always been a strong emotion among supporters of missionary or philanthropic enterprise.[7] In the reviving anti-slavery movement, although the old school of philanthropists represented by Henry Fox Bourne of the Aborigines Protection Society remained instinctively distrustful towards secular authority, those who were most moved by the passionate pleading from eastern Africa of men like Mackay increasingly favoured the use of force in the name of justice and humanity. Men whose religious and philosophical beliefs had little in common except an intensely moralistic patriotism began to see the expansion of the Empire and the "elevation of inferior races" as a solemn duty, often a personal challenge. Frederick Lugard, agnostic son of missionary parents, who landed at Mombasa in 1889 as the military agent of the Imperial British East Africa Company, may in retrospect seem to personify that shallow moral consensus which would eventually provide an ethical code for the rulers of a British African empire.[8]

Since the new imperialist ethic was invariably expressed

with intense national pride, it soon began to affect the language of political controversy. Since the Parliamentary reform of 1867 aspiring politicians had begun to learn that patriotism could provide a most valuable source of "texts" from which to address an enlarged but still potentially deferential electorate.[9] As far back as the Abyssinian expedition of 1867–8, it has been powerfully argued, Disraeli may be observed attempting, not only to assert British power and prestige in an increasingly competitive world, but to use that assertion as a means to secure political unity in a nation potentially divided by class conflicts.[10] After 1874, Disraeli in office experimented further with this political tactic, applying it not to African colonies (cf. *Prelude*, pp. 169–89) but to the prolonged Near Eastern crisis which introduced the word 'jingoism' to the English language. In the election of 1880 imperialist rhetoric did not prove a winning card, and in 1885–6 it was directed principally towards Ireland; nevertheless perceptive politicians began to apply the new intellectual perspectives – and the older concern to maintain national 'prestige' (vol. I, pp. 28–30) – to problems created by "destabilisation" in Africa. Joseph Chamberlain, whose first intention in the "Suez crisis" of 1882 was to guide and support any "legitimate expression . . . of resistance to oppression", quickly became a powerful advocate of forcible British intervention, not only in Egypt but elsewhere.[11]

His fellow radical Dilke was simultaneously extending British territorial claims in west and east Africa. (*Prelude*, p. 304). John Seeley's Cambridge lectures on *The Expansion of England*, first published in 1883, inspired Lord Rosebery's growing attachment to "the cause of real patriotism and the essential unity of the empire",[12] as well as his political perception that "the democracy are just a vitally interested as any other portion of the State, if only for the purposes of commerce, in the maintenance of the name and of the honour of Great Britain".[13] From about 1892 younger politicians, seeking to win votes without subverting the social order, increasingly aligned themselves either with Rosebery, as Liberal Imperialists, or with Chamberlain, as imperially minded Unionists; divergences between these groups came to centre on the economic and fiscal policies appropriate to an expanded and consolidated British Empire, rather than on the social and political relevance of expansion itself.[14] Slightly later than in France and Germany, the politics of social imperialism were developing in Great Britain also.

Lord Salisbury, whose statesmanship always combined a realistic concern for concrete national interests with a deflationary scepticism towards vulgar rhetoric, had little sympathy for creeds of indiscriminate imperial expansion. In a well-known speech of 10 July 1890, defending the exchange of Heligoland for German concessions in eastern Africa, he drew sensibly pragmatic conclusions from the changing African situation.[15]

> Up to 10 years ago we remained masters of Africa practically, or the greater part of it, without being put to inconvenience by protectorates or anything of that sort, by the simple fact that we were masters of the sea, and that we have had considerable experience in dealing with the native races . . . we left enormous stretches of the coast to the native rulers in the full confidence that they would go on under native rulers, and in the hope that they would gradually acquire their own proper civilisation without any interference on our part.

But the interference of other powers made it impossible to rely on policies of "masterly inactivity" underpinned by diplomacy, or to expect "the pacific invasion of England" to bring about gradual progress;[16] it had become "impossible that England should have the right to lock up the whole of Africa, and say that nobody should be there except herself". Negotiation and compromise, without grandiloquent rhetoric, might ensure that partition took place with minimum damage, not only to British commercial prospects, but to relationships with her European neighbours. Yet even Salisbury recognized that it would become increasingly necessary publicly to justify compromise to sections of British society who believed their interests might be affected, and to those whom they might persuade to support them.

Salisbury's biographer tells us that he did not favour discussing overseas policy before public audiences, except in the formal setting of Guildhall or Mansion House; it was a subject, he believed, "about which we must all think a great deal and speak very little".[17] He nevertheless knew that Imperial, even more than European, policy had to reflect concerns of the electorate. His own perceptions of national interest and public opinion meant that when Salisbury began to pursue more vigorous African policies priority, after Egypt, was given to the south and east of the continent. There was, as Fergusson had confirmed in August 1888, widespread humanitarian revulsion against the internal slave trade of this region (see p. 5); and many Christians were deeply concerned for the safety of Protestant missions. In 1889 Salisbury discreetly encouraged the expression of Scottish protest in order to impress the Portuguese;[18] and it was after receiving the freedom of Glasgow on 20 May 1891, that Salisbury made his broadest public exposition of African policy. Although he began by explaining that "The Foreign Office necessarily performs its duties in silence", and ended with a powerful plea that external policy should be insulated from party politics, he devoted much of his speech to predicting the early exclusion of Portugal from the Nyasa highlands, hinting that public subsidies to a Uganda railway might be an effective measure against Muslim slave traders, and indicating the excellent prospects which the Niger Company enjoyed in its "wonderfully fertile" sphere of influence.[19]

Outside that sphere, which Goldie's enterprise seemed to have made secure, Salisbury seems to have perceived no British interest in West Africa sufficient to justify widespread public concern. Although in 1888 he had encouraged Harry Johnston to publish his blueprint for partition (vol. I, pp. 238–9), he had made no serious diplomatic effort to implement it. The Africa Department of the Foreign Office had so many urgent and politically delicate problems under its direct responsibility that Salisbury can have had little time to examine the bulky dossiers concerning West African tariffs and boundaries which the Colonial Office continually forwarded for comment. But even if the lost opportunities of which the West African merchants complained in November 1891 were of merely minor importance, Salisbury could not ignore the protest; the injured interests were located in a city of great importance to the Conservative party, and A. L. Jones seemed quite prepared to publicize his frustrated ambitions as an example of lost Imperial opportunities. Even after the deputation had been disposed of, merchants worried by the latest cyclical recession of trade continued to seek African outlets for surplus production; some of the 137 British and Colonial Chambers of Commerce which met in congress in London on 28 June 1892 were clearly thinking imperially.[20]

Although Salisbury could do little to recover lost ground in Sierra Leone or the Ivory Coast, and was reluctant to become deeply involved in Liberia, he accepted the need to respond publicly to the demand for stronger action in West Africa. He declined to expose the rivalry with France on the public platform; a pre-election speech to the Primrose League on 6 May employed only the meaningless slogan of "Empire and Liberty", and though at Hastings on 18 May Salisbury again spoke ominously of the need to guard against foreign tariffs he also observed "absolute calm" in foreign affairs.[21] Salisbury's defence of his West African policy was not contained in his election address of 28 June but in the despatch to Dufferin published on the same date, which (like *The Times* article of 21 December 1891 which foreshadowed it) was by no means "social imperialist" in tone. Salisbury argued that his government had "made substantial progress", at small cost in money and lives, through its "policy of advance by commercial enterprise", and implied that the French military advances which worried the merchants were misguided rather than menancing. In fact his Colonial Minister had recently made a more substantial response to mercantile concern by military action of his own – but against African opponents whom the French had agreed to exclude from their sphere. In the Ijebu expedition of May 1892 the British West African empire took the offensive in the interests both of commercial expansion and of the new-style "civilizing mission".

THE EGBA AND THE IJEBU

After years of restraint, the British government had in 1888 cautiously sanctioned Moloney's plan to create a sphere of British influence in Yorubaland through Treaties of commerce and friendship; and the Agreement of 1889 provided safeguards against French intrusion (vol. I, pp. 162–3, 224–6). But Moloney's plan assumed a degree of common purpose among the Yoruba. In fact the roots of historic conflicts continued to be fertilized by the combined effects of structural economic change and short-term commercial depression, and the Lagos government lacked the power to control the intermittent fighting which continued (vo. I, pp. 129–34). Although during the six years following the partial armistice of 1886 exports of palm-oil and kernels increased by more than one-third,[22] merchants eager for expansion still blamed Moloney for over-indulging the political susceptibilities and desires of African rulers. It had always been recognized that social progress and commercial expansion were interdependent; now it was widely felt that both might require a more strongly enforced British *pax*. There were increasingly calls for action to settle the civil war, to reduce or remove tolls and taxes imposed by African authority, to extend on the mainland that recognition of property-rights in land rather than persons which had proved so rewarding at Lagos,[23] and to induce a dramatic reduction in transport costs through railway building. During the years 1889–92 the British government, gradually accepting such objectives, began to abandon the delicate and elaborate diplomatic procedures which had recently characterized its relations with Yoruba rulers.

A favourite target for complaint by frustrated merchants and ambitious pro-consuls remained the restrictions imposed on trade by African "middlemen" (cf. vol. I, pp. 112–6). Yet middlemen of one sort or another were essential to the whole West African commercial system. The most powerful were the shippers and commission agents of Manchester and Liverpool, who used their knowledge of the complex weaving industry and associated finishing trades to control relations between producers in Lancashire and their markets overseas. Next in the chain came the import–export merchants on the Lagos Marina – increasingly local branches of European companies, but including Africans like R. B. Blaize who had been fortunate in their early acquisition of landed property; until 1894, when A. L. Jones, after an uncertain start in 1891, founded the Bank of British West Africa with the right to import British silver coins, they were the major source of trading capital for the smaller African middlemen who actually engaged in buying and selling.[24] Conspicuous among this group were Yoruba repatriates from Sierra Leone or Brazil; returning to their region of origin with experience and a little capital accumulated elsewhere in the Atlantic economy, they were well-fitted to establish commercial contracts with their countrymen, either by opening shops or small businesses in Lagos or by seeking to re-establish themselves in their former homelands. But equally important were those indigenous Lagosian chiefs called *baba isale* who "acted as patrons and representatives of specific towns and villages on the neighbouring mainland and islands and in return enjoyed special, sometimes monopolistic, privileges over all others in access to their markets and trade routes";[25] D. C. Taiwo was the most outstandingly successful of these (vol. I, pp. 8–9).

None of these four sets of middlemen was universally popular, but each of them discharged functions which the others recognized as necessary. Attempts to lower costs by eliminating middlemen therefore tended to concentrate on the mainland suppliers of African produce and their rulers. The Egba and Ijebu peoples had hitherto assumed that they had natural rights to control the terms on which trade might pass through, or be conducted within, their territories.[26] In return for the tolls which they levied on transient traders they provided some security for their safe passage; in return for the duties charged in their markets and the controls they exercised over prices and conditions of sale the Egba and Ijebu authorities provided facilities for the orderly intercourse of buyers and sellers, with some safeguards against molestation, defecting debtors, and fraud. These sovereign attributes the European merchants now called into question.

The two Yoruba states which (besides producing oil-palm themselves) controlled the direct routes between Lagos and the dissolving empire of Oyo, were of very different character. The Egba state which centred on Abeokuta developed as a loose confederation of communities displaced by the northern wars; the titular chiefs of its constituent townships were controlled partly through the complex oligarchy of the *ogboni*, partly through the military power of the *ologun*. The Alake, elective chief of the senior township, held no executive authority, and power was shared by an elderly triumvirate (vol. I, pp. 155–61). Since the 1840s the new immigration of displaced persons from Sierra Leone had brought Christianity and literacy, new skills and new ideas of government, which were selectively absorbed into Egba society, and Protestant missionaries wrote jubilantly of 'sunrise in the tropics"; but the expanding power of Lagos made the Egba fear that missionaries were acting as *ajeles*, or British political agents. Egba opinion (including that of the "Saro") became deeply divided over whether to resist or to collaborate with the new forces of commerce and Christianity.[27]

The Ijebu had enjoyed a much longer period of relative isolation and stability within the tropical forest. Here too power was diffused through a complex oligarchical constitution; the power of a sacred ruler, the Awujale, was checked by the *ogboni* (here known as *oshugbo*), by trading chiefs and market supervisors (*pampas*), and by a political council, the *ilamuren*, drawn from the palace associations of Ijebu Ode;[28] some autonomy was also enjoyed by provincial rulers, like the *akarigbo* of Ijebu Remo. Traditional religious cults remained strong, especially that of Agemo, a deity whose worship may have been established in the country before the arrival of the Yoruba, and who required annual sacrifices of human victims.[29] In Ijebu Christian missionaries were received with hostile suspicion. In 1878 the chief of Iperu worshipped privately with the household of an Anglican convert, but when asked by the Reverend James Johnson (himself of Ijebu descent) to authorize a mission, he declared that other chiefs would be hostile, and that in any case the consent of the Awujale would be needed. Johnson and his Christian host were later summoned before a court of twenty-six elderly Ogboni chiefs and given an uncompromising refusal.[30] Even Islam, though professed by some Hausa slaves, made no impact on the Ijebu until about 1879.[31] Emphasizing such conservative forces, Professor Ayandele describes Ijebu's nineteenth century as an era of "splendid isolation".

Foreign trade however was actively encouraged, provided it remained under firm Ijebu control; and by the 1880s trade had produced greater ambivalence towards the Lagos colony. Aboki Tumwase, who became Awujale in 1886 after some years of internal upheaval about which we remain imperfectly informed, could see possible benefits in missionary advice. Soon after his accession he invited Father Chausse, a Yoruba-speaking priest of the *Société des Missions Africaines* to Ijebu Ode, arranged for him to be interviewed by leading chiefs, and told him that he hoped, after his coronation, to authorize a missionary initiative. His people, he told Father Chausse, distrusted all foreigners, especially the British; but he was convinced they would now accept a French Catholic Mission.[32] But Ijebu prejudices against foreign Christians were not easily overcome; when Chausse returned in November 1887 Tumwase still lacked authority to confirm his offer, and not until 1890 could the Fathers establish themselves in Ijebu Ode.[33] Even Sierra Leoneans of Ijebu origin were not encouraged to resettle, although close contacts were maintained with Lagos residents like James Johnson and J. Otonba Payne; in 1889 they persuaded Tumwase to admit a Black Anglican missionary, and a year later Payne preached in the capital from the text of Matthew 6, 24. But such innovations were still highly suspect, not only to "the old conservative Ijebu authorities who are the counsellors of the nation",[34] but to younger men. Freedom of trade and transit, which Christians tended to demand, would jeopardize the commercial interests of the Ijebu, and might enable their warlike northern neighbours in Ibadan to accumulate armaments.

Such pressure nevertheless increased. On 23 September 1889 Acting Governor Denton received a deputation of leading Lagos merchants, European and Saro, who blamed the closure of roads by both Egba and Ijebu for the alleged decline of the colony's trade. Denton and Moloney continued to rely on moral suasion, through eloquent letters and lengthy palavers with Yoruba delegations to Government House, and they succeeded in persuading the *akarigbo* to open an alternative market at Shagamu; but the Colonial Office was now tiring of the sporadically continuing Yoruba wars.[35] In January 1890 Knutsford instructed the Acting Governor to send an official, Alvin Millson, to investigate conditions in the interior; the report of this dogmatic and irascible man confirmed the growing European view that the key to political order and economic progress lay not with the coastal middlemen, but in "Yoruba proper". Millson argued that, if Lancashire could invade this market for cotton cloth (estimated precisely at 31 200 000 yards annually), the energies of Yoruba weavers would be released "for more extended agricultural pursuits", and British trade would quickly rise to the value of £500 000 a year. The obstacle lay in the Ijebus' fear and jealousy of Ibadan; "the interference of a weak and idle race" alone prevented access to "the friendly and faithful Yoruba country". Visiting Ijebu Ode on his homeward journey, Millson found that rumours of his intentions had outweighed any disposition on Tumwase's part to compromise; Millson was compelled to deny publicly that the country had been offered to England, and his private audience was cut short after one minute by Tumwase's words: "So long as my house is in order and at peace nobody has a right to say anything to me. My people are calling me. Go to your house." Millson therefore returned humiliated to Lagos, advocating a military expedition to Ijebu Ode: also a supply of firearms to Ibadan, which would enable Balogun Ajayi to finish the war in six months.[36]

Even Moloney, on his return from leave, reflected this new impatience with moral suasion; although he rebuked Millson for interfering in African politics, privately he began to "fear that eventually force will be the only remedy" for obstruction by the "ignorant and degraded" Ijebus.[37] On 13 June J. D. Fairley, leading an all-British mercantile deputation, suggested that the growing "disposition on the part of merchants here and elsewhere in Africa to penetrate into the interior" would justify increased taxation to pay for a travelling commissioner (the instrument of penetration recently adopted at Freetown). Moloney put them off by pointing out that military intervention to open markets actually damage the substantial trade which continued by other routes; but later in the year mercantile pressure resumed.[38] On the initiative of G. W. Neville, the enterprising agent of A. L. Jones, the Lagos Chamber of Commerce was reconstituted with greatly increased Saro participation;[39] on 2 December its Secretary wrote to complain of the "unjustifiable exercise of power" by the Ijebu in closing markets and obstructing communication with the interior, and to demand more "active interference" in the British sphere, at this time "when so much activity is being displayed elsewhere in Africa".[40]

Moloney remained committed to moral suasion, and on 19 December he at last persuaded the Ijebu to re-open the major waterside market of Ejinrin. Aboki had closed this in 1886, in reprisal against Lagosian settlers who had supported his dynastic rival and withheld insignia necessary for his installation; Moloney's patient and complex negotiations had involved both the *baba isale* and Lagos Saro of Ijebu origin. He took the opportunity to renew his lectures on the harmony of interests. "We do not want your country", he assured Ijebu messengers, "so long as you behave yourselves and prove your capacity for managing it without resorting to fiendish practices such as human sacrifices . . . Ijebu and Lagos are commercial peoples, are largely dependent upon one another, and should assist one another commercially as far as possible". But Moloney now added a warning:

> The question of middlemen – mark my words – will be, unless you change your commercial policy, the rock upon which Ijebu will split, and upon it will shipwreck be some day made of its independence. It may be soon or late, but if Ijebu persists in remaining as a block in the way of progress, Ijebu will lose its independence.

"There is a great cry in Europe at present for commercial highways in Africa", Moloney warned, "and the anxiety for them is not entirely selfish."[41]

Selfishly or not, on 27 January the Lagos merchants renewed their demand for a travelling commissioner, and they now incited their colleagues in the Manchester and Liverpool Chambers to approach the Colonial Office directly to complain against Ijebu.[42] Denton, acting as Governor, decided on a personal approach to the Awujale; but any conciliatory dispositions he had detected were neutralized when his armed party of one hundred crossed the lagoon.

Ijebu patriots rallied to the support of the *pampas* who felt their control of the markets threatened; Denton had to agree to proceed to Ijebu Ode without his escort; and when he arrived Tumwase felt obliged to reject his demands and refuse his presents, for fear of appearing to accept some derogation of sovereignty. Denton, though somewhat pompous, does not seem to have been a belligerent man; but he returned humiliated and anxious to retaliate by an armed expedition or a blockade.[43]

His call for action was taken up by Augustus Hemming, always the most vigorously expansionist of Colonial Office officials. Until September 1890 Hemming had assumed that military expeditions were "not to be thought of", but after studying Millson's report he concluded that "if anything is really to be done towards restoring peace and thereby reviving trade in the interior, it will be necessary to begin by coercing the Ijebus".[44] Denton's fiasco seemed to provide a suitable occasion.

> It accords a fitting opportunity for breaking open the trade monopoly which the Jebus arrogate to themselves and which is extremely prejudicial to the interests of Lagos and prevents the proper development of the resources of Yorubaland . . . we ought not now to hesitate to use force against Jebu.[45]

But Meade and Knutsford did hesitate, and refused to sanction any retaliation without consulting Moloney, about to move on to British Honduras. His advice, when it finally reached Whitehall late in October, was somewhat equivocal. While refusing to take the rejection of Denton's presents too seriously, Moloney agreed that some determined action was needed, but preferred a blockade to a military expedition, and only after a further attempt to negotiate with Ijebu representatives in Lagos.[46]

Despite these hesitations, it was becoming apparent that British policy was moving towards a stronger assertion of power in Yorubaland. In August 1891 the Egbado town of Ilaro, with the neighbouring districts of Ado and Igbessa, was at last incorporated in the Lagos protectorate (vol. I, pp.

157–8, 162). Moloney had proposed accepting the chief's offer of protection the previous year, suggesting this would check Dahomean raids into western Yorubland;[47] but as Ogundeyi (who controlled the tolls of the town) correctly perceived, it was also a means of bringing pressure on Abeokuta. Egba chiefs had again begun to menace Protestant missionaries and their followers, and to threaten closure of the trade routes, and the Onlado had renewed his attempts to re-open commercial links with the French at Porto Novo (vol. I, pp. 155–60).[48] Ilaro would also be a key point on any projected railway. Although the Lagos merchants did not renew their interest in this plan until 1892, Meade noted in September 1891, with reference to Millson's report, that

> There seems more hope here for a railway than any other point of the West Coast – an easy road and large traffic already waiting to be carried if only the middlemen could be arranged.[49]

Given this general sense of pending change, Hemming was able to argue that ultimate discretion should be left to the man on the spot, and to secure Knutsford's signature to instructions which authorized the new Governor, Gilbert T. Carter, "to take such measures as may be necessary to enforce compliance with these demands".[50]

Carter was a vigorous man, who had left the navy for colonial service in 1870 and taken part in the Asante war of 1873–4. Eager to see economic development and intolerant alike of Islam and of "fetishism", he was disposed to over-ride African resistance in the cause of economic development; as Administrator of The Gambia since 1886 he had been active in establishing British authority within the narrow territory left to him (vol. I, pp. 83–5). Like Moloney, Carter was eager to see rubber exports from Lagos develop, as they had done from Bathurst, and actively encouraged merchants to finance this.[51] He shared the conviction of Hemming, a friend and fellow-cricketer with whom he corresponded privately, that "we are bound to extend, by the pressure of circumstances, up to the borders of Yorubaland – if not, ultimately, over it",[52] and his determination to resolve the ambiguities which

Moloney had tolerated. Convinced that the proposed grand gubernatorial tour of Yorubaland would not succeed "unless a big thing is made of it and the interior people are made to realise that there is a strong and capable force at the disposal of the Governor", Carter decided to postpone this until the dry season of 1892–3 in favour of a drive to open the roads and markets of Ijebu.[53]

In reply to a peremptory ultimatum from Carter of 16 December, the Awujale reluctantly sent twenty-two representative messengers to Lagos. On 18 and 21 January, confronted with displays of Imperial pomp and power, and peremptorily lectured by Carter, these delegates apologized for insulting Denton and agreed verbally that all roads should be open and free. Carter interpreted this to mean, not merely the "free and unmolested passage" which he had demanded in his letter to the Awujale, but the abolition, in return for a fixed annual payment of £50, of the transit tolls from which many Ijebus profited. According to Carter, the messengers assented to this, but insisted that their instructions forbade them to sign any document lest this should unwittingly prejudice Ijebu sovereignty. Eventually two Lagos Ijebus, who had been counselling acceptance, signed in recognition that the messengers had heard the treaty read, and assented to its terms.[54] It is worth noting that James Johnson, Carter's fiercest critic, accepted this curious procedure as "a formal arrangement".[55]

The treaty roused intense and angry opposition in Ijebu Ode, and fears that the open roads would be used to strengthen their northern enemies. On 3 February, Rev. T. Harding, a CMS missionary, was delayed on his way to Ibadan; six days later his returning carriers, according to Ijebu sources, "began to pillage and plunder the Jebus and ill-treating their wives, take things in the market and refuse to pay, saying that the white man Governor of Lagos has purchased the Jebu country and their people and that whatever the Yorubas take from the Jebus they are not to pay for". The Ijebus, confirmed in their suspicions of Lagos, retaliated violently. Another missionary, Herbert Tugwell, stormed up to Ijebu Ode; he struck a representative of the Awujale who delayed him at the gate, and proceeded to lecture the Awujale's Council. "He did not behave as a missionary", one of the Lagos Ijebus sadly commented, "he acted more as the agent of Captain Denton to get a case against the Jebu." This enraged the "young men", and when Major Stanley was sent to investigate the missionary complaints he was not allowed to enter the capital.[56]

After his lecture to the Ijebu delegates Carter had confidently left on a visit to Ondo; he returned to find that his optimism was misplaced. Not only did it appear that the "younger party" had taken control in Ijebu; but the Egbas, angered by the occupation of Ilaro and worried by Carter's new tone, had closed their roads to the coast. Carter therefore concluded that Egbas and Ijebus were acting in collusion, on "pernicious advice from certain disloyal parties in Lagos" who wished to maintain existing trade monopolies, to frustrate government policy. Eventually, he warned Knutsford, the British would have to occupy both Abeokuta and Ijebu Ode; immediately, either a blockade or an expedition was necessary to the interests and prestige of Lagos.[57] When Carter's warning arrived the British government, chastened by the merchants' protest against its weakness further west, was disposed to take a more assertive line in west Africa. Throughout February the Colonial Office had been inundated by representations from the Liverpool, Manchester and Birmingham Chambers of Commerce, following up their deputation by demands for territorial extension, and action to secure "free commercial intercourse with the interior".[58] When news arrived that trade had been stopped, first by the Egbas, then by the Ijebus, the Lancashire lobby reacted indignantly; they wanted military action, not a prolonged blockade which could injure themselves more than their customers. On 8 March a meeting in Liverpool, attended by merchants from Manchester and Glasgow, demanded immediate action against the Egbas; there was even, as A. L. Jones reminded the government, a suggestion from Manchester of a deputation to enlist support from Gladstone and the Liberals.

At this point it becomes clear that the "fiendish practices" about which Moloney had warned the Yoruba might help to justify an expedition. Jones had argued in Liverpool that the Egbas had closed the roads to prevent their slaves deserting; hence "the sooner the British showed their abhorrence of such a thing as slavery the better'.[59] On 11 March Hemming, taking the cue, suggested that Knutsford should "take the bull by the horns and settle the question once for all by the subjugation of Abeokuta. It is a nest of slave dealers and intriguers and it would be well to break it up." Meade and Knutsford doubted the justification, and perhaps the military feasibility, of action against the Egbas; but Meade pointed out that moralism could be turned in a different direction. "Against the Jebus we have sufficient justification for coercion as they insulted the Queen's representative and have now broken their engagement." Hemming, anxious for action somewhere, now switched to this tactic, and on 18 March Carter was sounded about coercion of Ijebu: "H.M.G. are disposed to treat the cases separately and deal with Jebu first, which will very probably produce good effect on Egbas."[60] A few days later Knutsford confirmed this disposition; Colonel Francis Scott, a veteran of the Asante war, began to prepare an expeditionary force based upon 150 Hausas of the Lagos Constabulary and a similar contingent from the Gold Coast, and reinforced, as a precaution against Egba intervention, by one company of the West Indian Regiment from Sierra Leone.[61]

Knutsford's willingness to respond to mercantile pressure by authorizing the coercion of Ijebu (but not Abeokuta) must have been influenced by conclusions drawn from recent events around Sierra Leone, that the selective use of military force could lead to considerable expansion of trade and British influence with a minimum increase in the political responsibilities of the colony. The short sharp military campaigns against the Yonnies in late 1887 and against the Mende war-chief Makaia a year later, had been followed by two peaceful years with exports of palm produce and rubber rising to record levels; it seemed that Governor Hay's "frontier road", lightly garrisoned by the new Frontier Police force and supervised by a travelling commissioner, was providing the basis for an effective and economical *pax*. European merchants opened new branches in the estuaries; African entrepreneurs experimented with new crops (vol. I, pp. 175–6, 196–9; above, pp. 65–7). Although these developments themselves created new tensions, the full political implications were not yet apparent; Hemming and Meade saw chiefly the "gratifying results of . . . the expeditions which certain people in the House of Commons, out of the depth of their ignorance, recently took occasion to condemn".[62]

To some extent it was a matter of chance where the weight of Imperial power would make itself felt; public opinion was becoming more ready to be convinced of the moral justification. The reviving anti-slavery campaign pulled British philanthropists in two directions; military coercion of Africans might actually seem a moral duty where it was a question of slave-dealers, or other fiendish practitioners. Elderly lawyers like Knutsford might still question the justification for attacking the Egbas because they imposed tolls on their own territory, yet approve a therapeutic invasion of Ijebu in the wider interests of civilization.[63] His new Governor did after all believe that Ijebu resistance to Christian missions, and their continued practice of human sacrifice, meant that "the existence of this race, in its present wilful disregard of all attempts at enlightenment, is a blot on the civilization of the Colony".[64] African supporters for coercion could also be found. John Payne Jackson, a Liberian disciple of Blyden, was an ardent supporter of Carter's policies, as well as a grateful recipient of his patronage. His *Weekly Record* voiced the opinions and interests of many Oyo Yorubas settled in Lagos, who welcomed the new Governor's resolve to cement relations with their kinsmen in the interior.[65] The existence of such Empire Loyalists in the coastal colonies made it possible to claim that the new imperialism served African interests.

Other citizens of Lagos, however, still stood by their Egba and Ijebu kinsmen. On 13 April James Johnson led a deputation to Carter to suggest further attempts to negotiate with Ijebu;[66] three days later a private deputation of chiefs and traders from Lagos set out under J. P. Haastrup, a prominent Saro who claimed membership of the *oshugbo*. At a mass meeting in Ijebu Ode on 22 April Haastrup, making eloquent use of Yoruba proverbs and prayers, warned the Ijebu to adapt to changing times by opening their roads and welcoming missionaries and their schools. The British government, he suggested, would hold the military threat from Ibadan in check; and traders would still need Ijebu middlemen:

> A man who carried a pot of oil or a bag of kernels from Ibadan to Lagos and pays canoe-freight will soon find it to be a losing game, then they will halt at your markets to trade with you and you will not be known as the one stopping them.

Ijebu leaders appeared to be impressed, but declared that they would have to consult opinion throughout the country, and that the roads could not be re-opened in less than thirty days. Haastrup urged them to "divide thirty days in two";[67] but no response reached Lagos before the expedition was ready to leave on 12 May, and Carter did not even report the Haastrup mission to London. On 13 May Colonel Scott's force made a surprise landing at Epe; on the 19th it defeated the Ijebu army at Imagdon, in a bravely fought battle which Scott found as severe as anything in the Asante war. Next day the invaders entered Ijebu Ode.

This exercise of military force to resolve problems which earlier governors would have felt obliged to settle through diplomacy was widely recognized as marking an ominous change in British policy. Nine years later a distinguished Lagosian of Oyo origin recalled how

> the taking of Ijebu sent a shock of surprise and alarm throughout the land. Men felt instinctively that a new Power had entered the arena of Yoruba politics, that a new era was about to dawn on the land, and they were much exercised in mind about what the omen was likely to be. Not the least cause of anxiety was the employment of Hausa soliders which recalled the unhappy days of Afonja and his Jamas.[68]

Although Carter's suggestion of declaring a formal protectorate was rejected as contrary to public promises, Tumwase henceforth ruled under supervision by the British garrison, and his lagoon-side markets were incorporated in the Colony.

Under these provisional arrangements the Ijebu began to open their country, not merely to the free movement of traders but to the missionary religions and their schools, and to the new ideologies and attitudes which accompanied them.[69]

As Carter and Hemming had hoped, the effect on the Egbas was equally striking. After much internal debate, in Lagos and Abeokuta, they agreed unconditionally to re-open the roads, and in return secured a substantial reprieve of independence. When Carter made his long-delayed journey to the interior in January 1893 he took a draft treaty authorizing fairly close British control over the Egba state; but he finally agreed, after negotiations, that so long as Abeokuta kept open the roads and protected missionaries "its independence shall be fully recognized". The Egbas thus secured, until 1914, guarantees of autonomy which would shortly appear quite exceptional; but the conditions proved to involve "opening the roads" to capitalist penetration in fundamentally new ways. Carter's party included an engineer instructed to survey routes for railways into the interior; three years later, following further British pressure on the Egba authorities, construction began on the line from Lagos to Abeokuta and Ibadan.[70]

Even British officials appreciated the full significance of the new era only gradually. Now that both the obstructive "middleman" states had agreed to collaborate in commercial expansion, they believed that the people and rulers of the interior would welcome the new opportunities. Though they realized that there had been a shift in the delicate balance between collaboration and force – the twin bases of informal empire – they hoped to avoid the responsibilities of direct control. Hemming rejected Carter's arguments for establishing formal Protectorates in Yorubaland; his model for the exercise of British authority remained the system of light and economical supervision which Hay had established at Sierra Leone. When Carter obtained the agreement of the chiefs of Ibadan to the presence of a hundred Hausa troops, under a Resident with undefined responsibility for political supervision of Yorubaland, this appeared a satisfactory terminus for those extensions of responsibility which Hemming had long advocated.

> the policy which has been adopted at Ibadan of stationing a resident officer and force there is what we really want in Ashanti. We have neither assumed nor declared a protectorate over Ibadan, nor need we do so over Coomassie – but we want some one on the spot to watch the movements of the King and Chiefs, and to keep us in touch with them and with the people.[71]

But the delicate balance between force and collaboration could not be so easily stabilized.

THE LOGIC OF AN IMPERIAL POSITION

Political developments at home temporarily reinforced the reluctance of the administrators to undertake great new responsibilities. In the General Election of July 1892 Salisbury's "great law of the pendulum" produced a Liberal majority, though a narrow one, and hence a Liberal government.[72] But despite the anti-expansionist principles of Gladstone and his older colleagues, this result could hardly be interpreted as a decisive rejection of African empire. Rosebery, the new Foreign Secretary, inherited a brief which clearly established that, if some of the merchants' territorial claims were "fantastic", Britain's interests on the Niger were of primary importance;[73] and he soon showed himself ready to defend the Imperial cause as forcefully as any member of the previous government.

The division within Liberalism crystallized not over West Africa but over Uganda; by September 1892 Sir William Harcourt, the new Chancellor, who believed that "we have already as much Empire as the nation can carry", was fiercely denouncing "the policy of annexation and conquest and international rivalry" in which the Foreign Office was engaged.[74] When Lugard returned to England in October 1892 and undertook "the task of publicly explaining our duties and responsibilities in Africa",[75] the controversy over Uganda made the partition of Africa a subject of fierce political debate, at least within a limited political elite of businessmen, philanthropists, politicians, and "service gentry".[76] In this Rosebery, whose Imperial faith had long been maturing, was prepared to intervene publicly in scarcely veiled opposition to his own Prime Minister.

> "We have to look beyond the chatter of platforms and the passion of party", he told the jubilee dinner of the Royal Colonial Institute in March 1893, "to the future of the race to which we are at present the trustees, and we should in my opinion grossly fail in the task which has been laid upon us did we shrink from responsibilities and decline to take our share in a partition of the world which we have not forced on but which has been forced upon us."[77]

Less ostentatiously, the new Leader of the Opposition had already recognized that African policy had entered a new phase. On 4 February, after opening the new overhead railway in Liverpool, Salisbury addressed a deputation from the Chamber of Commerce, still much concerned about the effects of increased foreign tariffs. After hinting that British governments might need to retaliate fiscally, Salisbury agreed that in these new conditions territorial extension should no longer be regarded as "a mere sentimental freak, something like the love of a man to have a larger estate than he can possibly manage". "A great change has come over the political mind", Salisbury declared, "and has extended to both parties . . . we cannot suffer more than we can help that the unoccupied parts of the world where we must look for new markets for our goods should be shut from us by foreign legislation". The parliamentary Committee of 1865 was largely responsible for past inactivity in West Africa:

> it never occurred to them that if we left it alone other nations would not do so. . . . We imagined that the whole benefit of leaving the territory alone should be reserved to us and to the rest of the world, and that we could leave it independent and open to all the world. We did not lay our account from the fact that foreign nations would also awake to the advantages of colonial possessions, and that colonial possession in their mind was something much more exclusive and much more injurious to their neighbours than it is to ours.[78]

Even with Gladstone in Downing Street, the political climate was encouraging the rapid growth of British imperialism.

The changes in "the political mind" to which Salisbury referred were not simply a reflection of anxiety about markets. They also reflected new perceptions of empire in a period when, as Meade reminded the incoming Secretary of State, someone in every village had friends or relatives in the colonies.[79] In West Africa, there was increasing readiness to accept what one contemporary called "the logic of an Imperial position"; once it was recognized that British power could no longer be confined to the coastal colonies but must extend to their "hinterlands" it was difficult to set limits to the activities of zealous pro-consuls. Governors of course had always tended to claim that they could secure the financial solvency and political security of their colonies through modest territorial acquisitions, but now Whitehall too was more ready to accept such arguments. As already noted, hope of solving the commercial crisis by improving and cheapening access to inland markets had led Meade to favour a Lagos railway even before the local merchants returned to this idea; and before leaving office Knutsford had authorized surveys to discover the technical and financial feasibility of government railways in all three major West African colonies.[80]

Politically, the appointment of British agents in the interior invariably proved a stepping-stone towards deeper commitment, not a substitute for it. Hemming originally envisaged that Captain R. L. Bower, the Constabulary officer appointed as Resident and Travelling Commissioner at Ibadan, should simply "watch over" the conduct of the recently warring Yoruba rulers. The charter for this activity was a treaty concluded by Carter on 3 February 1893, by which the lawful overlord of the region, the Alafin of Oyo, agreed to accept the Governor of Lagos as ultimate arbiter of all disputes; since many of these disputes precisely concerned the respective rights of the Alafin and of subordinate rulers, Bower was soon involved in litigious palavers which neither temperament nor experience equipped him to handle. On such issues as the right to punish adultery by castration, Victorian officers like Bower were separated from the moral world of Yoruba statecraft by a gulf which they could bridge only by categorical denunciations of "fiendish practices" such as were returning to fashion at home. By November 1895 Bower lost patience and resolved to demonstrate British predominance; a minor judicial dispute became a "struggle for sovereignty" and ended in a savage bombardment of Oyo town. Thereafter the Alafin, Adeyemi, accepted reinstatement as a British client; neighbouring rulers took warning, and a "new Oyo empire" was instituted under British control.[81] Many Yorubas who had suffered from civil war were indeed able to profit commercially from the new *Pax Britannica*, and eventually from the railway; but the political consequences of their loss of independence also became progressively clearer.

Other scholars have spelled out the stages by which the logic of Britain's imperial position lead to the gradual substitution of force for collaboration. In the Niger Coast Protectorate also Nana, the Itsekiri "merchant prince" with whom Hewett and Johnston had collaborated in the later 1880s (vol. I, pp. 121–3) found his powers being gradually circumscribed by acts of the new Protectorate administration. Finally in 1894 the acting Commissioner, condemning Nana's interference with trade and hinting at unsubstantiated "atrocities" during his brother's funeral, launched a military attack and destroyed the basis of Nana's power; after an improvised trial at Old Calabar, this able ruler was sent into exile until 1906.[82] For present purposes this may serve as a parodigm case of how, with greater or less degrees of military violence, the Protectorate government gradually extended its direct control of the sphere which diplomacy had reserved for it. Campaigns against Brass in 1895, against Benin in 1896–7, a long series of military operations in the Igbo interior from 1896 onwards, successively consolidated the revolution in Anglo-Nigerian relations which the Ijebu expedition had heralded.[83]

RENEWED FRENCH CHALLENGES

The Agreement of 1889, by fixing a boundary as far north as the ninth parallel, had enabled the British to conduct their advance into Yorubaland without fear of French interference. And the Declaration of 1890 had sketched Nigeria's future northern boundary, though not unambiguously; while Britain recognized French influence to the north of the imaginary Say–Barruwa line, the only explicit reference to regions further south was that the Niger Company's sphere included "all that fairly belongs to the Kingdom of Sokoto" (cf. above p. 27). But a vast middle-belt, covering the southern section of the savanna region, remained untouched by diplomacy, and little visited by Europeans. Between the headwaters of the Niger and the countries traversed by Barth in the 1850s there had been little to limit the exercise of cartographical imagination until Krause's journey to Macina in 1886, quickly followed by political reconnaissances of the Voltaic kingdoms by von François in 1888 and by Binger in 1887–9 (vol. I, pp. 87, 92, 221–2). The British reacted by attempts to protect the southern and western approaches to Hausaland by exercises in political geometry. Having ensured continued commercial access to Salaga by the "Neutral Zone" agreement with Germany of 1888 (vol. I, p. 216), they half-heartedly attempted in 1889 to persuade the French to draw a diagonal boundary to Burrum on the middle Niger (vol. I, pp. 243–6, 250).

Though this suggestion proved unacceptable, French diplomatists were by no means opposed to bold political geometry; they knew that the colonial party, and especially the Sudanese military, were embarrassingly liable to plant the tricolour in faraway places and invoke national honour as an imperative reason to keep it there. In July 1890 Ribot – advised by Gabriel Hanotaux, a distinguished historian who had returned to the Quai d'Orsay as *sous-directeur des protectorats* after losing a seat in Parliament – suggested complementing the Say–Barruwa agreement by offering Germany a demarcation line passing between the White and Black Volta rivers to reach the Niger on the borders of Gwandu. This was primarily intended to secure the field for three military missions which Archinard had launched after the fall of Segou: those of Lieutenant Mademba Sy to the Tokolors of Macina, of Captain Quiquandon to Tieba at Sikasso, and of Dr Crozat to Mossi (see Map 1). But Ribot's proposal would have set limits to the future advance of the colonial army, to both British and German advantage; it might also have precluded the hopes which Etienne was beginning to form of advancing northwards through Borgu to the Niger after a future conquest of Dahomey. So the colonial department succeeded in killing the project.[84]

During the spring of 1892 the Quai d'Orsay, worried about the effects which the growing influence of the *parti colonial* might have on Anglo-French relations, made a new attempt to avoid friction in West Africa through comprehensive geometry. Hanotaux, promoted to the Directorship of Consular and Commercial Affairs, suggested that, although the diplomatic aftermath of the 1889 Arrangement was far from settled, an Anglo-French Commission should proceed to implement the 1890 Declaration in the Niger area. His desire for a speedy agreement was shared by the new Counsellor responsible for African negotiations in the British Embassy; Constantine Phipps, a descendent of one of the less distinguished British Foreign Secretaries, hoped to make his diplomatic reputation by speedily solving these tiresome African disputes. Unfortunately Hanotaux's initiative came precisely when Salisbury, stimulated by his commercial critics, had decided to take a stronger line in defence of British West African interests (see above, pp. 81–2). The Prime Minister showed his new pugnacity when on 22 April Phipps complained that Captain Lang's zeal to defend the claims of Britain's African subjects in the Gold Coast Boundary Commission was prejudicing his own attempt to "mediate and smooth down differences"; "I like Capt. Lang's tone", Salisbury bluntly commented.[85] Meanwhile he extended the area of Anglo-French rivalry by sending a talented young African agent, George Ekem Ferguson, to collect "treaties of free commerce and friendship" which would preclude the establishment of foreign protectorates to the north of the Gold Coast.[86]

Between 25 April and 1 October Ferguson, though he was unable to reach Mossi, gathered valuable information and established British influence more strongly in Gonja and Dagomba – former tributary provinces of Asante, where since 1874 many rulers and contenders for rule were ready to look for external support. Ferguson, trained in surveying and geology, was an African patriot who like Parkes favoured the expansion of the British empire. He reported enthusiastically on market opportunities, and tempted ambitious chiefs to sign treaties in hope of obtaining "the luxuries of civilization".[87] Ferguson's patriotic vigilance extended far beyond the countries he was able to visit. He reported that Ahmadu, exiled from Segou to Bandiagara, and his Tokolor kinsmen in Macina, were "anxious to have direct intercourse with us, the friend of [Turkey] and Conqueror of Ashanti";[88] and he claimed that, since Dagomba extended to the borders of Borgu, his treaties linked up with those of the Niger Company.[89]

Had Gonja and Dagomba been centralized polities whose treaties were readily recognizable by European chanceries, Ferguson might indeed have made substantial gains for the British empire. But since the weakening of Asante power in 1874, authority in the region had increasingly devolved to provincial rulers, thus preparing the ground for repartition by Europeans.[90] Indeed, parts of eastern Gonja and southern Dagomba were already included in the arbitrary Anglo-German Neutral Zone, an arrangement which Ferguson had some difficulty in explaining in central Gonja.[91] He was a skilful and sympathetic negotiator, and secured treaties – on this and subsequent journeys – which were of some value in diplomatic negotiations with France and Germany. But imperialistic governments were becoming less willing to accept African "treaties" without critical scrutiny. On this occasion, Salisbury's determination to concede no possibly valid claims on the eve of the election led him to miss the opportunity of an extremely favourable compromise.

When the Niger Commission met on 11 May Hanotaux told Phipps that, provided Britain would recognize French rights north of a line from Bonduku to Say (drawn to pass along the northern border of the Anglo-German Neutral Zone), she could have a free hand in unannexed territories to the south. Although it is not clear how far this would have restricted French claims after the conquest of Dahomey, all historians agree that Salisbury was unwise to quibble over terms almost as advantageous as his own suggestion of 1889.[92] Even

Anderson and Lowther, the parliamentary Under-Secretary, were delighted with the offer. But Salisbury had allowed Goldie to brief Phipps,[93] who dutifully insisted that the Niger Company held valid treaties covering not only Borgu, but the whole of Gurma, a politically indetermine country which appeared to be bisected by the French line. Hanotaux forcefully argued that it was better to rely on simple political geometry than on attempts to assess the value of African treaties – his own drawers, he said, were full of them; but Salisbury had made up his mind to be stubborn. "We should not accept any such proposal rashly," he minuted. "The French will be very tired of W. African acquisitions after the Dahomey war."[94] He could not have been more wrong; the French offer was quickly withdrawn and a more intensive period of African rivalry followed.

Ever since Salisbury's Guildhall speech of November 1891 had seemed to rule out any move to appease French desires for the evacuation of Egypt, Ribot had feared that he was aggravating Anglo-French relations with the intention of making Egypt a *cheval de bataille* at the elections.[95] Even before Ferguson's mission, a series of minor colonial disputes contributed to Ribot's irritation – Samori's arms purchases at Freetown, the difficulties of the Sierra Leone and Gold Coast boundary delimitations, the failure to conclude the promised customs agreement at Porto Novo, the British occupation of Aldabra, disputes over French jurisdiction in Madagascar, the departure for Fez of a new British minister (Euan Smith) suspected for his earlier record at Zanzibar. None of these was a popular cause. But from April 1892 reports began to reach France of the deaths of many Baganda Catholics, and of serious damage to the missionary work of the White Fathers, in what seemed an atrociously bloody civil war. As missionary reports blamed the intervention of Captain Lugard and the forces of the Imperial British East Africa Company, public indignation mounted; on 31 May D'Arenberg angrily questioned the government about "this violation of the rights of man". Responding to this new anglophobia, the French government pressed for compensation, attributing to the British government a responsibility for the actions of IBEA which most British politicians remained reluctant to accept.[96]

The cumulative effect was to quench the conciliatory dispositions of Ribot and Hanotaux; on 10 June Phipps reported that both men had recently delivered "jeremiads" against British African policy. The last straw came with the publication of Salisbury's depreciatory remarks about French colonial policy in his rhetorical despatch to Dufferin (see above pp. 82–3); on 20 June Hanotaux refused to reconvene the Niger Commission until the outstanding disputes over the Sierra Leone and Gold Coast borders had been settled.[97]

In June 1892 the colonialist coalition of interest-groups and ideologues moved on to the Parliamentary stage; ninety-two deputies, drawn from all parties except the Socialists, announced the formation of a "colonial group", with Etienne as President and D'Arenberg and Vallon as Vice-Presidents.[98] Within eighteen months this became the second largest inter-party group, second only to the agricultural interest.[99] In order to overcome the persistent anti-colonial prejudice which had recently been manifested over the Dahomey campaign (see below, pp. 161–3) and obtain support for their various colonial causes, the leaders appealed freely to anglophobic nationalism. While it may be true that "this Anglophobia did not correspond to any profound wave of public opinion",[100] a good deal of irritation, anger and frustration was provoked by the publicity given to recent British behaviour. Reassured diplomatically by the growing Franco-Russian rapprochement, and politically by signs of increased public acceptance, the *parti colonial* now became ready to change the unwritten conventions under which the scramble for Africa had so far been conducted, and in particular to challenge the *chasse gardée* of the Niger Company.

The means of doing this were pointed out by two explorers whose exploits were prominently featured in the colonial publicity campaign. Lieutenant Louis Mizon had first been sent to the Benue in 1890 by Tharel's *Syndicat français du Haut Benito* (see above, p. 29); his activities had predictably led to bitter conflict with the Niger Company, and had stimulated a somewhat embarrassed Quai d'Orsay to re-assert France's right to free navigation of the Niger and its tributaries.[101] But Mizon's eyes had also been fixed on Bornu – a country not explicitly mentioned in the 1890 Declaration – and he learned that attempts by the Niger Company's agent David MacIntosh to negotiate a treaty with Shehu Hashimi had failed.[102] Meanwhile experience in the emirates of Muri and Adamawa suggested more immediate possibilities of exploiting African hostility to the company. In June 1892 Mizon, having travelled from Yola through Ngaundere to the Congo, returned to a tumultuous welcome in France, orchestrated by leaders of the colonial party: since Crampel's mission had during the summer of 1891 been destroyed by Rabih Fadlallah, the rising power of the central Sudan, the Benue route now seemed to offer the best hope of securing access to Lake Chad. In August the British were informed that "a certain number of merchants and industrialists", organized in the *Compagnie française de l'Afrique centrale,* had sponsored a new Mizon mission, of an "essentially commercial and scientific character"; its political objects were deliberately concealed, possibly even from Jamais, the new Colonial Under-Secretary.[103]

The exploits of this second expedition produced an international sensation. In December Mizon, to secure a treaty from the Emir of Muri, joined with his modern weapons in a slave-raiding expedition; in May 1893 this atrocious act was denounced in the French press by one of his own companions, Dr Henri Ward. The outcry led to Mizon's recall by the French government; but before obeying he returned to Adamawa. Emir Zubairu, already facing internal threats to his authority from Mahdist sympathizers, ethnic minorities and his own vassals, was by now seriously worried by increasing pressure from agents of the Niger Company (themselves reacting against French and German attempts to penetrate this province) (vol. I, p. 107). Mizon, who in 1891 had been accompanied by Algerian Muslims and had made generous promises of firearms, seemed to Zubairu to represent a less objectionable and dangerous group of *Nasar'en;* when he returned in 1893 (bringing the promised firearms, in disregard of the Brussels Treaty) Zubairu not only signed his commercial treaty, but agreed to accept the Algerian Muhammed Mekhan as French Resident, with a small military escort.[104] Goldie's questionable agreements with the Sultan of Sokoto, even where reinforced by treaties with subordinate Emirs, no longer seemed sufficient to prevent foreign intrusion.

Further demonstrations of the gap between the Niger Company's claims and political actualities followed Monteil's arrival in Tripoli in December 1892 at the end of his great journey across the western Sudan. In Muslim areas Monteil had experienced growing suspicions of European activity; and though these had been most strongly fuelled by knowledge of the French aggression against Ahmadu, they clearly extended also to the Niger Company. In Sokoto Monteil convinced himself that the British had no valid treaty with the Sultan, and very little trade with territories which depended directly on him (as against those administered through Gwandu). Though precluded from seeking a political treaty himself, he concluded a commercial agreement on 28 October 1891.[105] In Bornu, where the theocratic structures established by al-Kanemi had been gravely weakened by political rivalries, plague and famine, and by the rising challenge of Rabih, Monteil found anti-European feelings even stronger; though he could secure no treaty himself, by confirming that MacIntosh had also failed to obtain one he gave new hope to Mizon's sponsors.[106]

When Monteil returned to France he received a hero's welcome. His disinterested courage and patriotism were contrasted by the colonial party with the behaviour of politicians and financiers recently implicated in the Panama scandals. "It is rather strange", wrote *L'Illustration*, "that with Dodds, Monteil, Lavigerie, Africa should console us for Europe." That sceptical imperialist Colonel Frey warned Monteil that profiteers and railway speculators were to be found among his own admirers; but his return provided an ideal opportunity to identify the colonial cause with that of French patriotism.[107] And, by exposing the highly dubious nature of those claims of the Niger Company which had been so hastily accepted in 1890, Monteil suggested apparently vulnerable targets for colonial ambitions.

Monteil, and the Colonial Department, reluctantly acknowledged that the 1890 Declaration had left to the Niger Company "all that fairly belongs to the Kingdom of Sokoto";[108] dubious though Goldie's treaties might be, to contest them would violate the diplomatic conventions which had, for example, obliged Britain to recognize France's protectorate over Samori. But there were other countries which, though south of the Say–Barruwa line, did not belong to the Caliphate. Bornu remained the colonialists' prime target in the east; but with Rabih's forces approaching there was little to be done there. The most hopeful route for penetrating Goldie's monopolistic empire therefore seemed to lie through the little-known country of Borgu (or Bariba). Goldie at first rested under the mistaken impression that Borgu was under the suzerainty of Gwandu, and so covered by Thomson's treaties; but, as reinsurance, one of his agents had in January 1890 secured a treaty with the ruler of Bussa. This, Goldie believed, "completes the protection of the Middle Niger from the possibility of French interference, either overland from the upper Niger or from Dahomey".[109] He was over-optimistic; as would emerge later, Bussa was only the senior polity within a confederation of impoverished but fiercely independent communities, over which the ruler of Nikki exercised more effective authority.[110] But this area – as vital as Muri and Adamawa to Goldie's claim to control the lower Niger navigation – would become accessible to France only after she had settled the unfinished business of relations with Dahomey.

NOTES

1. A. E. Ekoko, "British Defence Policy in Western Africa, 1878–1914", PhD thesis, University of Aberdeen, 1976; cf. vol. I, pp. 185–6.
2. This sentence represents an extension of the concept of "stabilizing factors" used by G. N. Sanderson, "The European Partition of Africa: Coincidence or Conjuncture?", in E. F. Penrose (ed.), *European Imperialism and the Partition of Africa* (1975).
3. Andrew Porter, "Cambridge, Keswick and late-nineteenth century Attitudes to Africa", *Journal of Imperial and Commonwealth History,* v, 1976; A. F. Walls, "Black Europeans, White Africans: Some missionary motives in West Africa", in D. Baker (ed.), *Religious Motivation: biographical and sociological problems of the Church historian* (Cambridge, 1978) pp. 339–48. Cf. vol. I, pp. 201–2.
4. Michael Howard, "Empire, Race and War in pre-1914 Britain", in H. Lloyd-Jones (ed.), *History and Imagination* (1981) pp. 346 ff; cf. Preface, pp. xii–xiii.

5. W. Winwood Reade, *The Martyrdom of Man* (20th edn., 1912) pp. 503–13.
6. On Social Darwinism, cf. B. Semmel, *Imperialism and Social Reform* (1960) ch. II with H. A. C. Cairns, *Prelude to Imperialism* (1965) ch. III, and p. 238.
7. Cairns, *Prelude to Imperialism,* ch. VI.
8. For some discussion of the assumptions on which late Victorians were brought up, see M. Howard, "Empire, Race and War", p. 341.
9. The reference is to the Introduction to the second (1872) edition of Walter Bagehot, *The English Constitution* (World's Classics edition, 1928, p. 271).
10. Freda Harcourt, "Disraeli's imperialism, 1866–68: a question of timing", *HJ,* 23, 1980, pp. 87–109.
11. C. H. D. Howard (ed.), Joseph Chamberlain, *A Political Memoir, 1880–92* (1953) pp. 70–6.
12. Rosebery Papers (National Library of Scotland) Letter Book 88, f. 93; Rosebery to Lady Seeley, 18 June 1895.
13. Rosebery, speech at Sheffield, 25 October 1894; *Lord Rosebery's Speeches* (1896) pp. 265–6.
14. H. C. G. Matthew, *The Liberal Imperialists* (1973); cf. Semmel, *Imperialism and Social Reform,* p. 51.
15. Hansard (Lords), 10 July 1890, 1265–71.
16. The phrase is from Salisbury to Temple, 2 September 1878, quoted in G. N. Uzoigwe, *Britain and the Conquest of Africa* (Ann Arbor, 1974) p. 16. For an example of Salisbury's practice in the Asian context for which the phrase was coined, see J. L. Duthie, "Some Further Insights into the Working of Mid-Victorian Imperialism: Lord Salisbury and Anglo-Afghan Relations: 1874–1878", *JICH,* VIII, 1980.
17. G. Cecil, *Life of Robert, Marquess of Salisbury,* IV (1932) p. 162 cf. A. N. Porter, *The Origins of the South African War* (Manchester, 1980) pp. 21–6.
18. R. Oliver, *Sir Harry Johnston and the Scramble for Africa* (1957) pp. 136, 151; cf. J. D. Hargreaves, *Aberdeenshire to Africa* (Aberdeen, 1981) pp. 36–7.
19. *The Times,* 21 May 1891.
20. Hynes, *Economics of Empire,* pp. 109–14.
21. *The Times,* 7, 19 May 1892.
22. Lagos exports (calculated from vol. I, p. 253):

	1880–5 total	*Annual average*	*1886–91 total*	*Annual average*	
Palm-oil	12 952 835	2 158 805	17 805 060	2 967 510	gals
Kernels	165 424	27 570	228 007	38 001	tons

23. A. G. Hopkins, "Property Rights and Empire-Building: Britain's Annexation of Lagos, 1861", *Journal of Economic History,* XL, 1980, pp. 777–98. See also two fundamental earlier works by Hopkins "Economic Imperialism in West Africa: Lagos, 1880–92", *Econ. HR,* 2nd series,, xxi, 1968: *Economic History,* esp. pp. 154–7.

24. R. Fry, *Bankers in West Africa* (1976) ch. 2; P. N. Davies, *Sir Alfred Jones*, pp. 56–7; A. G. Hopkins, "Richard Beale Blaize, 1845–1904: Merchant Prince of West Africa", *Tarikh*, I, 1965.
25. P. D. Cole, *Modern and Traditional Elites in the Politics of Lagos* (Cambridge, 1975) pp. 24–31, 56–8.
26. "God, who made the world, has also made divisions. The white men got the sea, and the natives the lagoon, and Jebu. They need not interfere with Lagos, nor Lagos with Jebu . . . there is nothing left but to play together". Balogun Nafokan to Denton, 15 May 1891 (CO 879/36, CP African 428, no. 1).
27. A. Pallinder-Law, "Government in Abeokuta, 1830–1914", (PhD thesis, University of Göteborg, 1973); idem, "Aborted Modernization in West Africa? The Case of Abeokuta", *JAH*, xv, 1974, pp. 65–72; J. H. Kopytoff, *Preface to Modern Nigeria: the Sierra Leonians (sic) in Yoruba, 1830–1890* (Madison, 1965).
28. P. C. Lloyd, "Political and Social Structure", in S. O. Biobaku (ed.), *Sources of Yoruba History* (Oxford, 1973) pp. 215–18.
29. O. Ogunba, "Agemo in the Religious System of the Ijebu People", Seminar paper, University of Ibadan History Department, 28 January 1971.
30. CMS Archives CA2/056, James Johnson to Wright, 21 June 1878.
31. M. O. Abdul, "Islam in Ijebu-Ode", paper presented to the 16th Congress Historical Society of Nigeria, December 1970, p. 3.
32. Archives, Société des Missions Africaines, Rome, [S.M.A.] 14/802.02, Chausse to Planque, 15 October 1886.
33. Ibid. Chausse to Planque, 1 May 1888; Pellet to Planque, 3 March 1896.
34. CO 879/33, CP African 399, No. 44 encl. 3, Samuel Johnson to Moloney, 29 September 1890; *Payne's Lagos Almanack*, (1893) 23 February 1890; cf. E. A. Ayandele, "Ijebuland 1800–1891: Era of Splendid Isolation", Seminar paper, History Dept., University of Aberdeen, 6 December 1971, pp. 19–21.
35. CO 879/33, CP African 399, No. 1, Denton to Knutsford, 11 October 1889; No. 12, do. 6 January 1890, enclosure 6, interview of 4–5 November 1889.
36. CO 879/33, CP African 399, no. 23, encl. 1, Millson (Ikirun), 14 February 1890; no. 27, encl. 1, Millson (Oshogbo) Conf. 30 March; no. 31, encl. 18, 19, Millson, Conf., 22, 25 May 1890; cf. C. A. Moloney, "Cotton interests, foreign and native, in Yoruba, and generally in West Africa", *Journal of the Manchester Geographical Society*, v, 1889, p. 3.
37. Ibid, no. 23, Moloney to Knutsford, Conf., 5 April, encl. Conf. Minute 29 March; nos. 26, 27 Moloney to Knutsford, Conf., 19 and 30 April 1890.
38. Ibid, no. 29 encl. 3, Report of deputation, 13 June 1890; cf. no. 26, Moloney Conf., 19 April.
39. A. G. Hopkins, "The Lagos Chamber of Commerce, 1888–1903", *JHSN*, III, 1965, pp. 242–4.

40. CO 147/77, Moloney to Knutsford 402, 10 December 1890, encl. Lagos C of C, 2 December.
41. CO 147/77, Moloney to Knutsord, 401, 10 December: 409, 26 December 1890.
42. CO 147/79, Denton to Knutsford, 42, 7 February 1891: CO 147/83, M/cr C of C to CO, 31 March, Liverpool C of C to CO, 6 April 1891.
43. CO 879/36, CP African 428, nos. 1, 2, 4: Denton to Knutsford, 141, 21 May: Conf., 22 May; Conf., 9 June 1891.
44. CO 147/75, Hemming minute 2 September 1890 on Moloney Conf., 24 June; cf. CO 147/74, Hemming minutes 18 May, 22 June on Moloney, Conf., 5 April, 30 April.
45 CO 147/80, Minute by Hemming 9 July on Denton 141, 21 May 1891.
46. CO 879/36, CP African 428, no. 5, Minute by Moloney, Belize, 9 October 1891.
47. CO 879/33, CP African 399, nos. 38, 39: Moloney to Knutsford, Secret 30 August; Conf., 13 September 1890; cf. Hopkins, "Economic Imperialism . . .", p. 595, for a reference to problems of Lagos traders.
48. SMA 14/802.02, Francois to Planque, 17 March, 29 May, 2 July, 10 July, 24 September 1890, 12 February 1891.
49. CO 147/83, Minute by Meade 3 September 1891 on Millson, 21 August; cf. O. Omosini, "Railway Projects and British Attitude towards the development of West Africa, 1872–1903", *JHSN*, v, 1971, p. 504.
50. CO 879/36, CP African 428, Knutsford to Carter, 5 November 1891; cf. CO 147/83, Minutes and Drafts on Moloney, 9 October 1891.
51. P. N. Davies (ed.), *Trading in West Africa* (1976), pp. 145–6, interview with W. K. Findlay; W. N. Geary, *Nigeria under British Rule* (1927) pp. 56–7.
52. CO 147/84, Hemming, 29 April 1892 on Carter, Tel., 29 April.
53. CO 147/81, Carter to Hemming, Pte., 7 November; CO 147/82, Carter to Knutsford 375, 10 December 1891; CP African 428, No. 15, Carter to Knutsford, 379, 17 December 1891 (encl. Carter to Awujale, 16 December): Conf., 18 December 1891.
54. Ibid., no. 22, Carter to Knutsford, 25 January 1892.
55. Rhodes House Oxford, Mss Br.Emp.S.18: Anti-Slavery Papers, C151/178, James Johnson to Fox Bourne, 12 February 1892.
56. Hastings Report, April 1892; CP African 428, nos. 39, 80, Denton to Knutsford, 63, 20 February 1892, Conf., 3 March 1892; Anti-Slavery Papers, G18; anonymous MS, "The Jebu Matters".
57. CP African 428, nos. 42, 86, Carter to Knutsford, Tel. 16 March, Conf., 18 March 1892.
58. These may be studied in CO 147/88, in CP African 428, and in CO 267/397. Cf. Hopkins "Economics Imperialism", pp. 601–2: Hynes, *Economics of Empire*, p. 123.
59. CO 147/84, cutting from Liverpool Courier, 9 March; cf. Elder Dempster to Bond, 12 March 1892.
60. CO 147/84, Minutes by Hemming, 11 March, Meade, Knutsford, 14 March on Carter, Tel., 10 March; by Knutsford, 15 March, on Denton

63, 20 February: by Hemming and Meade, 17 March, on Carter, Tel., 16 March. CO 879/36, CP African 428, no. 43, Knutsford to Carter, Tel., 18 March 1892.

61. For the military preparations and operations, see Robert Smith, "Nigeria–Ijebu", in M. Crowder (ed.), *West African Resistance* (1971). Cf. A. A. Aderibigbe, "The Ijebu Expedition, 1892", in *Historians in Tropical Africa.* Proceedings of the Leverhulme Inter-Collegiate History Conference, 1960 (Salisbury, 1962).
62. For Hay's reports to Knutsford, and official comment, see CO 267/381, Hay 40, 14 February 1890; 75, 28 February with minute by Meade; CO 267/383, Hay 248 and 249, 6 June 1890, with minute by Hemming; CO 267/385, 441, 8 November 1890; CO 267/386, Hay 549, 9 December 1890, CO 267/389, Hay 204, 15 April 1891 shows Hay congratulated by the merchants.
63. Aderibigbe's criticism of Knutsford ("The Ijebu Expedition, pp. 273–4) fails to note that his Minute of 14 March refers to the Egba and not the Ijebu.
64. CO 879/36, CP African 428, Carter to Knutsford, 149, 5 May 1892.
65. F. I. A. Omu, *Press and Politics in Nigeria, 1880–1937* (1978) pp. 32–3, 121–3; cf. Aderibigbe, "Ijebu Expedition . . .", pp. 279, 267–8.
66. CP African 428, No. 109, Carter to Knutsford, 129, 20 April 1892.
67. Anti-Slavery Papers, G18. J. P. Haastrup, printed "Report of the Deputation of the Native Inhabitants of Lagos sent to Ijebu Ode, April 1892".
68. Lagos Institute, Proceedings, 20 November 1901; the Hon. Dr Obadiah Johnson, BA MD, "Lagos Past" in RCS Library.
69. E. A. Ayandele, "The Ideological Ferment in Ijebuland, 1892–1943", *African Notes*, University of Ibadan, 1970.
70. A Pallinder-Law, "Government in Abeokuta", pp. 56–61.
71. CO 147/91, Minute by Hemming, 16 January 1894, on Carter 260, 11 December 1893.
72. Liberals 272; Conservatives 268; Liberal Unionists 46; Irish Nationalists 81; others 3. For "the great law of the pendulum", see Salisbury to Cranbrook, 19 October 1900, A. E. Gathorne Hardy, *Gathorne Hardy, First Earl of Cranbrook* (1910) II, p. 374.
73. FO 84/2256, "Notes from the African Dept.", August 1892.
74. Harcourt to Rosebery 23, 27 September 1892: A. G. Gardiner, *The Life of Sir William Harcourt* (1923) II, pp. 193–7. Cf. R. R. James, *Rosebery* (1963) pp. 259–68, for further evidence on the conflict in the Cabinet.
75. Lugard's Address to Royal Scottish Geographical Society, 15 November 1892, *Scottish Geographical Magazine*, VIII, 1892. See D. A. Low, "British Public Opinion and 'The Uganda Question', October–December 1892", in his *Buganda in Modern History* (1971) pp. 55–83.
76. For this phrase, see J. L. Duthie, ". . . Lord Salisbury and Anglo-Afghan Relations, 1874–1878", *JICH*, VIII, 1980, p. 200 and n. 134.
77. *The Times*, 2 March 1893.
78. *The Times*, 6 February 1893.

79. Meade to Ripon, 15 September 1892, quoted in J. S. Galbraith, *Mackinnon and East Africa, 1878–1895* (Cambridge, 1972) p. 219.
80. P.P. 1905, LVI, Cd.2325, p. 23; Lyttleton circular, 5 December 1904.
81. J. A. Atanda, *The New Oyo Empire* (1973) ch. II, App. C for the 1893 treaty with Oyo.
82. O. Ikime, *Merchant Prince of the Niger Delta* (1968).
83. For general views of this process by modern Nigerian historians see J. C. Anene, *Southern Nigeria in Transition* (1966); O. Ikime, *The Fall of Nigeria* (1977) Fuller accounts of particular episodes include J. E. Flint, "The Revolt of the Brassmen", in Flint, *Goldie*, ch. 9; A. F. C. Ryder, *Benin and the Europeans* (1969) pp. 260–94; P. Igbafe, *Benin under British Administration* (1979) ch. 2; R. Horne, *City of Blood Revisited* (1982); E. Isichei, *A History of the Igbo People* (1976) ch. 9.
84. ANSOM, Afrique VI/84 Etienne to Ribot, 18 June, 23 July; Ribot to Etienne, 29 July, encl. Herbette to Ribot, 19 July; Etienne to Ribot Conf. 3 September 1890. See also A. S. Kanya-Forstner, *The Conquest*, pp. 157–8. For the three missions, cf. Meniaud, *Les Pionniers du Soudan*, I, pp. 525–7.
85. FO 84/2208, Phipps to Anderson, Pte and Conf., 22 April 1892; with Minute by Salisbury.
86. Ferguson's instructions and reports are in CO 879/38, CP African 448; his main report is printed and annotated in K. Arhin (ed.), *The Papers of George Ekem Ferguson* (1974). See also R. G. Thomas, "George Ekem Ferguson: Civil Servant Extraordinary", *THSG*, XIII (i), 1972, pp. 181–215.
87. Arhin, pp. 78, 83–5: the king of Bule "wants trade to make him a big man".
88. Arhin, pp. 76, 83.
89. Arhin, p. 79.
90. For indications of the structure of Asante rule, see I. Wilks, *Asante in the Nineteenth Century* (Cambridge, 1975) esp. pp. 66–8. For developments in Dagomba, M. Staniland, *The Lions of Dagbon* (1975) pp. 7–10 and ch. 2.
91. Arhin, p. 84.
92. B. Obichere, *West African States and European Expansion* (New Haven, Coun., 1971) pp. 150–1; Flint, *Goldie*, pp. 217–18 fails to note Goldie's responsibility for the failure.
93. FO 84/2208, Minutes by Salisbury, Anderson, on Dufferin to Salisbury, 103 Africa, 9 May 1892.
94. FO 84/2208, Dufferin 108 Af, 13 May 1892, enclosing Phipps report of Niger and Lake Tchad Commission no. 1, 11 May, with Minutes by Anderson, Salisbury, Lowther; Dufferin, 109 Af, 16 May, enclosing Niger Commission no. 2, 15 May, with Minute by Anderson.
95. DDF, IX, nos. 62, Waddington to Ribot, 10 November; 70, 71, Ribot to Waddington, 17, 18 November 1891; 158, Ribot to P. Cambon, 17 January 1892; cf. Cecil, *Salisbury*, IV, pp. 395–6.
96. JO (Chambre, 1 June 1892); M. Perham, *Lugard: the Years of Adventure 1858–98* (1956) ch. XVIII.

97. FO 84/2208, Dufferin, 137 Af, 11 June, ending Phipps, 10 June; Phipps to Salisbury, 142 Af, 20 June 1892.
98. H. Brunschwig, *Mythes et Réalities*, (1960) pp. 113–16; C. M. Andrew and A. S. Kanya-Forstner, "The French Colonial Party", *HJ*, XIV, 1971, esp. p. 107; H. Sieberg, *Eugène Etienne und die französiche Kolonial-politik* (Köln, 1968).
99. Sieberg, *Etienne*, p. 97.
100. H. Brunschwig, "Anglophobia and French African Policy", in P. Gifford and W. R. Louis, *France and Britain in Africa* (New Haven, Conn., 1971) p. 27.
101. DDF, ix, no. 2. Waddington to Ribot, 1 September 1891. For the bitterness of this controversy, see D. J. M. Muffett, *Empire Builder Extraordinary: Sir George Goldie* (Douglas, 1978) pp. 148–57.
102. Flint, *Goldie,* pp. 168–72; L. Brenner, *The Shehus of Kukawa* (Oxford, 1973) pp. 120–2.
103. DDF IX, no. 435, Ribot to Waddington, 8 August 1892; cf. Kanya-Forstner, *Conquest*, p. 238n; Person, *Samori*, III, 1387.
104. Sa'ad Abubakar, *The Lamibe of Fombina* (Zaria, 1977) pp. 135–43. Flint, *Goldie,* pp. 172–9; R. A. Adeleye, *Power and Diplomacy,* pp. 149–58.
105. Yves de Tessières, "La mission Monteil de 1890–1892", *RFHOM*, LIX, 1972, pp. 374–5; P. L. Monteil, *De Saint-Louis à Tripoli* (1895) p. 253.
106. Tessières, pp. 376–81; Monteil, ch. XII; L. Brenner, *The Shehus of Kukawa,* ch. VII.
107. H. Labouret, *Monteil*, pp. 130–1, 136; Frey to Monteil, 22 December 1892. Cf. Tessières, pp. 387–90.
108. Tessières, pp. 393–7.
109. FO 84/1997, Goldie to Anderson, 17, 18 June 1889; FO 84/2087, RNC to FO, 22 July 1890. Flint, *Goldie,* pp. 160–2.
110. M. Crowder. *Revolt in Bussa* (1973) ch. I gives conflicting traditions of Borgu. The fullest study of its political structure is J Lombard, *Structures de type "feudal" en Afrique noire* (1965) cf. R. Cornevin, *Histoire du Dahomey* (1962) ch. v.

10 The Fall of Dahomey

BAYOL AND BEHANZIN

Even when Franco-Dahomean conflicts began to escalate during the 1880s, few Frenchmen felt any imperial mission to conquer Gelele's Kingdom, least of all those who actually operated on its soil. Despite vast cultural differences and profound mutual misunderstandings Franco-Dahomean relations rested on a basis of real but limited mutual interest. The merchants could obtain palm-oil in quantity and at reasonable prices; the Kings of Dahomey received in return fire-arms and consumer goods, which fortified the power of the monarchy. The conditions they imposed at Whydah, the traditional port of trade, included stringent control on the movements of foreigners, and enforcement of Dahomean commercial regulations;[1] but the merchants accepted this for the sake of good business, confident that they would never be squeezed to the point of unprofitability. Régis indeed was often the arbiter of Franco-Dahomean relations, advising both the French Government and Gelele on their policy, and facilitating settlement of the British blockade in 1876–7 at his own expense.[2] "In all grave circumstances the sovereigns of Dahomey have always approached us for advice", his firm claimed, with justification.[3]

Inter-European rivalries, which elsewhere in West Africa often upset the balance of similar mutually advantageous relationships, had only indirect effects in Dahomey. The local roots of French imperialism were to be found in Porto Novo, where the different perspectives of French commercial agents and missionaries began to lead them, and some of their administrators, to denounce Fon barbarism, and to advocate action against it (vol. I, pp. 163–9). The Ministry would have been better able to resist such pressures had it not been for the dispute over Cotonou, which handled an increasing trade as palm forests in the Wheme valley were opened up. By the early 1890s, 80 per cent of Porto Novo's imports (valued at between £150 000 and £200 000) consisted of spirits and tobacco destined for Aja or Yoruba country; about one third passed through Lagos, paying a reduced rate of duty to the British, the rest was trans-shipped across the dangerous bar at Cotonou.[4] The colonial administration wished to improve landing facilities at this port, recouping the cost by imposing its own tariff. The difficulty was that the Treaties of 1868 and 1878 which they believed entitled them to do this had not been authorized by Gelele: the monarchy would never accept cessions of Fon territory, especially at a major trading port. Settlement of this dispute was to be the first concern of Lieutenant-Governor Jean Bayol.

This volatile Provençal had now served nine years in West Africa, and for seven had been France's senior representative in her southern dependencies. Bayol was a convinced Republican partisan of Etienne and the Gambettist remnant,[5] and a believer in the secular mission of the Republic in those parts of Africa which he now believed he knew well. As originally drafted, his instructions left him wide discretion to decide, after studying the situation on the spot, what measures were needed "to re-establish our diminished prestige at Porto Novo and to improve our situation *vis-à-vis* Dahomey".[6] Though authorized to consider the deportation of Tofa to Gabon, Bayol had almost certainly already rejected such a course in discussion with Etienne in Paris, and returned resolved to fortify the King's position. The instructions also gave high priority to settling the problem of Cotonou. Bayol was authorized to consider occupying Whydah, and other ports in southern Dahomey, if necessary applying for naval assistance and for an additional company of *tirailleurs*.

Although these draft instructions emphasized the need for tact and circumspection, the Foreign Ministry, given less than a week to comment, feared they might lead Bayol to commit the French government. Diplomatic worries concentrated on the danger of new conflicts with Lagos: a suggestion that Viard might be employed on new treaty-making expeditions towards the Niger was deleted from the draft, and the general injunctions to prudence were emphasized. But even as amended the instructions left large powers of initiative with

Bayol. On 20 October he arrived at Porto Novo, where he was "awaited like the Messiah",[7] and confidently announced his intention to act resolutely to solve the Colony's problems.

The euphoria of the French community soon subsided; Bayol's first action was to appoint the unpopular d'Albeca as Resident in place of Captain Tautain, who had gained the confidence of Catholic missionaries and Creole traders by advocating more direct French administration in Porto Novo as a preliminary to an early military expedition to Abomey. Tofa's cowardice in 1889 had left him few friends. "All, Whites, Creoles and natives, are anxious to have done with a King who is good for nothing but stirring up quarrels", wrote Pied in April, and this view was only partially modified when Tofa began to put in occasional ceremonial appearances at Mass.[8] Yet Bayol seemed to be reverting to old policies. Tofa, despite his frivolous tastes in fancy hats and alcohol, was a shrewd enough politician to understand the importance of rehabilitating himself with the French; on Bayol's arrival he demonstrated his loyalty, and his religious eclecticism, by commissioning special prayers in the Tijani mosque. Bayol reciprocated by confirming his intention to maintain Tofa on the throne. Apart from the difficulty of replacing him, Bayol feared:

> the embarrassment in which the Government representatives at Porto Novo would be placed if the natives, who are accustomed to being kept in their place by very severe rules, should without any transitional period find themselves enjoying the liberty granted by our laws.[9]

Bayol was thus committed not only to securing Fon recognition of France's claim to Cotonou, but to supporting a *protégé* whom the Fon regarded as a revolted upstart. To suppose that peaceful diplomacy could reconcile Gelele to this required an exceptional combination of conceit and ignorance; Bayol himself prepared for failure by studying a possible military advance on Abomey by the Whemé valley. Nevertheless, after an inconclusive exchange of letters, he decided to negotiate in person and so "make it impossible for the King to avoid a precise reply". On 16 November, having warned

Etienne to disregard rumours which interested parties might spread during his absence, the Lieutenant-Governor left for Abomey.[10]

His arrival had a decisive though unintended effect on the power struggle which marked the declining years of Gelele's reign. Fon from the coastal areas most involved in the oil-palm trade had long favoured conciliatory policies towards Europeans, involving gradual reform in the institutions and tradition of the state: in Abomey they were represented by Vissegan, Gelele's senior wife, and by Topa, one of his younger sons; they saw no future in confrontation with the French, and even favoured allowing them to occupy the coastline on payment of rent, as the British did at Lagos. Against them, *féticheurs* who feared the influence of Christian missions and other intransigent traditionalists, were led by Kondo, the heir-apparent. Bayol's blunt demands now tipped the balance at court in favour of those who were prepared to destroy the palm-trees which brought so much wealth to the monarchy rather than compromise on questions of Dahomean sovereignty or territorial integrity.[11]

In negotiating with Bayol,[12] Kondo assumed that the Treaties of 1868 and 1878 had no validity whatever as bases for French rights at Cotonou (cf. *Prelude*, pp. 120, 208–10); far from signing any new document or authorizing France to levy customs duties, he demanded that Bayol should formally renounce any claim to do so. Bayol simply could not grasp the possibility that the treaties might be invalid (although Tautain had understood this clearly);[13] he repeated that they had been duly ratified by the French Republic (as if this procedure could validate forgery) and suggested submitting them to Portuguese arbitration. Kondo's ironical response drove this good Republican to impotent fury; since France now seemed to be governed by *de jeunes gens irrefléchis*, would it not be wise to abolish the Republic and restore sane monarchial government?[14]

Far from accepting Bayol's demands, Kondo went over to the diplomatic offensive. He rehearsed the litany of complaints against the French which had first been heard earlier in the year, and brought it up to date by alleging that the former Resident Beckmann had publicly declared an intention of occupying Cotonou regardless of Dahomey's attitude. More ominous still was Kondo's view of the Porto Novo question:

> He declared to me (Bayol reported] that this country belonged to Dahomey; that Tofa had been named King by his father; that he asked me to replace him, or better still to send him as a prisoner to Abomey.[15]

Bayol fumed at this treatment; but he could do nothing to escape it. Like earlier European visitors to Abomey he was kept a virtual prisoner at Abomey, conscious that customary human sacrifices were taking place elsewhere in the royal palace, and that those decapitated included Porto Novo prisoners of the April campaign, "snatched from a territory under French protection". He dared not risk sending messengers to Porto Novo, even when offered facilities to do so; and his confident warning against crediting rumours from Abomey had precluded any possible action by his countrymen to expedite his release. Eventually on 27 December Bayol complied with Kondo's demand that he should accept a document declaring that the alleged treaties regarding Cotonou were void, and proudly asserting Dahomey's equality of international status:

> In Dahomey white men are not killed; white men are not struck; no harm is done to white men. The King of Dahomey gives his country to no-one. God has given the white men their share; when God gave everyone his share, it was Dahomey which had this place. The man who comes to take the country of Dahomey without the King's permission will die.[16]

Having signed this document "as witnesses", Bayol and his party were allowed to leave the capital, carrying a meagre present of four cloths for leading French ministers. (A supplementary offer of three women for the use of President Carnot had been declined.)[17]

Bayol had cut a pathetic and ridiculous figure in Abomey; but his arrival served as a warning that the Fon needed to close their ranks against a mounting threat to their territory.

On 31 December, the day that Bayol thankfully reached Cotonou, Gelele's death was announced, and Kondo's succession in the regnal name of Behanzin.[18] The new king continued to identify himself with "the integral maintenance of traditional values and independence" by taking as his heraldic symbol "the shark that troubled the bar", thus evoking those predatory fish which had long harassed French lighters in the Atlantic surf at Cotonou (*Prelude,* pp. 210, 295). Vissegan, and those who supported her readiness to accept a French occupation of Cotonou, were imprisoned on charges of treason; but Behanzin attempted to maintain unity in defence of the national patrimony by appointing his brother Topa as Meu or second Minister.[19]

Indeed, as Fon traditions emphasize, Behanzin was too shrewd a ruler not to see the perils of confronting the French; as the *yavogan* is said to have warned him, "it was the whites who made the guns".[20] Documentary evidence confirms his readiness to seek honourable compromises, and his skill in exploiting internal disagreements of the French community, about which his subjects on the coast seem to have kept Behanzin well-informed. The enlarged litany of complaints emphasized the personal failing of Bayol (in sending no message of sympathy on Gelele's death, for example), thus implying a prospect of better relations under other governors. Despite his fury against Tofa and his continued support of Soigbe, Behanzin did not invade Porto Novo territory. And he does not seem to have seen any inherent incompatibility between maintaining his claim to Cotonou and encouraging the French to trade there. It was Bayol who found these ambiguities in Franco-Dahomean relations intolerable, and on his return to Porto Novo determined to resolve them by force.

On 4 January 1890 Bayol wrote an indignant letter to Etienne, suggesting alternative sanctions. His "pacific solution" implied abandoning Cotonou in favour of the beach further east known as Porto Novo *plage*; but although this would deprive Dahomey of customs revenue of 100 000 francs annually, it would create new commercial difficulties, and given the growing share of German merchants in Dahomean trade might prove ineffective. Bayol clearly preferred the "radical solution" of an expedition to Abomey.[21] His eagerness to destroy a slave-trading despotism was not however shared in Paris; most of Etienne's colleagues cared nothing for Dahomey but feared the political repercussions of any request to Parliament for credits. On 16 January, before Bayol's full account of his experiences in Abomey had arrived, an alarmist telegram warned of an imminent attack on Cotonou and proposed a pre-emptive expedition to Abomey; Etienne replied that the Council of Ministers, though determined to protect French establishments and property, would not sanction any major expedition requiring parliamentary approval.[22] But their request for an estimate of forces required allowed Bayol to propose operations which went far beyond the needs of local defence. A modest reinforcement from Senegal of two companies of *tirailleurs* and four mountain guns, he cabled, would suffice to occupy not only Cotonou, but Whydah, and the smaller Dahomean ports of Avretété, Godomey and Abomey Calavi. Sufficient customs revenue could then be collected to defray all costs of the operation.[23]

Had the Colonial Department still been attached to the Ministry of Marine, these rash estimates might have been more carefully scrutinized; as it was, Etienne accepted Bayol's prescription. Two companies of *tirailleurs* and the guns were sent from Dakar in the *Ariège*; and the *Sané*, arriving from Gabon on 16 February, brought an additional detachment.[24] Yet the Navy accepted only limited responsibility for the projected operation. Captain Fournier of the *Sané* thought Bayol's plans optimistic and feared the fighting might escalate into something as serious as the Anglo-Asante war; the Admiralty, determined not to become involved in dangerous and unhealthy operations on shore, formally forbade him to land a single sailor or assume any responsibility for the operations in which he was to assist.[25] This divergence of outlook between land and sea forces was reinforced by difficulties of communication; the two services shared no signal code, and naval officers rarely crossed the difficult and dangerous Cotonou bar for fear that bad weather, or industrial action by the Mina canoemen, might make early return impossible.[26] But the Navy's initial scepticism quickly gave way to alarm for French prestige.

Bayol had miscalculated Dahomean military strength. On 21 February, the reinforcements having reached Cotonou, he despatched a defiant letter to Behanzin, repudiating his signature of 27 December. France, Bayol declared, would maintain her commitment to Tofa, and her interpretation of the Cotonou treaties; "henceforth, Cotonou will be French territory".[27] The *tirailleurs* occupied the town, killing a number of Dahomeans; fifteen Fon office-holders were arrested and taken as hostages to Tofa at Porto Novo.[28] But within two days the Dahomeans strongly counter-attacked, wounding two defenders; their vigour clearly surprised Bayol, who desperately demanded reinforcements.[29] While Dahomean troops could be heard distantly singing songs which threatened death to the French, the *Sané* was reduced to firing into the bush in an aimless manner, which impressed the young Joseph Conrad by its futility.[30] On 4 March a new counter-attack cost the defenders nine dead and nineteen wounded; Terrillon, their commander, decided to destroy most of the African town and concentrate his forces around the European factories.

The most immediately serious consequence of Bayol's coup was to endanger French subjects elsewhere in Dahomey. Agents of Fabre and Régis, experienced in collaborating with Fon authorities at Whydah, Avretété, Godomey and Abomey Calavi, did not share Bayol's moral indignation; they may even have suspected that they could be worse off under French control. The Fon, well aware that foreigners based on their soil had different interests and attitudes from those at Porto Novo, had not molested them during the 1889 campaign, and Fournier did not expect reprisals now.[31] When Bayol suggested that all French subjects should withdraw to Cotonou on receiving the codeword *requin,* the traders hesitated; besides the damage to business and goodwill, they feared that a general exodus of foreigners would rouse the suspicions of Fon officials. They preferred to await the relief which Bayol led them to believe would reach Whydah within a few days; when the codeword arrived prematurely on 15 February, five French commercial agents and two missionaries (later joined by two new arrivals and by German colleagues) barricaded themselves in the consular agency (Fabre's factory). By this initiative merchants and missionaries implicated themselves in Bayol's hostile designs; as relief failed to arrive, they were faced with signs of increasing hostility from their besiegers. On 24 February they were persuaded to emerge for discussion with local officials; the Frenchmen were seized, chained, and three days later sent inland to Allada. The Fon now held hostages too.[32]

French Ministers were increasingly alarmed by the consequences of Bayol's rash optimism. On 23 February Etienne personally drafted a warning telegram:

> What motive did you have for seizing Cotonou by force? Have you been attacked? I remind you of my orders to protect nationals and not proceed to offensive.[33]

On 4 March he expressed pained surprise at the news of the capture of the hostages; this was shortly reinforced by representations from Mante *frères* and Fabre, who after expressing concern about the safety of their agents indicated their strong intention to claim compensation from the Government, not only for any damage to their property but for stoppage of their trade.[34] On 8 March Etienne answered a Parliamentary question from François Deloncle, emphasizing that France's primary aim was to secure respect for treaties and to protect her citizens: but when he went on to mention a possible need to take "more energetic measures", Deputies became worried by the danger of being drawn into a crusade against Dahomey.[35] A further infantry company was sent from Senegal, which Etienne hoped would permit the occupation of Whydah; but on 13 March the Tirard government, about to fall, formally rejected Terrillon's suggestion of providing sufficient reinforcements to advance on Abomey.[36]

Half-measures could not resolve the impasse into which Bayol had blundered. On 25 March Terrillon, attempting an armed reconnaissance towards Godomey, was ambushed by Dahomean troops, who inflicted the heaviest casualties of the campaign. Terrillon now quarrelled fiercely with Bayol, accusing him semi-publicly of having underrated the enemy; Bayol replied by suggesting that the campaign to relieve Whydah should be entrusted to Fournier.[37] But the composite force of marines and *tirailleurs*, increasingly stricken by disease and by low morale as they awaited the rains in their impoverished bivouacs, now seemed incapable of even that limited operation.

French politicans now feared that Etienne had lost control. On 17 March the Ministry was reconstructed under Freycinet, who since the Egyptian affair of 1882 had special reasons to fear disapproval by the Chamber on overseas issues; two weeks later responsibility for Dahomey was transferred to the Minister of Marine, Edouard Barbey. Bayol, who was replying to demands for precise information with wild generalities and requests for promotion, was ordered to return to Paris; his plan to march on Whydah was abandoned, and instead a blockade was declared over the Dahomean coast, in hope that this might induce Behanzin to release the hostages and negotiate about France's status at Cotonou and Porto Novo.[38] The Governor's powers, with operational command on land and sea, passed to Fournier, lying off-shore at Cotonou, pending the arrival of Rear-Admiral Cavelier de Cuverville. These officers were instructed to avoid new military commitments, and seek negotiations with Behanzin on any terms which might save France's face. The starting point was to be the release of the French hostages and recognition of the status quo "as it exists today" (that is, since the French attack at Cotonou): but Fournier was authorized to offer generous financial compensation for Dahomey's loss of revenue, and even to agree that customs might still be collected by Fon officials.[39] At one point Barbey even contemplated deposing Tofa and replacing him by a chief mutually acceptable to France and Dahomey.[40] With the French negotiators instructed to seek peace at almost any price, Behanzin was now in a strong position.[41]

CONQUEST OR COMPROMISE?

Bayol's aggression at Cotonou had tipped the balance in favour of the intransigent party within Dahomey, and strengthened Behanzin's resolve to resist. On 2 March he wrote to Wilhelm II proposing an expansion of trade, with the evident intention of using German merchants to re-equip his army with modern firearms.[42] But the "commercial" party still retained some influence, and Behanzin himself avoided provoking unnecessary conflicts by attacking the weakly held French posts at Aghwey and Great Popo. On the same day as his approach to the Kaiser, Behanzin wrote to his old friends in Marseille, reproaching them for allowing their captive agents to become involved in Bayol's plot, and suggesting that new men should be sent to re-open the factories on the old basis.

> as you well know, gentlemen, in my territory it is a law never to harm Europeans nor pillage their factories, and so you have left many million pounds worth of merchandise in your factories at the beach without white supervision, and you have never suffered any loss; yet with such laws Europeans think fit to attack me!

Mante *frères* concluded that Behanzin wanted to use them as intermediaries in negotiation, and this view was later confirmed by the receipt of letters which the French hostages wrote at the direction of their captors; praising their good treatment in Abomey, they indicated that their release might be arranged in exchange for the Fon officials whom Bayol had seized at Cotonou.[43]

Fournier responded to this overture by sending messengers, who reached Abomey about 18 April;[44] meanwhile he remained deeply worried by the presence of the Fon army in the lower Wheme valley. On 20 April it fought a prolonged battle at Atchoupa, a few miles from Porto Novo, against a force of *tirailleurs* and Porto Novan levies. Casualties were particularly heavy among the latter, including Tofa's commander Gbenou, and as in 1889 the capital was seized by panic. Fournier, seriously alarmed himself, sought and obtained permission to send Marines ashore, fired four warning shells around the town of Whydah, and called for reinforcements from France.[45] But Fon casualties at Atchoupa had also been heavy, and Behanzin reacted by authorizing the exchange of hostages, which took place at Whydah on 8 May. (Unhappily nine of the fifteen Fon prisoners were drowned as the French despatched them across the bar.) Before releasing the French hostages, Behanzin harangued them, blaming Bayol and Tofa for the conflict, but emphasizing that thunder would strike him if he abandoned his right to Dahomean territory at Cotonou.[46] Though the return of the prisoners relieved the immediate political apprehensions of the French Cabinet, who faced a Parliamentary interpellation two days later, it did nothing to resolve the basic conflict about French sovereignty at Cotonou.

Once the exchange was completed the Fon army marched rapidly to Egba country and about 21 May resumed its old policy of raiding villages for prisoners.[47] The object was to obtain the means of remunerating German merchants for the expected supplies of firearms. Since exports of palm produce could not be rapidly expanded, and had in any case been reduced by the war,[48] it was necessary to return to an older form of economy and expand the export of slaves (accepted by their purchasers in the more delicate guise of indentured labourers). During the 1880s the Portuguese had revived this trade to serve their cocoa plantations in Sao Thomé and Principe; German entrepreneurs, already interested in providing labour gangs for the Congo Free State, now found a new customer in the government of Kamerun, which required carriers, soldiers and labourers to support a more active colonial policy (see below, p. 191). In July 1890 Ernst Barth, a Swiss merchant trading out of Hamburg, travelled from Lagos to Abomey, escorted through the Wheme valley by supporters of Soigbe; he was promised Behanzin's patronage if he opened trade at Whydah, and received a certain amount of coin in advance.[49] Though he denied it to Moloney, Barth's trade would be basically in firearms; other German firms were already supplying these through Togoland.

Such developments strengthened Fournier's scepticism about the prospects for satisfactory negotiations,[50] and on 10 May he sent two despatches to the Ministry of Marine. One proposed a fairly exacting set of negotiating terms; the other submitted Terrillon's detailed plan to advance on Abomey with a force of around 3000 men, once conditions for navigating the Wheme became favourable during October.[51] Like most Frenchmen at Porto Novo, Fournier was now convinced that the conquest of Dahomey would in the end prove necessary, and positively advantageous to commerce and humanity.[52] But the French government still shrank from the political risks. In the Chamber on 10 May, Deputies who had read press reports emanating from French traders[53] expressed concern about the way the Dahomean situation had been handled, and fear that France might again be drawn into a major colonial war by a policy of *petits paquets*.[54] The government's response was to re-iterate their limited objectives; Etienne's unexpectedly vigorous attempt to link the maintenance of French prestige in Dahomey with the prospects of creating a great colonial domain in North and West Africa held no attractions for Freycinet and his senior colleagues (see above, pp. 24–5). They preferred to respond to Behanzin's hints and try to restore Franco-Dahomean relations to their old commercial basis, if only they could find a formula which would save their face, and their finances.

Two channels of negotiations seemed possible. On the one hand Mante *frères,* encouraged by Behanzin's letter of 2 March, offered to send back a former agent in Dahomey, Siciliano, who it may be supposed was to use financial inducements as a mode of negotiation. On 16 May their representatives saw Freycinet, who somewhat unenthusiastically agreed that Siciliano might be semi-officially authorized to negotiate, under Cuverville's supervision, to induce Behanzin "to respect our position and *leave us in peace* at Porto Novo and Cotonou". Although Fournier feared that Siciliano might abuse his position in order to obtain private commercial privileges, he was provided with ministerial letters, and joined Cuverville at Dakar.[55] Meanwhile Fournier on 21 May renewed direct peace proposals to Abomey through Bernardin Durand, a Catholic Creole of dubious reputation. But when Admiral Cuverville reached Cotonou early in June he found little reason for optimism about the prospects for an honourable negotiated settlement.[56]

* * *

Cuverville, a devout Breton Catholic, had four years earlier concluded that France ought eventually to extend her control over Dahomey; though not a bellicose man, he arrived seeing no ultimate alternative to military conquest. While accepting that "before undertaking a *decisive expedition* we shall have to *exhaust* the possibilities of conciliation"[57] he had no confidence in Siciliano, whom he suspected of seeking some discreditable deal through the commercial underworld of Whydah, and forebade him to go beyond Cotonou and Porto Novo.[58] With no news of Durand's mission, negotiations were making no progress. But Cuverville found the prospects of mounting an expedition to Abomey little better. As the rains came on the sick-rate among European soldiers rose to around 40 per cent, and there was little hope of receiving reinforcements from France.[59]

An alternative was to arm and train a local African army. Father Planque, head of the Lyon Fathers, had in 1889 proposed seeking French volunteers to re-organize the Porto Novo army; but Tofa had rejected his offer.[60] Cuverville hoped to find recruits at Atakpamé, north of Aghwey, but found that the mission post which was to serve as recruiting agency had been withdrawn.[61] Rather stronger hopes were placed on Dahomey's traditional enemies at Abeokuta, where Catholic missionaries retained influence. Victor Ballot, Resident at Porto Novo, had sent messengers, with presents of guns, to seek Egba support, and they brought back vaguely encouraging responses towards the end of March.[62] But any chance of the Egba oligarchy agreeing to send troops to Porto Novo disappeared when Dahomean raids on their own territories resumed in May.[63] On 30 June new French messengers offered to arm and train an Egba force of 2000; after much discussion in Abeokuta, the Onlado apparently promised to send men by the end of July, but only three Egbas arrived eventually to offer their service. Cuverville also hoped to recruit Hausas, but they were greatly in demand by British and German recruiters and were equally scarce.[64]

If the missionaries could not raise an army they might at least provide better channels than the traders for negotiating with Dahomey. Although Father Pied and his colleagues at Porto Novo were bellicose, the branch of the mission which since 1884 had been re-established at Whydah had inevitably acquired a more sympathetic understanding of Fon attitudes. In certain Breton parishes, the Church had shown a capacity to incorporate and transform pre-Christian customs, beliefs and rituals, which may help to explain why some priests regarded Dahomean "savagery" more tolerantly; those accustomed to ceremonies venerating the dead may have been more disposed to understand the purpose underlying sanguinary "customs".[65] Father Alexandre Dorgère, born at Nantes in 1855, was an energetic and temperamental extrovert who had acquired some working knowledge of Fon language and culture; already in 1886 Cuverville had warned him against becoming too involved in African affairs.[66] Dorgère had been one of the hostages taken from Whydah to Abomey, and his personality had impressed some of his captors, including an influential *ifa* priest or *bokono*; his involvement in Dahomean politics now began to seem a possible asset, and by 23 June Cuverville was wondering whether to accept Dorgère's patriotic offer to return to Abomey as French envoy.

> His mission will be to go and find prince Kondo (whom I will not recognize as king until we have obtained the satisfaction we seek) in order to make known our government's conditions and to show him that before taking action we wish to remove all misunderstandings. The *man of peace* will do his work, while making it clear that, failing *immediate* results, force will have the last word (to the great profit of civilisation). . . . These people have a religious sense, and the role of priest commands their respect.[67]

Cuverville regarded such an embassy as a means of convincing Paris that military action was unavoidable rather than as a serious policy. While keeping Dorgère by him in the role of military chaplain, he prepared for the Ministry a detailed plan (based on that of Terrillon) for an expedition to Abomey through the Wheme valley. In order to use the high waters for navigation it would be essential to establish an advance base at Fanvié by early September, and to begin the advance a month later; French forces should be brought up to around 3000 by Foreign Legionnaires, Algerian *tirailleurs*, or seasoned volunteers from the Marine Infantry, with detachments of artillery and other specialists.[68] Dorgère was to test the possibilities of negotiation in sufficient time for failure to be followed by execution of this plan in 1890. In early July the priest accepted this mission in the interests "of our dear fatherland and of the glory of God", and Cuverville proceeded to draft instructions.[69] But it took time to obtain clearance from the Fon authorities; Dorgère had left for Abomey only at the end of the month, on the clear understanding that if he were not back by 1 September France would resume bombardment of the Dahomean coast. Cuverville warned the Minister that he expected failure, in which case "you will doubtless decide whether the *status quo* is compatible with the dignity of our country and with the maintenance of the legitimate influence which it has so long exercised in these waters".[70] Meanwhile he telegraphed for permission to occupy Fanvié, asking for reinforcement by five hundred Foreign Legionnaires.[71]

But ministers refused to be stampeded into what they rightly sensed would be an irreversible step towards Abomey. Father Planque, who had frequently visited Paris during the summer to lobby ministers and to plant anonymous articles in the press, reported that Barbey and others who favoured an expedition had failed to overcome the opposition of Freycinet and Ribot.[72] The Cabinet categorically refused Cuverville's proposal; and this meant that there could be no major campaign in 1890. Cuverville complained bitterly about this lost opportunity to repress an "odious regime" and at the same time occupy a magnificent country of great potential wealth; but he obediently acquiesced and did not carry out a privately expressed threat to resign.[73] There was now no obvious alternative to relying on Dorgère to find some new basis for co-existence with Dahomey.

Dorgère had been provided with a draft treaty containing three contentious demands, together with more general proposals. French rights to Cotonou were to be explicitly recognized; Dahomey was to be allowed pecuniary compensation for surrendering control of the Cotonou customs, but this would at least partly be offset against a war indemnity. Secondly, Behanzin was to promise to respect the territory of the Porto Novo protectorate. Thirdly, as a "touchstone" of

Dahomean intentions, France would re-occupy her fort at Whydah with a garrison of one hundred. In addition France would appoint a Resident, with rights of jurisdiction over French subjects; French trade was to receive most-favoured-nation treatment; Behanzin was to encourage French missionaries and to work for the suppression of human sacrifice.[74]

Although these proposals for a thinly veiled French protectorate over the Dahomean court stood no chance of acceptance as they stood, Behanzin did not reject negotiation outright. His opponents were reported to have launched an abortive "revolution" on 1 August;[75] and though this was suppressed the king was anxious to show the "peace party" that he took the French commercial connection seriously. Indeed, he was himself anxious to profit from that connection, always provided that the fundamentals of Dahomean sovereignty were respected.

> God [he informed Cuverville at the end of Dorgère's mission] has created Black and White, each to inhabit its designated territory. The White man is concerned with commerce and the Black man must trade with the White. Let the Blacks do no harm to the Whites and in the same way the Whites must do no harm to the Blacks.[76]

So Dorgère, escorted into Abomey on 7 August by the king's nephew Zizidogué and by Guédo, the Cussugan or commercial superintendent of Whydah, was received with state honours and long salutes of gunfire.[77] His warm personality and good reputation quickly secured the release of Bernardin Durand and his companions (who had been held in ineffective seclusion since their arrival) and of twenty-seven African employees of French merchants, who had been retained as hostages after the release of the Europeans.[78] But political negotiations proved very tough indeed.

Porto Novo created little immediate difficulty; despite his bitter grievances against Tofa, Behanzin recognized that he would have to respect the territory of France's protégé. (The exact limits of this territory were still highly contentious, and Behanzin reasserted claims to the Whemé valley which would cause serious trouble later; but Dorgère did not complicate a difficult negotiation further by trying to define a boundary.) On Cotonou, while Behanzin would consider practical compromises, he firmly rejected French juridical claims. Cotonou was Fon territory, and Fon officials must return there; but he was prepared to allow the French not only to trade but to collect the customs in return for a payment of £1500 a year. The demand for a French garrison at Whydah was flatly rejected; to Cuverville's embarrassment, Behanzin countered a demand for equal treatment with Portugal by suggesting that Portugal should withdraw her small garrison from her own fort. The only response to the more far-reaching proposals about future Franco-Dahomean relations were suggestions of a non-aggression treaty, and of arrangements for the reciprocal extradition of criminals – a point certain to cause embarrassment in view of the wide divergence between Fon and French schools of jurisprudence.[79]

Cuverville thus greeted Dorgère's return to the coast on 24 August with mixed feelings. Relief that his envoy had been received honourably and secured the speedy release of the African prisoners produced *une très grande détente*; but on substantive issues the Admiral saw little hope of anything better than an armed and precarious peace, and that only after further difficult negotiations. After meeting Dorgère on 10 September Cuverville grew slightly more optimistic;[80] but other Frenchmen, including Dorgère's missionary colleagues, did not share his modest hopes. Father Pied reported that the population of Porto Novo remained alarmed and despondent; he joined with the Apostolic Prefect, Father Lecron, in deploring government policies which involved the national humiliation of collaboration with "this abject tyrant, who personifies the most absolute despotism, the most bestial cruelty, the most insensate pride, and the vilest passions that can be imagined". God, Pied concluded, was imposing upon France the duty of conquering Dahomey.[81] But after laborious negotiations at Whydah during the long wet month of September, Cuverville and Dorgère came briefly to glimpse another version of France's mission.

Cuverville, unwilling to descend personally to detailed bargaining, sailed away to Libreville, and on 16 September a French delegation landed at Whydah under Captain

Montesquiou-Fezenzac of the *Roland*. Bewildered by "this strange country where it is not easy to understand anything"[82] Montesquiou relied heavily on Dorgère's advice. Dahomean interests were represented by Zizidogué and the Cussugan, apparently working under narrow guidelines imposed by Behanzin. There was rapid progress on the practical issues which had caused the original conflict: the Fon representatives speedily agreed to respect the French protectorate at Porto Novo and to recognize France's right to occupy Cotonou indefinitely, accepting in return an annual indemnity reduced to 20 000 francs (£800). But even this meant leaving unresolved underlying questions of right. Although all previous Franco-Dahomean agreements were stated to remain in force Behanzin would not explicitly recognize the treaties of 1868 and 1878 which France claimed as the basis of her position at Cotonou. Still more seriously, there was no attempt to define Dahomey's boundary with Porto Novo. Although Behanzin had clearly staked extensive claims in the Wheme valley,[83] the French still hoped to extend Tofa's control in this productive region.

The main stumbling-block was Cuverville's demand to instal a token garrison in the old French fort at Whydah; at first the Fon representatives refused flatly to discuss this. When Dorgère hinted that such a garrison would avert any future danger of a German or British protectorate (writing to his friend the *bokono* to emphasize this) Zizidogué did agree to submit the proposal to Abomey; but Behanzin refused to budge. When Cuverville returned to Whydah late in September to find the negotiations deadlocked he began to think again, emphasizing the difficulty of maintaining this garrison in face of possible Dahomean hostility and of "that same general who cost us San Domingo – fever".[84] He offered, as an act of apparent generosity, not to install the garrison provided that France's *right* to do so was recognized; but Behanzin stubbornly refused to make such a potentially dangerous concession. By 3 October Cuverville's patience gave out; he accepted an "Arrangement" which did not mention garrison rights at Whydah, and shelved the other disputed points by an ambiguous recognition that *traités et conventions ultérieures* remained in force. In a secret clause the Fon promised not to accept protection from any power other than France; in return Cuverville conceded the principle of reciprocal extradition of fugitives from the common law. As officials noted, "the common law of Dahomey has nothing in common with that of France", and Cuverville seemed naively unaware that this could provide a means of returning fugitive slaves for export or immolation.[85]

This "Arrangement", hurriedly signed after what had often been for both sides a dialogue in the dark, seemed to many Frenchmen a barely honourable truce, a *drôle de paix* forced on them by the pusillanimity of Paris.[86] Only Cuverville claimed to see virtue and promise in the conditions he had reluctantly accepted; with apparent sincerity he began to describe it as a just and generous settlement, which could open the way to the *conquête morale* of the "valiant little people" of Dahomey.[87] Dorgère seems somehow to have convinced this Catholic patriot that there was an honourable alternative to conquest: that Dahomey might yet be civilized by the peaceful penetration of French influence, above all that of missionary priests.

This notion that Church and Republic could work together to extend Western civilization in Africa was already taking shape on the frontiers of empire, anticipating in practice that *ralliement* of Catholics to the secular state which Lavigerie would publicly advocate in November 1890 (see above, pp. 32–3). The Porto Novo missionaries, who in 1886 had claimed to be "neither French, British nor German . . . but simply Catholics, working as a mission for one single cause",[88] were by 1889 co-operating with Masonic officials to extend French civilization on the Slave Coast. On 14 July 1890, an official Mass, followed by a reception at the French Residency, and attended by Tofa resplendent in his own Order of the Black Star, had provided Father Pied with a glimpse of Church and State reconciled for the glory of God and of *patrie*.[89] But in Dahomey itself, Dorgère, whose readiness to encounter traditional religion on its own ground was far ahead of its time, saw a different future. Many orthodox Catholics were shocked when on Sunday, 5 October Fon officials paraded with palm fronds through the church at Whydah to give thanks for peace, while French warships fired a salute off-shore.[90] Yet Cuverville, perhaps recognizing some exotic form of *pardon*, seems to have become sincerely convinced of the possibility of converting Dahomey from within; Behanzin, he told a colleague, showed a nobility of sentiment of which Tofa was incapable, and the guarantees he offered for French interests should be taken seriously.[91] Dahomean society might appear impenetrable as well as repulsive; but Behanzin's firmness in negotiation and bravery in battle had convinced the Admiral that it was worth penetrating, and that Dorgère was capable of doing so. "*Le curé* is indispensable to us here; he is the pivot of our influence and our only serious source of information." The main thrust of French penetration should be through Dahomey – Porto Novo was only an armed camp and trading post where French influence was superficial – and the October arrangement provided a starting-point. "Let us favour by all possible means the development of Catholic Missions and the teaching of the French language, let us multiply schools and create little agricultural colonies, away from the factories and under the direction of the Reverend Fathers who are evangelizing this country."[92]

Cuverville therefore assisted the Fathers to obtain land at Whydah to extend their school, and encouraged them to open new ones at Cotonou and Great Popo. As French replaced the colloquial Portuguese which still served as the commercial and diplomatic language the Mission would nurture "a new Dahomey";[93] Behanzin might eventually become its Clovis. On the political front Cuverville directed the civilian Resident of Porto Novo, Victor Ballot, to undertake a formal mission to Abomey, to try to reconcile Tofa with Behanzin, and to present the gifts which the relieved French Cabinet had spontaneously offered to Behanzin.[94] This bold and quixotic enterprise depended heavily on the personality of Dorgère, an untypical missionary in his tolerance towards traditional religion. Even though Behanzin might be prepared to use missionary contributions to strengthen his state, the cultural gulf remained enormous; and it soon became clear that in Paris, where support from a devoutly clerical Admiral was liable to prove counter-productive, there would be little enthusiasm for attempts to bridge it.

* * *

On 15 November a relieved Council of Ministers decided to submit the Arrangement of 3 October for Parliamentary ratification, although plenty of precedents existed for ratifying treaties with Africans by Presidential decree. It soon became clear that misgivings about France's role in Dahomey which had been expressed earlier in the year had not been removed, and that new ones had been created. The text was referred to a strong Committee under Admiral A. Vallon, a Breton-born naval officer who, after governing Senegal in 1882, had been elected as its Deputy in 1889, and later became Vice President of the Parliamentary colonial group. Vallon, who had visited Abomey in the later years of Gezo's reign, began a full-scale enquiry into the events of 1890; at his request the Colonial Department assembled a carefully edited dossier of 130 documents or extracts.[95] Meanwhile dissatisfaction with Cuverville's compromise developed from various sources. Cyprien Fabre, as President of the Marseille Chamber of Commerce, expressed the grievances of the two French firms, and began by demanding compensation for loss of trade and thefts from the occupied factories.[96] In January Fabre broadened his criticisms in a letter to Vallon, subsequently quoted in the Chamber, which denounced the agreement itself as *funeste pour notre prestige et compromettante pour nos interêts*. French merchants were returning to Whydah as after a defeat, to find three favoured German competitors where formerly there had only been one: to give the arrangement formal ratification would not only raise the prestige of *un roi nègre* still further, but would imply that Dahomey was a fully independent state, free to negotiate with other powers.[97]

This anti-German note gave the cue to right-wing critics who, though caring little for Africa, were always ready to taunt Republican Ministers with lack of patriotism. Déroulède continued to insist that the government had no right to send a single soldier to die beyond France's frontiers;[98] and the old Bonapartist Cassagnac ridiculed the ineffective way in which Barbey – "an ex-Lieutenant from the age of sailing-ship [who had] made a very honourable fortune in cotton bonnets" – had defended the honour of France and her navy.[99]

Anti-clericalism, fuelled by Cuverville's insistence on publicly decorating Father Dorgère with the cross of the Legion of Honour, and his identification of the national cause with that of the missionaries, was another early source of criticism; the "arrangement" had hardly been signed before it came under virulent attack from *La Lanterne*.[100] Such sentiments were encouraged by Etienne and his Republican associates in the colonial administration, who resented Cuverville's public denunciations of Bayol's bungling, as well as their own effective exclusion from his negotiations.[101] When he recovered responsibility for Dahomean affairs in December, Etienne seems to have felt bound to re-assert departmental autonomy by slighting the Admiral's Catholic associates, and excluding Dorgère from the forthcoming mission to Abomey.

Although the *Comité de l'Afrique française* as such took no strong line in Dahomey, the Report of Vallon's Committee on 22 April 1891 presented a negative view of Cuverville's compromise. They complained that the negotiations had been mishandled; the government should have insisted on occupying Whydah, refused to make payments which Behanzin was already using to finance rearmament, given more attention to the promotion of French commerce and the suppression of slave-trading and human sacrifice. Though there was little discussion of the nature of French interests in Dahomey, it was assumed that they had been defended in a manner barely consistent with national honour and prestige. Two deputies favoured total rejection of the arrangement, but the majority preferred simply to let it operate without formal parliamentary sanction; this would have provided "a character of solemnity and permanence which a sense of their own dignity has always led France and other European nations to avoid most carefully".[102]

When the Chamber discussed the Report on 28 November 1891 these criticisms were widely echoed. Although Cuverville was repeatedly attacked for actions necessitated by instructions from Paris, ministers showed no willingness to defend him on any grounds but those of short-term expediency, still less to persist with the policies which he now envisaged. His new enthusiasm for informal colonisation through missionary agency was not echoed even by Catholic deputies. There was no formal ratification of the October Arrangement; the

Chamber left it to the government to implement its provisions in the way most conducive to French interests. This, Cassagnac argued, was the proper patriotic course. The executive was competent to deal with Africans as it thought fit without Parliamentary sanction; "the government may give ten, twenty, a hundred thousand francs to other negro kings on the coast in the cause of French interests and we shall never criticize them".[103] These negative criticisms expressed the hesitancy towards African problems of politicians who no longer knew what sort of colonial initiatives their constituents would accept. Coalition governments worried about survival were unlikely to act decisively until the developing situation in Dahomey itself obliged them to do so.

THE FRENCH OFFENSIVE

While these debates were taking place in Paris the mission to Abomey, which Cuverville had hoped would initiate real collaboration with Behanzin, was being changed into a military reconnaissance. The Admiral originally intended that the mission should leave in mid-December; that it should be led by Ballot (who had been successfully working to induce Tofa to adopt more conciliatory attitudes); and that a leading role would be taken by Dorgère.[104] But after the Cabinet's original offer of gifts, nobody in Paris took much interest in this scheme. The Ministry of Marine slowly prepared to hand back responsibility; the resentful Colonial Department would take no action until this was done on 18 December, and then complained that they were still ignorant of Cuverville's intentions. By this time Ballot had been invalided home; command of the mission was transferred to a soldier, Commandand Audéoud,[105] and Etienne somewhat spitefully directed that Dorgère, they key figure in any real attempt to ally with Behanzin, should not form part of the mission.[106] Audéoud was to present the tawdry collection of gifts which marked the Cabinet's "ratification" of Cuverville's arrangement, and to escort Tofa's messengers of reconciliation; but he was to maintain strict reserve about future Franco–Dahomean relations, and especially the embarrassing "extradition treaty".[107]

The mission eventually left Whydah on 18 February 1891, escorted by Zizidogué and the Cussugan, and remained in Abomey from 23 February until 11 March. Each of its five French members prepared a report;[108] two of these, by Lieutenant Chasles and by Audéoud himself, concentrated on observations relevant to an eventual French military expedition along the Wheme route. All the reports reflect disdain for the Fon and their institutions, sharpened by impatience at the delays imposed by Dahomean protocol: yet all show a certain respect for Behanzin personally (and common contempt for Bayol),[109] with some recognition that the apparently despotic structure of the state was subject to complex controls of "public opinion", or at least the opinion of influential chiefs.[110] Departing with gifts of cloths and young slaves, the French officers reflected that Behanzin seemed sincerely anxious for peace and friendship.[111]

In the one serious political discussion, on 6 March, Behanzin reiterated the familiar principles of his diplomacy.[112] When asked to release relatives of the mulatto Béraud, he replied that these were Dahomean subjects over whom his jurisdiction was not open to discussion. The *ilaris* whom Tofa had been persuaded to send received a reiteration of old grievances, and of Behanzin's determination to protect Soigbe, still present in Abomey;[113] but, the King assured the French, "we shall no longer go to Porto Novo to make war since you are there, though we shall go elsewhere". Enquiring about the payment of his 20 000 franc indemnity, Behanzin repeated that "he could not cede Cotonou, that his fetish forebade him to give away an inch of his territory, but that as far as our occupation was concerned, things would remain as they were". However, recent rebuilding in the vicinity of the French post indicated that Behanzin had not recognized the specific concession of land contained in the "treaty" in 1878; and this was confirmed soon afterwards when the Yavogan who represented Dahomean sovereignty at Cotonou returned to resume his duties within this area.[114]

Besides re-affirming Dahomean rights, Behanzin emphasized his capacity to defend them by public parades and private boasts about the strength of his army. The French refused to be over-impressed: Audéoud tended to discount reports about the modern weapons supplied by the Germans, and Behanzin's claim to have a factory capable of making both guns and powder, as boasts intended to impress his subjects rather than the French.[115] But while the French officers' confidence in the success of a well-prepared campaign against Abomey was confirmed, it was tempered by recognition of possible difficulties and dangers and by some feeling that the destruction of Dahomey might not be the only way to advance French interests.

On their return to Porto Novo, however, any goodwill the officers may have felt towards Behanzin was dissipated by a humiliating discovery. Audéoud, dependent on interpreters he did not trust, had reluctantly been persuaded that the Fon would recognize a gesture of peace and reconciliation if a *tirailleur* and one of Tofa's *ilaris* were to parade at the formal reception with wreaths of palm-fronds around their necks. Only later did he learn that this gesture had rather signified a humiliating request by the French for royal pardon. Audéoud's anger, later loudly echoed by Parisian chauvinists, was largely concentrated against Father Dorgère who, excluded from the official mission, had made his own way to Abomey at Behanzin's request. Although Dorgère does not seem to have given any direct opinion about the palm-fronds, he was accused of having maliciously failed to prevent a humiliating *faux pas*;[116] furious officials were confirmed in rejecting his notions of collaboration with Dahomey. It was only a matter of time before some new incident would upset the Franco-Dahomean truce.

* * *

Behanzin, meanwhile, was seeking other European friends. In September 1890, during the difficult Whydah negotiations, Moloney received reports that Dahomean emissaries would like to be escorted past Porto Novo in a British launch; and on 25 October an unescorted party reached Lagos with a wordy letter of complaint about French behaviour.[117] The emissary was a Whydah mulatto, known to the French as Hendry Doscivo Kagandou, educated at mission school in Lagos, who had acted as interpreter both to Behanzin's son Fasinu in 1888–9, and to Barth in July 1890.[118] Lagos was at this time particularly disgruntled with the results of the boundary agreement of 1889; French officials were flatly refusing to expedite the "definitive customs agreement" it envisaged, since equalization of custom duties would destroy the trade and revenue of Porto Novo.[119] The French in turn believed the British could have done more to facilitate their communications through the lagoon during recent operations. But Moloney could not contemplate supporting Dahomey against France, and Hendry had to content himself with enlisting the sympathetic interest of Lagos Africans worried by the growing manifestations of European imperialism, notably the Liberian-born journalist, John Payne Jackson.[120]

So the best hope of European aid lay with the Germans. The Imperial government never contemplated political involvement, though a few exuberant officials in Togo may have been tempted. But the Hamburg house of Godelt, which in 1884 had tried to draw Bismarck into a commercial treaty with Dahomey,[121] had secured a consular agency for its Agent-General Witt; Behanzin may thus have seen political significance in his delivery of 408 *chassepots* in January 1891. notwithstanding the recently signed Brussels Convention, other Hamburg firms joined in providing modern firearms in return for the "indentured labour" required in Kamerun. (During the summer of 1891 the German colonial government contracted for 370 such labourers; two years later two-thirds of them were dead.)[122] The enterprising Barth, and another new firm, Tangott Sollner, imported nearly a thousand modern weapons between February 1891 and August 1892. Wölber and Brohm, long-established in Togo, supplied four Krupp cannons of various types and three *mitrailleuses*, besides 433 Winchesters and Peabodys;[123] and their agent Richter visited Abomey to instruct in their use.[124]

In order to re-equip his army in this way, Behanzin had to secure more slaves for export. And labour was needed for other purposes too. These were famine years in Dahomey; the mobilization of the army in 1890 had interfered with agriculture and 1891 saw severe shortages. It appears that Behanzin tried to increase production by slave labour on the royal plantations; so there was a double pressure to extend the old methods of procuring slaves by raiding neighbouring peoples.[125]

Behanzin seems first to have turned to traditional raiding grounds to the east and north: by September reports spoke of a "desert zone", where no more slaves could be obtained, around Dahomey's frontiers.[126] Some British officials, moved by accounts of suffering Yorubas, wanted to urge the French to take action; but Salisbury refused to endorse an interpretation of spheres of influence which might extend British liabilities elsewhere.

> to advance the contention that a State should be held responsible for the exercise of due control over all the countries within a sphere which by arrangement with another country, is held to be under its influence would . . . be dangerous; the argument might be applied against Great Britain as regards territories over which she has no control[127]

Indeed, the Foreign Office declined to interfere with Behanzin's arms supplies by enforcing the provisions of the Brussels Convention at Lagos before that treaty had been internationally ratified.[128] The only direct British response was to make the Dahomean raids a pretext for occupying Ilaro – a move intended to reinforce their pressure upon the Egbas rather than to relieve the Dahomean military threat (see above, pp. 114–15). But by confirming British views of Dahomey as a "nest of slavery and bloody superstition", the Dahomean raids helped to create a climate in which a French conquest would receive public acclamation.

By September 1891 the Dahomean drive for slaves was turning westward, towards the undemarcated hinterland of Great Popo, and there was a raid on an Ewe village near Athiemé. Ehrmann, the French Resident, responded cautiously. French forces in this part of their protectorate were negligible; the construction of a wharf and blockhouse at Cotonou (undertaken in 1890 to provide a base for future operations against Dahomey) was going slowly; and in France politicians were still debating past policy. Ehrmann's protest over the Athiemé raid was therefore mild and courteous; and when Behanzin's messengers arrived on the anniversary of the Whydah arrangement they were paid the 20 000 francs *rente*, a little late, with the express approval of Paris.[129] Towards the end of November a more serious episode caused a panic at Great Popo; Behanzin, pressed for deliveries by his German customers, raided the town of Atchicomé. Ehrmann's warning letter, though still measured in tone, received an alarming reply; Behanzin declared his intention to punish such of his neighbours as offended him without consulting the French, and claimed Great Popo itself, together with the Wheme valley, for his sphere of influence. Ehrmann was warned to show greater respect to the King, to recognize his continued sovereignty over Cotonou, and to "remain quietly at Porto Novo, do your trade, and stop troubling me."[130]

Dr David Ross thinks that the truculent tone of this letter may owe something to the interpreter Xavier Beraud, whose interest lay in provoking Franco-Dahomean conflict and in inflating his own importance;[131] but Behanzin was clearly committed to maintaining his hard line in defense of Dahomean sovereignty. A further letter of 16 January complained of bad behaviour by French soldiers at Cotonou (in requisitioning quarters, stealing pigs and chickens) and called for a return to African–European relationships based as formerly on mutual respect.[132] His economic situation was growing critical, as anti-slavery pressure upon the Belgian and German governments began to make it more difficult to dispose of slaves accumulated near Whydah.[133] In time the Fon peace party might have asserted itself; in fact Behanzin's difficulties pressed him into offering the provocation for which French colonialists had been waiting.

* * *

While French attention was concentrated on Great Popo the conflicting claims of Behanzin and Tofa in the Wheme valley remained unresolved. In this area support for the lineage of Mepon remained strong; the rebellion of Chief Kekédé of Dekamé had provoked Fon intervention, with its threat to

Porto Novo in 1889. In November 1890 Kekédé told Victor Ballot that he intended to make his peace with Tofa, and so become a French protégé; but he added that he would first have to discuss matters with Behanzin. Before he could do so the Whemé dispute had exploded into an open conflict (in which Kekédé was eventually to choose Behanzin's side).[134]

Some Dahomean notables favoured avoiding the Whemé valley in their slave-raiding expeditions, so as not to provoke the French; but apparently Behanzin was persuaded to accept the aggressive policies of his brother Guchili, who proceeded to lead a slave-raiding party into the Dekamé area.[135] When Ballot proceeded to investigate on 27 March the raiders fired on his armed launch *Topaze*, wounding five Africans. Ballot's protests were met by Behanzin's assertion that not only the Whemé valley but all Porto Novo belonged to him; armed with their new German weapons his warriors continued to advance; until 3 April Porto Novo town seemed in imminent danger of attack for the third time in three years. Then the Fon troops unexpectedly withdrew up the Whemé; but the French continued to feel vulnerable, even after reinforcements on 3 May raised their total strength on the coast to 942 *tirailleurs sénégalais* and local levies.[136]

It seems unlikely that Behanzin really wished to provoke a war with France. He had been compelled by famine and the demands of German arms-traders to activate claims which he had clearly affirmed in 1890 to the Whemé valley, his last easily accessible slaving frontier as well as the site of royal farms. A letter of 29 March appears to have amounted to a formal re-assertion of overlordship rather than a declaration of war; one of 10 April assumed that Ballot, had, perhaps inadvertently, broken the 1890 "arrangement" by his incursion. "Kindly remain calm and continue to trade at Porto Novo and we shall remain at peace as formerly," Behanzin declared (Indeed he later claimed that he had executed the men involved in the Whemé incident, even though they had only returned Ballot's fire.)[137] At Whydah the Lyon Fathers (only one of whom was actually a Frenchman) and the French commercial agents were placed under surveillance; but they were not arrested as in 1890, and three Sisters were freely allowed to leave.[138] Nevertheless Frenchmen in Porto Novo felt threatened, and their Government now finally decided to resolve the conflict with Dahomey.

* * *

The Colonial Ministry (re-attached to the Ministry of Marine for the duration of Emile Loubet's government, from 3 March 1892 to 17 January 1893) interpreted Ballot's first telegram as revealing a serious military threat: "Dahomey appears to have completed her period of re-armament, and a section of her troops is now armed and trained in the European manner", a Note of 30 March declared.[139] According to the Jesuit de Salinis (a usually well-informed observer, deeply prejudiced against Republican governments) a special committee including Loubet, Cavaignac the new Minister of Marine, and Emile Jamais the new Under-Secretary, together with Brière de l'Isle, Borgnis-Desbordes, Fournier and Audéoud, recommended a decisive expedition to occupy Abomey and overthrow Behanzin; but the Council of Ministers drew back, hesitating to commit itself to more than defensive operations.[140]

On 7 and 11 April the Radical Deputy Hervieu interpellated the government. Debate was somewhat clouded by the Government's insistence on combining discussion of Dahomey and of supplementary estimates for the Sudan; anti-imperialists like Hervieu, Pelletan and Deroulède mingled uncomfortably with civilian colonialists like Martineau and François Deloncle, who accused the *Soudanais* of "seeking gold braid and glory at the expense of commercial colonisation". Jamais, while requesting an additional three million francs to defend French interests in Dahomey, left the government's intentions in doubt, and the Parliamentary Committee which scrutinized the proposal suggested that forthright acceptance of a march on Abomey might be "the most economical solution, as well as that most in accordance with the dignity of France and the general interests of her African policy".[141] Discussion was further complicated by recriminations over the fiasco of 1890, and by allegations that Vallon's Committee had toned down its Report to the

Chamber under official pressure. But it is possible to detect in many speeches, especially by Catholic Deputies, a readiness for decisive action in Dahomey, which seems to foreshadow the formation of the cross-bench colonial group later in the year. In particular the former monarchist and ardent clerical Count Albert de Mun, (in a speech prominently featured by the *Comité de l'Afrique française*) called for a more open and positive colonial policy, to assert French economic and political interests in face of *la grande poussée de l'Europe vers le continent africain.* Although Hervieu's interpellation was rejected only by 270–232, the Chamber voted the additional credits by 314–177, and in the Senate the vote was unanimous.[142]

A valuable analysis of French periodicals has shown how, since 1890, the French public had been conditioned to applaud strong action against Dahomey.[143] After Bayol's mission Catholic papers, and journals exploiting popular tastes for the exotic, began to sensationalize Fon practices of human sacrifice. Descriptions of the exceptionally bloody funeral "customs" for Gezo in 1860 were resurrected, searched for gory details, and removed from the explanatory context of Dahomean cosmology and institutions in which mid-century authors had sometimes tried to place them. Enterprising journalists added new refinements, suppressing the distinction between royal funerary rites and the much less sanguinary annual customs, inflating estimates of victims, elaborating allegations of cannibalism and torture; (but suppressing references to similar practices at Porto Novo, which had been documented by one of the same sources in 1878). Slave-raiding, recently revived to meet renewed European demand, was attributed to the need of savage Dahomeans for victims to gratify their innate cruelty. Illustrators exercised their imaginations on this rich material. By 1892 many readers had come to accept and applaud military action against a ruler whom one Deputy called a "royal gorilla".[144]

So the Government moved hesitatingly towards a military campaign. On 21 April Cavaignac, as Minister of Marine, took over direct responsibility for Dahomean affairs from Jamais; on the 30th he appointed Colonel Alfred Amédée

Dodds, a Senegalese Eurafrican, as *Commandant Supérieur* in Dahomey. Dodds was to remain on the defensive "for the present", and to study alternative methods of "finally assuring our position in Dahomey", including an expedition to Abomey; on 14 May the Council of Ministers emasculated his draft instructions so as to require still greater caution.[145] Nevertheless, a task force was now in being. On 29 May Dodds assumed full civil and military powers at Cotonou, having recruited three extra companies of *tirailleurs* on his passage through Senegal; and on 11 July, after a debate in the Chamber, he was given command of the naval forces as well.[146]

* * *

French policy now took a more decisive turn. Dodds' first concern was to ensure the safety of three French citizens still in Whydah; after an exchange of letters with Behanzin they were conveyed to the French ship *Brandon*, and with Portuguese help exchanged for two Fon agents arrested in Porto Novo.[147] Behanzin's letter was conciliatory, agreeing to re-open roads to trade and suggesting that relations should continue as formerly; but he refused to abandon his territorial claims or withdraw his troops. On 15 June Dodds declared a blockade of the Dahomean coast and prepared for further operations. With the formation of the colonial group in Parliament and the public acclamation of Mizon (see above, pp. 129–31) ministers grew a little bolder; advised by Dodds that a limited operation against Whydah would prove indecisive, they agreed on 25 July (with the Parliamentary recess ahead) to authorize and expedition to Abomey if necessary.[148] Dodds now executed the plans drafted by Terrillon and Cuverville in 1890. Reinforcements of Senegalese and Foreign Legionnaires during August brought his fighting strength to over 2000; by 14 September an advanced base was established at Dogba; on 2 October the expedition crossed the Whemé and advanced towards Abomey.[149]

Dodds did not keep Paris closely informed of his progress; and his final report has been analysed by other writers.[150] It is clear that the numerically superior Dahomean army fought extremely bravely, but was not always able to make the most effective use of its modern German weapons, or to adopt its traditional raiding tactics to prevent the advance of the French square. The French had difficulty in obtaining supplies and drinking-water; their casualties were heavy, especially among officers,[151] and by 21 October Dodds had to await reinforcements under Audéoud (who had been attempting with little success to make a diversionary advance from Great Popo). On the other hand the French were assisted by Yoruba slaves from the palm plantations of the Whemé. On 5 November Dodds' force reached Cana and opened negotiations; by the 14th Behanzin agreed to cede his whole coastline, open all roads to trade, abolish human sacrifice, hand over all his modern firearms, and pay an indemnity of 15 000 000 francs. According to Bayol, now in disgruntled retirement, it was Ballot who insisted on rejecting these terms, judging that the chauvinistic spirit of the French Cabinet and public would prefer an occupation of Abomey.[152] On 17 November Dodds, claiming that insufficient arms had been surrendered, marched into that burning and deserted town. Reinforcements, arriving on the coast, occupied Whydah and the other ports, and the road through Allada was opened without further resistance. On 3 December Behanzin (who had retreated northwards with the remnant of his army) was declared deposed; the coastline was annexed and the rest of the kingdom declared a French protectorate.

AFTERMATH

Although the British government, France's traditional rival in Dahomey, did not attempt to obstruct the French conquest, some international complications continued. Portugal, though she had abandoned her claim to a protectorate over Dahomey, clearly intended to retain the fort at Whydah. Its commandant assisted in arranging the exchange of hostages in June, and in August the commander of the warship *Mindello* offered to collaborate in the French blockade. Captain Marquer of the French navy discerned an ulterior motive, the hope of being allowed to continue shipping *travailleurs libres* to Sao Thomé after the conquest; though one cynic in the Quai d'Orsay noted that Régis had been doing the same until 1865, French officials unanimously agreed not to tolerate this, hoping thus to destroy Portugal's interest in maintaining this costly outpost. However, they underrated the power of Portuguese imperial pride; in March 1893 a new Premier, Hintze Ribeiro, peremptorily refused to withdraw, and the tiny garrison remained throughout the period of French rule, until 1961.[153]

Complications with Germany centred on the Hamburg merchants who had been supplying Behanzin with modern weapons: and also, so Dodds believed, with technical and military advice. During the campaign rumours reached European newspapers that Germans were serving as officers in the Fon army; one such report, reproduced in a pot-boiling little book by a French officer, even named three Germans and a Belgian who had been taken prisoner on 7 October and summarily shot.[154] This sensational mess-gossip has been uncritically reproduced by reputable historians; the German government took no formal note of it, clearly accepting the view of a more reliable observer that "no white was captured, nor even sighted during the whole affair, but in all our colonial campaigns it has become a habit to see Germans and Englishmen leading our enemies".[155]

Dodds' somewhat milder suspicions were confirmed after the occupation of Whydah by captured commercial records of the German firms, including a letter of tactical advice from Barth to Behanzin.[156] He therefore arrested all the German agents and expelled them from the new French colony; and further proposed to prohibit all future trade by Wölber & Brohm and Barth & Joss on the grounds that they had sold modern arms to Behanzin after the start of hostilities.[157] The merchants found only limited sympathy in Germany, where the government stood by the principle of European solidarity when faced by African military resistance; the Foreign Ministry's representations against Dodds' arbitrary reprisals were limited to attempts to mitigate their long-term effects on Hamburg's trade.[158] There can never have been any notion of responding to the desperate plea for mediation which Behanzin addressed to Wilhelm II in October 1892.[159] Once France had undertaken her military commitment in Dahomey, no European government was prepared to interfere.

Behanzin, who with the remnants of his army withdrew to the northern town of Atcheribé, did not abandon hope of finding friends abroad. The French were worried by his contacts in both German and British colonies, noting that the fugitive forces could still import maize through Lagos;[160] but Behanzin's main intention was to excite sympathy for his cause among foreign critics of French imperialism. His emissary Hendry returned to Lagos, accompanied by three Fon notables, renewed contact with John Payne Jackson, and deposited silver coins to the value of £1000 with the Bank of British West Africa, recently established by A. L. Jones. Jackson, besides attacking French aggression in the *Record,* drafted a manifesto, which British newspapers published in March 1893, attributing the conflict to aggression by Ballot, and calling on the nations of the world to support an honourable peace on the terms provisionally agreed at Cana.[161] But despite French suspicions, Hendry received no encouragement from Government House.[162] Irritation with the French never led to any suggestion of abandoning the 1889 agreement, and most British officials, though apprehensive about further French expansion, felt it "decidedly to our interest, and to that of the neighbouring countries, that this nest of slavery and bloody superstition should be destroyed".[163]

Failing support from foreign governments, Hendry invested the remaining funds of the Dahomean treasury in appeals to French opinion. On 27 June and again on 24 July he despatched telegraphs to President Carnot, appealing for opportunities to negotiate in France for an honourable peace.[164] These might well have found some political response. Despite the patriotic and moralistic fervour which had been aroused to support the expedition of 1892, ministers hesitated to seek credits for a new campaign: "Our strict duty is to impose no sacrifice on our country which is not absolutely worthwhile (*utile*)", Delcassé, the new Colonial Under-Secretary, warned Dodds in February 1893.[165] In the Chamber the government still faced cautious sniping from critics of military expansion. On 28 March a short interpellation was conducted by two ex-Boulangist army officers, the Vicomte de Montfort and R. F. Le Herissé. Both argued that the Chamber had voted funds for Dodds' expedition with the aim of punishing Behanzin, not of remaining in Abomey; they cited the somewhat dated precedents of British campaigns against Kofi Karikari and Theodoros. Only de Mun, in the short debate, argued that France should retain Dahomey as a base for expansion. Delcassé, already embroiled with military empire-builders in the Sudan, took a conciliatory line; his objective in Dahomey was

> the simplest possible administration, whose mission would be to encourage and even stimulate private initiative and to support the individual efforts of those (who it seems to me ought to be numerous) who will found commercial establishments and agricultural colonies.[166]

Some colonialists at least were thus disposed to take the possibilities of negotiation seriously. In July the *Bulletin* of the *Comité de l'Afrique française* pointed out that in Dahomey, unlike the Sudan, France could not count on finding collaborators among rulers overthrown by their own opponents: "we are offering thrones and nobody among the princes of the royal family will accept them".[167] Next month the Cotonou correspondent of another colonial journal suggested, as the only alternative to another military campaign, that Behanzin's authority should be restored under French control.[168] On 20 July the Chamber approved without discussion a supplementary estimate of seven million francs for expenses of "occupation and administration" during 1893; but the military still doubted whether civilian ministers awaiting the August elections under the shadow of the Panama scandals could be trusted to see the campaign through. On 2 August Admiral Rieunier, Minister of Marine, warned Prime Minister Dupuy against "the partisans of generosity, who had keen representatives among certain of our officers, even at Cotonou".[169] Rieunier may have been thinking of sympathizers with Cuverville; but the article in *Le Figaro* which he cited proved to have been written by a young man who enjoyed close relations with advisers of both Etienne and Delcassé.[170]

But Behanzin's agents failed to establish contact with potential sympathizers. In October Hendry and the three Fon notables embarked for Liverpool and Paris, escorted by Jackson and by G. W. Neville, A. L. Jones's Lagos agent. By this time Dodds's second military campaign was under way; the French Embassy in London refused to receive the emissaries and when they reached Paris, half-frozen, on 10 November, they found no better response from President Carnot.[171] Jackson had over-estimated the willingness of European critics of colonialism to act on behalf of the Dahomean monarchy.

* * *

Dodds had not begun the new campaign without reluctance. Although the Fon army had been broken as a field force it was clear that populations in the northern part of the kingdom remained loyal to Behanzin; a prolonged guerilla campaign was likely, bringing few opportunities for martial glory, but grave difficulties of supply and communication, and probably heavy losses from disease. During 1893 there were various (ill-documented) attempts by Dodds, and by his temporary replacements, to bring Behanzin to negotiate personally at Whydah; but he, fearing treachery, invoked the convenient "tradition" against looking on the sea, and the French refused to deal with intermediaries. In late October the advance towards Atcheribé began.[172]

But although Dodds' army met little military resistance, it proved difficult to find Behanzin among his loyal subjects, and equally difficult to identify collaborators who possessed traditional authority and were prepared to put it at the disposal of the French. On 4 November the French received a letter in which Behanzin offered to disarm if he were allowed to retain the royal title, and substantial surrenders of armaments followed; but Dodds still insisted on negotiating with Behanzin personally, and it is clear that his intention was now to depose him. Some thirty chiefs and royals did indeed surrender, but Behanzin himself took to the bush, where for more than two months he eluded pursuit, thanks to a highly efficient intelligence network among his loyal subjects. Open military resistance had ended, but political deadlock seemed complete.

Nevertheless, both sides retained motives for compromise. Dodds wanted to withdraw his weary soldiers, reduce the occupied territory to order, and allow commercial exports to revive; the Dahomean chiefs, whichever side they had taken in earlier disputes, were united in seeking to preserve the monarchy, and above all to avoid the shameful danger (of which Behanzin appears to have been acutely conscious) that the French might seek to impose the arch-enemy Tofa.[173] According to Dodds, the Fon came to accept the idea of a new king for a variety of reasons: antagonism to Behanzin, war-weariness, ambition, and patriotism – "a sentiment", he acknowledged, "of which the Dahomeans are far from incapable".[174]

Fon oral traditions concerning this troubled period are confused and contradictory; some suggest that an ambitious faction led by a war chief called Soglo actually plotted to replace Behanzin by his brother Gucili, others suggest that Behanzin entered into a secret blood pact with Gucili, acquiescing in his own deposition in hope of preserving the monarchy itself.[175] (The fact that the leading *ifa* priest whom the French named Bokonou finally left Behanzin and acknowledged his successor may support the latter view.)[176] In any case, at a ceremony conducted under French auspices on 15 January 1894 Gucili was enthroned under the name of Agoli-Agbo ("the dynasty has not fallen"), and recognized by the French as King of Abomey. The Southern part of the kingdom was detached, and on 4 February Dodds installed a representative of the dynasty overthrown in 1724 at Allada. Behanzin, who surrendered on 25 January, was honourably exiled, and died in Algeria in 1906.

* * *

The conquered kingdom now became the nucleus of a larger French colony, which took its name. Initially, Dodds promised Agoli-Agbo to respect the laws of Dahomey, except as regards human sacrifice, and to tolerate the purchase of slaves; he seemed genuinely willing to use the monarchy as agent of French administration.[177] But this did not last long. The colonial rulers, short of resources, imposed growing burdens of taxation and forced labour, and enforced their orders through the harsh régime of the *indigénat*; chiefs who collaborated closely with them became discredited, those who failed to do so were deposed. In 1900 Agoli-Agbo, having already been deprived of the province of Agony, followed his brother into exile, and his territory was divided into arbitrary *cantons*.

Elsewhere, too, it became clear that collaboration with the French could secure only limited freedoms. Yoruba slaves, employed on royal plantations, welcomed the French as liberators, and at first Dodds was glad to use them as armed auxiliaries and porters. But once they discovered they were to be left under Fon control they reacted strongly, and Dodds soon had to disarm and repatriate these levies.[178] The Yoruba states which had been conquered by Abomey seemed more reliable partners; protectorate treaties promised that Ketu and Sabe would be "governed according to the manners and customs of the country, whose institutions will be respected".[179] But after 1900, as the French administration gathered strength and confidence, this renaissance of Yoruba chieftaincy was soon reversed.

In Porto Novo, which remained the administrative capital of the new colony, Tofa's uneasy alliance with the French survived the strains of 1889–92 with some difficulty. Growing opposition among his subjects had been exploited by Soigbe, under Behanzin's patronage – and also by the British, who encouraged Gun traders to migrate to Badagry.[180] Cuverville, Ballay, Ehrmann, all reported Tofa's unpopularity, and recommended the deposition of this cruel despot.[181] Nevertheless the French did not feel they could safely change collaborators during these dangerous years; on 7 June 1894 Tofa achieved one of his main ambitions when acting-Governor Dumas recognized his son as heir-apparent. But the powers and perquisites of monarchy in Porto Novo diminished rapidly as French control became assured. In August 1899 the French imposed head-tax in Porto Novo, bypassing

Tofa and collecting it directly through village chiefs; increasingly they administered the district through Brazilian Creoles rather than those Gun notables who remained loyal to Tofa. When he died in 1908, Tofa had clearly become a prisoner of the French; with his grandiose funeral ceremonies, say the traditional historians, the Porto Novan monarchy came effectively to its end.[182] For French imperialists at least, it had served its purpose well.

NOTES

1. ANSOM Dahomey 1/1/b. Bayol to Etienne, 20 February 1890 – Dahomeans insist that kegs of French-made power shall be full to the top, although Fabre claims that it is heavier than British powder because better dried. E. Chaudoin, *Trois Mois de Captivité au Dahomey* (Paris, 1891) pp. 66–7, for reduction in size of the standard measure of palm-oil. This work gives a good vivid impression of the Whydah trading community.
2. *Prelude*, pp. 203–7.
3. ANSOM, Dahomey, v/3/a. Mante to Etienne, 23 April 1890. Although the Marseille firm of *V Régis ainé* had been absorbed by *Mante frères et Borelli*, the old name persisted on the coast.
4. C. W. Newbury, *The Western Slave Coast*, p. 124.
5. ANSOM Dahomey 1/1/b, Bayol to Etienne, 12 October 1889 closes with congratulations on the election results.
6. Etienne to Bayol, 13 August 1889. Two drafts are in ANSOM Dahomey 1/1/a: cf AE Afrique 125, Etienne to Spuller, 5 August, Spuller to Etienne, 13 August, 1889.
7. SMA, 12/802.00, Pied to Planque, 12 January 1890.
8. Ibid, Pied to Planque, 4 April, 7 May, 5 June, 4 September 1889; E. Foa, *Le Dahomey* (1895) pp. 280–4.
9. ANSOM Dahomey III/1, Bayol to Etienne, 14, 10 January 1890; cf Vol. 1, pp. 168–9.
10. ANSOM Dahomey I/1/b, Bayol to Etienne, 4 November 1889; cf his later account of 10 January 1890 in Dahomey III/1.
11. ANSOM Dahomey, III/2/a. Béraud to Ehrman, 12 March 1891. D. A. Ross, "The Autonomous Kingdom of Dahomey, 1818–94", PhD Thesis University of London, 1967, pp. 308–18; M. L. Garcia, "Archives et traditions orales", *CEA*, XVI, 61–2, 1976, pp. 196–200. I am indebted to M. Garcia for personal discussion of his extensive studies of Fon oral traditions. His thesis on "La France et la Conquête du Dahomé, 1875–1894" was submitted to the Sorbonne in 1983, after the completion of this work.

12. Bayol's fullest account is ANSOM Dahomey iii/1, Bayol to Etienne 14, 10 January 1890; this was written after his return to Porto Novo and calls for an early military campaign. Dahomey I/1/b Bayol to Etienne, Tel. 1 January, Letter 4 January 1890, give more immediate and summary reactions. Although in the letter Bayol complains that he has no time to analyse the political situation, he spends some time describing the Amazons for the benefit of Mme Etienne. Dahomey iii/1, Angot to Bayol, 5 January 1890, is a diary apparently written in Abomey; cf Dahomey v/1, Bayol to Etienne, 6 December 1889 (not sent until 4 January 1890 for fear it would be read by the Fon messengers).
13. ANSOM, Sénégal iv/124/b, Tautain to Thomas, 1 June 1889.
14. ANSOM, Dahomey iii/1, Bayol to Etienne, 14, 10 January 1890.
15. Ibid.; cf vol. 1, p. 167.
16. ANSOM Dahomey v/1, Gelele's letter enclosed in Bayol to Etienne, 4 January 1890.
17. ANSOM Dahomey i/1/b, Bayol to Etienne, 4 January 1890.
18. Vol. 1, p. 143 reports Dr David Ross's view that Gelele may already have been dead. M. Garcia feels this view feasible, but unlikely; he suggests rather that Bayol's mission may have provided the opportunity for Kondo to poison his ageing father, op. cit. pp. 199–202.
19. ANSOM Dahomey, iii/2/a, Béraud to Ehrmann, 12 March 1891; Garcia, pp. 197–9.
20. M. J. and F. S. Herskovits, *Dahomean Narrative* (Evanston 1958), p. 376; cf the traditions reported by Behanzin's brother Agbidinoukon in App. I of A. Le Herissé, *L'ancien Royaume du Dahomey* (Paris, 1911).
21. ANSOM Dahomey, i/1/b, Bayol to Etienne, 4 January 1890.
22. ANSOM Dahomey i/1/c, Etienne to Bayol, Tel. 16 January 1890.
23. AE Afrique 126, Etienne to Spuller, 16, 21 January 1890 quotes the relevant telegrams.
24. ANSOM Dahomey i/1/c, Etienne to Bayol, 10 February 1890.
25. ANSOM Dahomey i/3/a, Fournier to Marine, Tel. 8 February 1890, Dahomey i/3/b, Marine to Fournier, Tels, 10 February, 2 March 1890.
26. AM BB[1] 1989, Fournier to Marine, 5 April 1890.
27. ANSOM Dahomey iii/1, Bayol to Bedanzin [sic] 21 February 1890.
28. ANSOM Dahomey i/1/b, Bayol to Etienne, Tel. 22, 25 February; Despatch, 5 March 1890. Dahomey iii/1, Bayol to Etienne, 14 December 1890, cf Garcia, p. 199.
29. For these operations, see ANSOM Dahomey i/1/b, Bayol to Etienne, 5 March, 4 April 1890, and numerous telegrams.
30. J. Conrad, *Heart of Darkness* (ed. L. F. Bean, Englewood Cliffs, NJ, 1960) pp. 10–11, 95n. "There wasn't even a shed here and she was shelling the bush . . . There was a touch of insanity in the proceedings, a sense of lugubrious drollery in the sight . . ."
31. AM BB[4] 1989, Fournier to Marine, 8 February 1890.
32. The clearest account is AE Afrique 126, Bontemps, Report on Events, 15 February–8 May 1890. For Bayol's subsequent defence, ANSOM Dahomey iii/1, Bayol to Etienne, 14 December 1890. Another account

by one of the hostages is E. Chaudoin, *Trois mois de captivité au Dahomey* (Paris, 1891).

33. ANSOM Dahomey i/1/c, Etienne to Bayol, Tel., 23 February 1890.
34. Dahomey i/1/c, Etienne to Bayol, Tel. 4 March, Dahomey V/3/a, Mante frères to SSEC, 8 March 1890; Fabre to SSEC, 29 March 1890, referring to interviews with Etienne.
35. JO (Chambre: Dêbats) 8 March 1890, pp. 486–7; cf. *Journal des Débats*, 9 March.
36. ANSOM Dahomey i/1/c, Etienne to Bayol, Tel., 13 March 1890.
37. ANSOM Dahomey i/1/b, Bayol to Etienne, 26 and 28 March mentions five French dead; but SMA 12/802.00 Pied to Planque, 8 April, puts the dead at 18 (including 8 whites) with 32 wounded.
38. ANSOM i/3/b, Barbey to Fournier, Tel., 5 April 1890. An article in *Le Temps* by Henri Mager, 29 April 1890, gives Etienne's view of these events (cf ANSOM Dahomey, V/3/c).
39. AM BB^4 1988, Barbey to Cuverville, 8 April 1890. Barbey to Fournier, 8 April 1890. These documents are faithfully reproduced in a polemical work by a Jesuit admirer of Cuverville, A. de Salinis, *La Marine au Dahomey: Campagne de la Naiade 1890–1892*, (Paris, 1901), pp. 22–6.
40. AM BB^4 1988, Draft Tel. to Fournier, 8 April 1890.
41. ANSOM Dahomey I/3/a, Fournier to Barbey, Tel., 9 April 1890.
42. Behanzin to Wilhelm II, 2 March 1890, in M. Kalous, "Some Correspondence between the German Empire and Dahomey in 1882–1892," *CEA*, vii, 32, 1968.
43. ANSOM Dahomey v/3/a, Behanzin to Mante, 2 March 1890 (copy) encl. in Mante frères to Etienne, 23 April 1890; Hostages to Carnot, 4 April; Bontemps to Fabre, 4 April 1890 encl. in Fabre to Etienne, 22 May.
44. AM BB^4 1989, Fournier to Barbey, Tel., 11 April 1890; AE Afrique 126, Report by Bontemps, May 1890.
45. ANSOM Dahomey I/3/a, Fournier to Barbey, Tels 21, 22 April 1890; SMA 12/802.00 Pied to Planque, 24 April 1890; A. Akindélé and C. Aguessy, *Contribution à l'étude de l'histoire de l'ancien royaume de Porto-Novo* (Dakar, 1953) p. 87.
46. AE Afrique 126, Bontemps Report, May 1890; Chaudoin, *Trois Mois de Captivité* pp. 244–49; cf ANSOM Dahomey, V/3/a, Behanzin to Ballot, 2 May 1890.
47. SMA/14/802.02 François to Planque, 29 May 1890; CMS G3/A2/06. Wood to Lang, 11 June 1890. CO 879/33. CP African 399, No. 30a, Moloney to Knutsford, Conf. 17 June 1890.
48. See the figures in C. W. Newbury, *The Western Slave Coast*, p. 123 (which presumably include the exports of Porto Novo).
49. CO 147/76, Moloney to Knutsford, Conf. 27 August, 22 September 1890, including Barth's notes. ANSOM Dahomey, v/4/6, Ballay to Etienne, 3 October 1890, gives the version received by the French.
50. ANSOM Dahomey, i/3/b, Barbey to Fournier, Tel., 11 May 1890; Dahomey i/3/a, Fournier to Barbey, Tel., 21 May 1890.

51. AM BB^4 1989, Fournier to Barbey (two despatches), 10 May 1890.
52. SMA 12/802.00, Pied to Planque, 8 May, 21 May 1890.
53. Copies of some of these are in ANSOM Dahomey, V/3/c.
54. JO (Chambre: Dêbats), 10 May 1890, pp. 747–54.
55. AM BB^4 1990, Freycinet to Barbey, 16 May 1890: BB^4 1989, Fournier to Barbey, Tel., 17 May.
56. AM BB^4 1989; Cuverville to Barbey, 23 May (Dakar), 27 May (Dakar: extracts in Salinis, pp. 35–8), 10 June (Cotonou).
57. SMA 12/802.00, Cuverville to Lecron, 23 June 1890 (emphasis in original).
58. AM BB^4 1989, Cuverville to Barbey, 10 June, 3 July, 19 September 1890; BB^4 1990, Siciliano to Barbey, 10 September 1890.
59. SMA 12/802.00, Pied to Planque, 14 June 1890.
60. F. Renault, *Lavigerie, L'esclavage africain et l'Europe, 1868–1892*, Vol. II (1971) pp. 216–24. SMA 2 B 12, Planque to Pied, 10, 31 July 1889; 2 B 11, Planque to Tofa, 10 July 1889; 12/802.00, Pied to Planque, 4 September 1889.
61. SMA 12/802.00, Cuverville to Lecron, 7 June 1890; Lecron to Cuverville, 25 June.
62. SMA 12/802.00, Pied to Planque, 25 March 1890.
63. SMA 14/802.00, François to Planque, 29 May 1890.
64. SMA 14/802.00, François to Planque, 2, 10 July, 24 September 1890. AM BB^4 1989, Cuverville to Barbey, 19 September 1890.
65. G. Le Bras, *Etudes de Sociologie réligeuse* vol. I (1955) pp. 72–84, for a brief appreciation of Breton Christianity.
66. SMA 12/802.00, Menager to Planque, 17 February 1886. The SMA archives contain several drafts of a biography of Dorgère by Father R. F. Guilcher, based in part on the large and unclassified *Fonds Dorgère*.
67. SMA 12/802.00, Cuverville to Lecron, 23 June 1890; AM BB^4 1989, Cuverville to Barbey, 3 July 1890.
68. AM, BB^4 1989, Cuverville to Barbey, 3 July 1890; cf Terrillon, *Project d'expedition*, 6 May 1890, Fournier to Barbey, 8 May.
69. SMA, *Fonds Dorgère*, Dorgère to Cuverville, 10 July 1890; Cuverville to Dorgère, 11 July 1890. Cf Salinis, pp. 69–71.
70. AM BB^4 1989, Cuverville to Barbey, Tel., 30 July: Despatch 86, 1 August 1890. For his correspondence with the Fon, Salinis, pp. 71–9.
71. Ibid., Cuverville to Barbey, Tel., 7 August 1890.
72. SMA 2 B. 12.ff. 148, 165, 186; Planque to Pied, 22 May, 2 July, 10 September 1890.
73. AM BB^4 1989, Cuverville to Barbey, 88 bis, 11 August, 1890 (cf Salinis, pp. 81–2); SMA 12/802.00, Pied to Planque 8 August 1890. Cf ANSOM Dahomey I/6/b, Cuverville to Ballot, 31 October 1890.
74. AM BB^4 1989, Cuverville to Barbey 86, 1 August 1890, encl. draft treaty. Cf SMA *Fonds Dorgère,* Cuverville to Dorgère, 13 August 1890.
75. ANSOM Dahomey V/4/a, Durand to Ballot, 15 September 1890.
76. AM BB^4 1989, Behanzin to Cuverville, 18 August 1890, encl. in Cuverville 113, 5 September 1890; printed by Salinis, pp. 95–9.

77. AM BB^4 1989. Dorgère to Cuverville, 9 August 1890 (partial text in Salinis, pp. 90–2). There is a brief journal up to 13 August in the *Fonds Dorgère*.
78. ANSOM Dahomey v/4/a, Durand to Ballot, 15 September 1890.
79. AM BB^4, 1989, Dorgère to Cuverville, 9 August; Behanzin to Cuverville, 18 August 1890.
80. Ibid, Cuverville to Barbey, 114, 5 September 1890: 124, 11 September 1890.
81. SMA 12/802.00, Lecron to Planque, 7 August (sc September) 1890; Pied to Planque, 9 September 1890.
82. Copies of Montesquiou's reports are enclosed in Am BB4 1989, Cuverville to Barbey, 137, 5 October 1890; they are summarized in Salinis, pp. 107 ff and form the basis of these two paragraphs.
83. Salinis, p. 130.
84. AM BB^4 1989, Cuverville to Barbey 176, 7 November 1890; cf Salinis, p. 104.
85. Ibid., Cuverville to Barbey, 137, 5 October 1890, with marginal note. The text of the Arrangement is enclosed with this despatch; its open clauses are in ED IX pp. 101–2.
86. SMA 12/802.00, Pied to Planque, 9 November 1890.
87. Ibid., Cuverville to (?) Lecron, 11 October, to OC Tps, 29 October 1890. Cuverville to Montesquiou, 30 September, Salinis, p. 125: AM BB^4 1989, Cuverville to Barbey, 146, 9 October 1890.
88. SMA 12/802.00, Ménager to Planque, 17 February 1886.
89. SMA 12/802.00, Pied to Planque, 23 July 1890.
90. AM BB^4 1989, Cuverville to Barbey, 137, 5 October 1890. The manuscript Life of Dorgère by Father Guilcher (SMA) XI 33, contains this description of the ceremony:

    > On vit entrer sous le toit délabré toutes les autorités païennes de la ville venues pour remercier Dieu du bienfait de la paix. Elles commencaient par se prosterner, puis s'étant levées elles défilaient devant une statue du Sacré-Coeur, entourée de palmes et de lumière, qu'elles saluaient la main levée.

91. AE Afrique 126, Cuverville to Vice-Admiral Vignes, Pte, 11 October 1890.
92. AM BB^4 1989, Cuverville to Montesquiou, 21 November 1890.
93. SMA 12/802.00, Cuverville to (?) Planque, 9 November 1890; AM BB^4 1989, Cuverville to Barbey, 183, 9 November 1890 (cf Salinis, pp. 191–3).
94. ANSOM Dahomey V/4/b, Cuverville to Ballot, 6 October 1890. AM, BB^4, 1988, Barbey to Cuverville, Tel. 4 October 1890.
95. ANSOM Dahomey V/2/b, Vallon to Etienne, 23 December 1890; Etienne to Vallon, 16 January 1891. JO (Chambre: Documents Parlementaires) 22 April 1891, pp. 608–14, no. 1235, *Rapport* by de Lanessan.
96. AE Afrique 126, Fabre to Ribot, 24 November 1890.

97. AE Afrique 127, Fabre to Vallon, 3 January 1891; Barbey to Ribot, V Conf., 27 January 1891, enclosing Fabre to Barbey, 27 January.
98. JO (Chambre: Débats) 28 November 1891, 2341.
99. Ibid., 2336–9: cf. 7 April 1892, p. 509.
100. AM BB[4] 1989, Cuverville to Marine, 390, 2 December 1891.
101. AE Afrique 126, Etienne to Ribot, 18 December 1890; cf Salinis, p. 183.
102. Lanessan Report, 22 April 1891.
103. JO (Chambre: Débats) 28 November 1891, 2328–45.
104. AM BB[4] 1989, Cuverville to Marine, 195, 22 November 1890.
105. ANSOM Dahomey III/2/a, Etienne to Ribot, 18 December; Barbey to Ribot, 21 December 1890; Ribot to Etienne, 10 January; Etienne to Ribot, 24 January 1891.
106. AE Afrique 127, Etienne to Ribot, 5, 12 February 1891.
107. ANSOM Dahomey III/2/9, Ballay to Audéoud, 9 February 1891.
108. Four of these reports are reprinted in ED IX: Rapport topographique présenté par le Sous-Lieutenant Chasles, pp. 102–5: Journal de marche rédigé par le Capitaine Decoeur, pp. 105–15: Rapport du Commandant Audéoud, pp. 115–25: Rapport politique, Capitaine Hocquart, pp. 128–34. The report of *aspirant* d'Ambrières is in ANSOM III/2/a, together with Decoeur's original journal; extracts quoted in Salinis, op. cit.
109. D'Ambrières, op. cit.
110. Audéoud, p. 120.
111. Decoeur, pp. 113–14. On the insistence of four of the officers on taking their new *protéges* to France, see ANSOM Dahomey I/5/a Ballay, Political Report 10 March–10 April 1891.
112. Except where otherwise stated, the source for this paragraph is Hocquart, pp. 131–4.
113. Cf Decoeur, p. 110; d'Ambrières.
114. ED, IX, pp. 138–9, Ehrman to Ballay, 8 May 1891.
115. Audéoud, cf pp. 118–21; also Decoeur, pp. 109–10.
116. ANSOM Dahomey III/2/a, Audéoud to Ballay, 3 April 1891. (printed in ED IX, pp. 126–8). The references to this episode in SMA *Fonds Dorgère* and in Father Guilcher's biography do little to clarify Dorgère's role.
117. CO 147/76, Moloney to Knutsford, Conf. 21 September, 31 October 1890.
118. References to Hendry are fragmentary and confusing; but see CO 147/93, FO to CO, 4 April 1893, encl. Bayol's article in *Le Temps* 26 March; Carter to CO, 23 May 1893; A. Le Herissé, *L'ancien royaume du Dahomey* (Paris, 1911) pp. 338–40; BCAF, December 1893. For his association with Barth, ANSOM Dahomey V/4/a, Durand to Ballot, 15 September 1890. See E. Dunglas, "Contribution à l'histoire du Moyen-Dahomey", *ED* XXI, 1958, p. 14 for a man of similar name acting as intermediary during the British blockade of 1877. Hendry also acted as Behanzin's German secretary; M. Kalous, "Some

Correspondence between the German Empire and Dahomey", *CEA*, VIII, 32, 1968.

119. ANSOM Dahomey I/5/a: Lieutenant-Governor Ballay's despatches of 1891–2 repeatedly insist that Porto Novo must keep its duties lower than those of Lagos, to compensate for geographical disadvantages.
120. On whom see F. I. A. Omu, "Journalism and the rise of Nigerian nationalism; John Payne Jackson, 1848–1915", *JHSN*, VII, 1974, pp. 521–39, cf. above, p. 119.
121. H. Washausen, *Hamburg und die Kolonialpolitik des Deutschen Reiches* (Hamburg, 1968) p. 79.
122. Adolf Rüger, "Der Aufstand der Polizeisoldaten", in H. Stoecker (ed.), *Kamerun unter deutscher Kolonialherrschaft* (E. Berlin, 1960) pp. 103–5.
123. Details of these purchases, extracted from captured records of German firms at Whydah in January 1893, are in Am BB[4] 1992.
124. ANSOM Dahomey I/6/c, Ehrmann to Ballay, 381, 8 November 1891.
125. B. Obichere, *West African States and European Expansion* (New Haven, Conn., 1971) pp. 94–5.
126. ANSOM Dahomey I/6/c, Ehrmann to Ballay, 282, 8 September 1891.
127. CO 879/31, CP African 386, No. 92, CO to FO, 1 May 1891; No. 95, FO to CO, 12 May 1891. CO 147/82 for minutes by Hemming and Meade.
128. CO 147/82, CO to FO, 16 January; FO to CO, 30 January 1891.
129. ANSOM Dahomey, I/6/c, Ehrmann to Ballay, 309, 29 September (encl. Ehrmann to Behanzin, 21 September); 334, 8 October 1891. Dahomey I/5/a, Ballay to Etienne, Tel., 6 October (annotated *Payez rente*); 650, 22 October 1891. Obichere (p. 87) is mistaken in saying this payment was never made.
130. Ibid., Ehrmann to Ballay, 431, 8 December 1891, *ED*, IX, pp. 154–6. prints Ehrmann to Behanzin, 10 December 1891, Behanzin to Ehrmann, 2 January 1892.
131. D. Ross "Autonomous Kingdom", p. 364n.
132. ANSOM Dahomey V/5/b, Behanzin to Ehrmann, 16 January 1892.

> God made Europe for the Whites and Africa for the blacks, and I am the King of Dahomey who rules the Negro nations. The monarchs of Europe and I have been friends for some time . . . Formerly when any white man, great or small, arrived on the African coast, he was respected out of consideration for the European monarchs; today they have themselves thrown all into disorder . . . It would be preferable for all the monarchs to agree that things should return to their former condition.

133. Ibid., Ballot to Ballay, 6 March 1892. Cf Dahomey I/6/c, Ehrmann to Ballay, 37, 3 February 1892; Dahomey I/6/d, Ballot to Ballay, 58, 1 March 1892.
134. Cf above vol. 1 pp. 142–65; AM BB[4] 1989, Cuverville to Marine, 195, 22 November 1890, encl. Ballot, 13 November.

135. According to traditions recorded by E. Dunglas, "Contribution à l'Histoire du Moyen Dahomey", *ED*, XXI, 1958, pp. 578. In 1905 an alternative, somewhat dubious, version was publicized by the West Indian journalist, H. Lara, *Pour Behanzin;* cf Cornevin, *Histoire du Dahomey,* pp. 360–2.
136. ANSOM Dahomey, I/5/a, Ballay to Jamais, 28 March, 2 April (Tels), 22 April; Dahomey I/6/d, Ballot to Ballay, 98, 8 April 1892.
137. Behanzin to Carnot, 24 October 1892, cit. M. Kalous, CEA, VIII, 32, 1968.
138. ANSOM Dahomey I/5/a, Ballay to Jamais 22 April (encl. Behanzin to Ballot, 10 April), 8 May 1892.
139. ANSOM Dahomey V/5/b, Note sur les affaires du Dahomey, 30 March 1892.
140. Salinis, *La Marine au Dahomey,* pp. 305–10.
141. JO (Chambre: Documents Parlementaires) no. 2069, *Rapport* by Chautemps.
142. JO (Chambre: Débats) 7, 11 April 1892; (Sénat Débats) 13 April 1892. cf FO 84/2208, Dufferin to Salisbury, 83 Africa, 20 April 1892, concluding that "The recent debate in the Chamber and the very general preoccupation of the Press . . . would appear to indicate the probable resumption of a more vigorous colonial policy.
143. This paragraph is based on V. Campion-Vicent, "L'image du Dahomey dans la Press française, 1870–95", *CEA,* VII, no. 23, 1967, pp. 27–58.
144. FO 147/87, FO to CO, 14 October 1892, citing Douville-Maillefeu.
145. AM BB[4] 1991, Cavaignac to Dodds, 4 May 1892, and amendment of 14 May.
146. JO (Chambre: Débats) 11 July 1892; ANSOM Dahomey I/8/d, Marine to Dodds, Tel., 14 July 1892.
147. Salinis, pp. 310–2, Dodds to Behanzin, 2 June, Behanzin to Dodds, 10 June 1892; ANSOM Dahomey, v/5/6, Jacquot to Dodds, 15 June.
148. ANSOM Dahomey, I/8/d, Marine to Dodds, Tel., 25 July 1892; cf Salinis, pp. 327–31.
149. ANSOM Dahomey, V/6/a, Dodds' final report on the campaign of 1892.
150. For example, David Ross, "Dahomey" in M. Crowder (ed.), *West African Resistance* (1971); R. Cornevin, *Histoire du Dahomey* (1962) pp. 339–49; B. I. Obichere, *West African States,* pp. 103–11.
151. Dodds' final report states French casualties as 11 officers and 70 men (33 *indigénes*) killed in action, 25 officers and 411 men (216 *indigènes*) wounded. Total fighting strength, including the October reinforcement, may be calculated as 91 officers and 2556 other ranks, giving approximate casualty of 40 per cent officers and 19 per cent other ranks.
152. Article in *Le Temps,* 26 March 1893; copy in CO 147/93.
153. AM BB[4] 1892, Marquer to Marine, 29 August, Dodds to Marine 9 September 1892; MAE to Marine, 14 February, 23 March 1893. AE,

Afrique 127, Delcassé to Deville, 21 April 1893, with annotation; AM BB[4] 1891, Marine to MAE, 27 April 1893.

154. Jehan de Riols (Comdt Riou) *La Guerre du Dahomey, 1889–92* (1893).
155. RFECE, XVII, pp. 75–6.
156. AM BB[4] 1992, Dodds to Marine, Tel., 6 June 1892; 48, 19 February 1893, encl. E. B. Moyca (=Barth) to Behanzin, 8 May 1892.
157. Ibid., Dodds, Tel. 21 December 1892, 14 January 1893; 15, 17 March 1893.
158. Ibid., MAE to Marine, 8 August, 3 September 1892, 21 January, 11 February, 18 March 1893.
159. M. Kalous, Some correspondence, *CEA*, VIII, 32, 1968.
160. ANSOM Dahomey, v/10/a, Dodds Report on Campaign of 1893–4.
161. W. N. M. Geary, *Nigeria under British Rule* (1927) pp. 62–3; *The Times* 25 March 1893; cf *BCAF* April 1893. According to French sources Jackson's sense of African solidarity was reinforced by financial retainers: ANSOM V/8/a, Dodds to Delcassé, 11 October 1893.
162. CO 147/93, Carter to CO, 23 May 1893.
163. CO 147/87, Minute by Hemming on FO, 3 May 1892. But cf Phipps to Dufferin, 6 October in FO to CO, 10 October 1892.
164. ANSOM Dahomey, VI/9/a, Bories to Marine, 30 June, encl. Behanzin to Carnot, 27 June; Dahomey VI/8/a, Bories to Delcassé, 30 June, Dodds to Delcassé, 11 October 1893.
165. ANSOM Dahomey I/8/d, Delcassé to Dodds, Tel., 22 February 1893; Note, Cabinet du Ministre de la Marine, 20 March.
166. JO (Chambre: Débats) 29 March 1893, pp. 1125–31.
167. *BCAF*, III, 1893, July 1893.
168. *RFEC*, XVIII, 15 August 1893, pp. 168–70.
169. ANSOM Dahomey, V/11/a, Rieunier to Dupuy, Pte, 2 August 1893.
170. Ibid., Interior to Marine, 18 August, 1 September 1893, with enclosures.
171. ANSOM Dahomey v/11/b, Decrais to Develle, 3 November, d'Estournelles to Develle, 5 November 1893; *BCAF*, III, December 1893.
172. The principal source for this campaign is Dodds' report in ANSOM Dahomey v/10/a, supplemented by the original *journaux de marche* in v/10/b.
173. It is not clear whether Dodds had any such intention; but after the fall of Abomey he used Porto Novan envoys to demand the surrender of the Fon, and presented Behanzin's gold throne to Tofa (J. de Riols, *La Guerre du Dahomey*, pp. 93–4).
174. Dahomey v/10/a, Dodds *Rapport*, f. 79.
175. L. M. Garcia, "Archives et tradition orale", *CEA*, XVI, 61–2, 1976, pp. 189–92, 202–4. Cf M. J. and F. S. Herskovits, *Dahomean Narrative*, pp. 383–4.
176. Dahomey v/10/a, Dodds *Rapport* f. 82.
177. Dahomey v/10/b, *Journal de marche*, 28 January 1894.
178. ANSOM Dahomey v/11/b, *Journal de Marche*, 13 January 1894; cf Soudan III/2, Toutée, *Notes Politquies*, 23 January 1896.

179. A. I. Asiwaju, *Western Yorubaland under European Rule, 1889–1945* (P, 1976) pp. 49–51, 85–8.
180. CO 147/77, Moloney to Knutsford, 414, 28 December 1890, encl. Ewart, 20 September.
181. AM BB[4] 1989. Cuverville, 21 November 1890; ANSOM Dahomey I/5/a, Ballay to Etienne, 9 March 1891; Dahomey I/6/c, Ehrmann to Ballay, 4 February, 8 September 1891; *ED*, IX, pp. 140–1, Ehrmann to Ballay, 8 May 1891.
182. Akindélé and Aguessy, *Contribution*, pp. 88–90. cf N. S. Senkomago, "The Kingdom of Porto Novo with special reference to its external relations, 1872–1968", PhD, University of Aberdeen, 1976, pp. 373–90.

11 Power Politics

Although the conquest of Dahomey had not been a primary objective of the French colonial party, the rationalizing logic of imperialism demanded that the new colony should expand: in the words of an armchair geographer, "il ne peut rester comme il est car il deviendrait une non-valeur ce qui est contraire aux principes mêmes d'une politique coloniale".[1] The obvious line of expansion was northwards towards the middle Niger; as early as December 1890 Cuverville had considered asking Behanzin to provide an escort for a French expedition from Grand Popo to Say, in hope of encouraging "les races fétichistes, bien plus accessibles à notre civilisation" to resist the Muslim opponents of the Sudanese army.[2] Such a thrust would not only gratify businessmen in Marseille, who were becoming interested in a possible northern railway, but fulfil the ambition which Etienne had cherished since 1890, of challenging Goldie's monopoly of the lower Niger. The region thus became the focus of the last and most bitter struggles of the European partition. The British and German governments, following French examples, increasingly accepted demands from colonial enthusiasts to support the expansion of existing colonies towards the imagined resources of the African interior. Though diplomatists still tried to exercise restraint, international rivalries intensified; and there were narrower opportunities for African statecraft to influence the outcome. As elephants fought, the grass was inevitably trampled.

THE BEGINNING OF THE STEEPLECHASES: BENUE, NILE AND NIGER

Antagonism between Goldie and the French colonialists had been rekindled by the provocations of Mizon's first journey, which revealed that the Niger Company had no treaty rights in Bornu and were encountering serious hostility in Adamawa. Advocates of the Chad plan now saw the Benue as the most vulnerable link in Goldie's defences (see above, pp. 131–2). But while Mizon began to discredit himself by the excesses of his second expedition Goldie, abandoning hope of totally excluding foreigners from Adamawa, attempted to bring in the Germans as a barrier to French penetration.

By 1892 the German colony of Kamerun was displaying a considerable capacity to generate its own expansion towards the supposed wealth of the Muslim north. Eugen Zintgraff had established an advanced commercial and political base in the Bamenda grasslands through a treaty with his chosen collaborator, Galega;[3] his earlier journeys into Adamawa had been followed up by Lieutenant Morgen (1890–1) and Baron Von Stettin (1892–3); the small armed police-force which had been created with Behanzin's help was undertaking its first operations.[4] In Berlin Dr Kayser was an increasingly effective champion of colonial expansion. Disturbed by French advances towards Chad, members of the *Deutsche Kolonialgesellschaft* now established a separate Kamerun Committee under the chairmanship of Ernst Vohsen. During the summer of 1893 Vohsen visited London and secretly agreed terms with Goldie for a partition of Adamawa. "The French and Germans will come into collision. We may benefit", Percy Anderson happily prophesied.[5] The Kamerun Committee then organized an expedition under Lieutenant Uechtritz and Dr Passarge, largely financed by the *Kolonialgesellschaft*, but with contributions from the Foreign Ministry and from private sources (including Krupps).[6] Travelling from Lokoja in a Niger Company vessel, this party reached Yola on 31 August; Passarge was present when the Company's agent Wallace (supported by an emissary from Sokoto) persuaded Emir Zubairu to order Mizon to quit Adamawa (see above, p. 131). Zubairu, though increasingly worried by the European influx, then reluctantly allowed Uechtritz to proceed up the Benue to Garua, where he began to reconnoitre the proposed partition line.[7]

By an Agreement of 15 November 1893, the two Foreign Offices confirmed the terms of Goldie and Vohsen. Faced with the French challenge, Goldie abandoned his claim to monopolize control of all river-banks accessible from the sea, and accepted a geometrical partition line which left Germany not only the greater part of Adamawa emirate but access to the Benue, with consequent navigation rights.[8] Besides retaining the Adamawa capital of Yola in their sphere the British secured German recognition of their claim to Bornu; but their greatest advantage appeared to be the exclusion of France. They expected that Germany's eastward expansion from the region whose western border had just been settled would certainly preclude French access to the Benue, possibly frustrate her thrust towards Lake Chad, conceivably (though it is an error to regard this as a prime objective) interfere with the plan which some French colonialists were now contemplating for a trans-African expedition from the Congo to the Nile.

During 1893 French colonialists gloomily contemplated these dangers. In May Marschall had suggested resuming the Franco-German boundary negotiations suspended in 1890 (see above, pp. 27–9), in order to reduce the risk of conflict between exploratory "missions"; but it soon became clear that these would make little headway until the Anglo-German agreement was complete. In July Marschall did offer to concede French access to Lake Chad: but only by a circuitous route, not, as France insisted, along the Chari valley.[9] The claims of some German colonialists went further, envisaging a vast Anglo-German zone embracing central Africa from coast to coast, which would cut off France's empire in west and north Africa from her Congo colony.[10]

However, not all Germans shared Vohsen's anglophilia. Many enthusiasts for *weltpolitik* already regarded the British Empire as the most formidable obstacle to the expansion of German power and German capital in the overseas world, and every example of British intransigence strengthened their influence. Some, conspicuously including Kayser himself, felt that Britain had driven a hard bargain in Adamawa and that Marschall had sacrificed too much for the sake of Anglo-German friendship. The lessons of European history, and the dominant voices of public opinion, still emphasized antagonism between Germany and France; but many who looked into the future already predicted a need for continental solidarity (cf. vol. I, p. 36). Although it would be premature publicly to advocate such a grand design, it was precisely in such marginal areas as Adamawa that foundations might be quietly laid. A few days after the Anglo-German agreement Kayser was hinting to the French Ambassador about "une entente générale . . . en vue d'avoir une politique commune contre les tendances égoistes et envahissantes de l'Angleterre dans le domaine colonial".[11]

However, when Franco-German boundary negotiations re-opened in Berlin in December they did not go well. The priorities originally defined by Delcassé were to secure control of the Sangha basin, and a northern route giving access to Lake Chad by the Chari valley; (this would automatically leave open a road towards the Nile) (see Map 4). But on 10 December his successor as Colonial Under-secretary, Maurice Lebon, after discussion with Mizon, decided to press for access to the Benue in Adamawa, if necessary sacrificing Brazza's claims in the Sangha. Monteil, appointed to negotiate by Delcassé as a hero of the *parti colonial*, advocated French claims so vigorously that by mid-December the negotiations seemed about to collapse.[12] On 18 December Kayser suddenly became more conciliatory. This change seems to have been prompted by a new burst of irritation with the British, who that day revealed that, by negotiating with Rabih, they had intruded into territory just recognized as a German sphere. Monteil later claimed that Wilhelm II intervened at this point, transferring control of the negotiation from Marschall to Chancellor Caprivi with the intention of promoting "a Franco-German alliance, offensive and defensive against Britain, in the colonial sphere". Whatever the motivation, on 21 December Kayser offered to accept a westward deviation of the boundary which would give France access to the Mayo Kebbi branch of the Benue at a place called Bifara, and to support her consequent claim to share in supervision of the Niger navigation under the Berlin Act. Monteil jumped at the prospect of joint pressure on the British; agreement on these lines was reached on 4 February and published on 15 March.[13]

In the long run, these triangular manoeuvres had important consequences only for those Africans who, years later, would

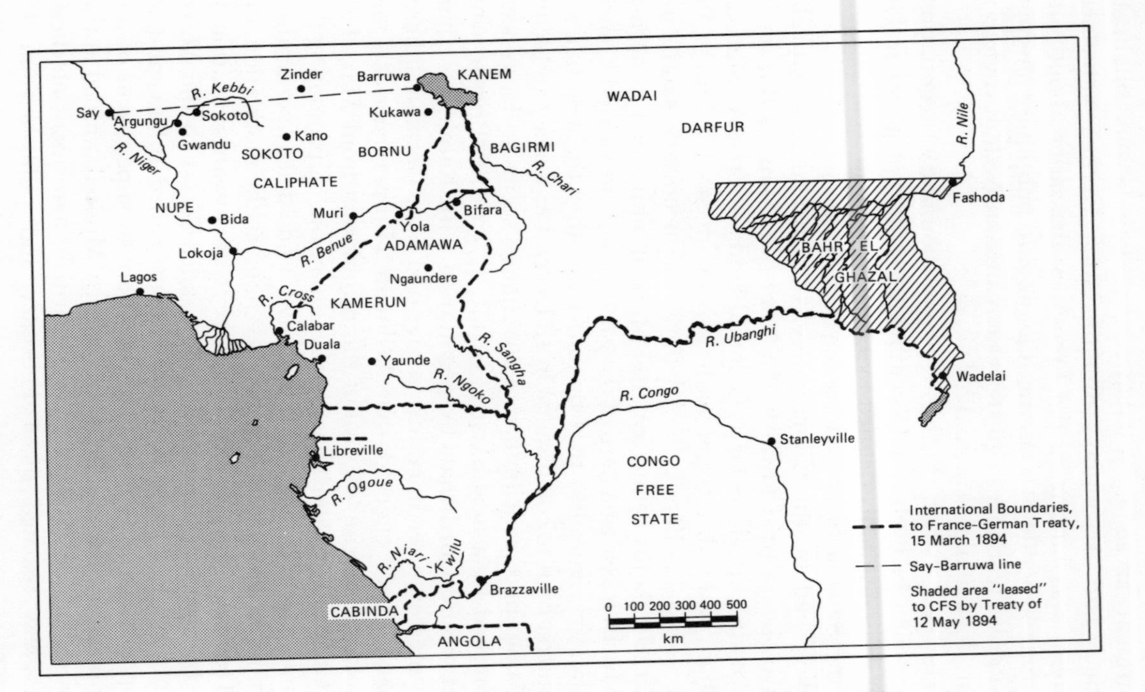

Map 4 *France and her rivals in Equatorial Africa, 1894.*

discover to which European master they had been allocated; Goldie resigned himself to modifying his navigation regulations without much difficulty.[14] But they did demonstrate that Britain could no longer rely on general German support for her African policies. On 7 March Kayser warned a British diplomatist that Franco-German co-operation to internationalize the Niger navigation might become "the next great African question"; on 17 April he drafted a despatch formally warning the British that such co-operation might result unless they paid more heed to German interests.[15] It appeared that in Germany too colonialists could now exercise sufficient leverage to affect the course of European policy; and this was shortly confirmed by a diplomatic crisis on the Nile.

* * *

In March 1894 the French Colonial Department was at last raised to full ministerial status. The first Minister, Ernest Boulanger, was an elderly jurist appointed to organize the transition;[16] but two months later he was succeeded by Theophile Delcassé. As *rapporteur* of the colonial budget in 1891 Delcassé had asserted that a successful colonial policy depended on European policy;[17] until his translation to the Quai d'Orsay in 1898 he contrived to make the African tail wag the dog of French diplomacy. He had not yet formed any long-term view of where that dog should eventually make its home; ten years later, when forced to choose between Britain and Germany, he would opt for the Entente Cordiale, but immediate colonial priorities led him to challenge British rather than German interests. As Colonial Under-Secretary in 1893 Delcassé had secured a narrow parliamentary majority for the establishment of the new Ministry;[18] from this base he actively pursued policies favoured by the civilian advocates of commercial colonization. Since July 1893 the major colonial banking and commercial interests had become organized in the *Union Coloniale française*, which, while disavowing any general policy of aggrandisement, pressed forcefully for the defence of existing French rights, often very widely interpreted.[19] Delcassé served some of these interests well. He seemed more willing than his predecessors to grant far-reaching economic concessions to private companies; he moved to break military control of the Sudan by appointing the controversial Albert Grodet as first civilian Governor;[20] and he set in motion the madcap plan of challenging British control of Egypt by a trans-African mission to Fashoda.

Since 1891 French and Belgian agents had been competing for influence among the Muslim rulers of the upper Ubanghi basin; but while Leopold II had definite ambitions to reach the Nile, Delcassé was the first French Minister to endorse this objective. During the spring of 1893 he had joined President Sadi Carnot (an engineer interested in the possibilities of hydrographic control) in persuading Monteil to undertake a secret mission directed towards Fashoda, with the aim of "re-opening the Egyptian question". But his departure was delayed by the skilful intrigues of Leopold II, whose network of French supporters was reinforced by the secret employment of Alis. Monteil was diverted to the diplomatic negotiation in Berlin; and when Delcassé returned to office in Charles Dupuy's government of 30 May 1894 he was confronted by an Anglo-Congolese agreement which interpolated, on the diplomatists' map, a vast barrier of Congolese territory between the Ubanghi valley and the left bank of the Nile.[21]

Historians generally agree that this treaty was a blundering attempt to relieve the growing pressure on perceived British interests by a piece of diplomatic legerdemain. It originated with the political triumph of the Imperialist wing of the British Liberal party – a loosely organized group of patrician activists whose concern for more positive policies of "National efficiency" implied commitment to a strong Navy, substantial continuity of foreign policy, consolidation of the "white" Empire, and a resolute defence of British interests in Africa and elsewhere.[22] On 3 March Rosebery, hero of this school of Liberalism, succeeded Gladstone as Prime Minister; as his own successor at the Foreign Office he designated the elderly Whig imperialist Lord Kimberley. Although Harcourt exacted a right to be consulted over foreign policy, the failure of his rearguard action against expansion in Africa was finally registered on 12 April, by public announcement that the government has decided "to establish a regular administration" in the Uganda protectorate.

A few weeks before the change of Premier the vigorous Percy Anderson had succeeded Sir Villiers Lister as Assistant Under-Secretary in the Foreign Office.[23] With the Uganda protectorate pending Anderson thought it essential to deal with problems likely to arise from the presence of forces of Leopold's Congo Free State at Wadelai in the Nile valley, and Rosebery had authorized negotiations on the basis that territorial claims in the Nile valley might be leased to the Congo state for Leopold's lifetime only. The primary motive was to preclude France succeeding to such territories on Leopold's death, under the right of pre-emption she had secured in 1884 (*Prelude,* p. 337); but Anderson quickly perceived a further ingenious possibility. By extending northwards this "lease" (of land which may have belonged to Egypt, but to which Britain had no legal title of her own) a huge tract of Congolese territory might be interposed in Monteil's path. And, not content with trying to kill two birds with one stone, Anderson aimed at a third. The Anglo-Congolese agreement reached on 12 April and eventually published (after slight amendment) on 21 May also provided that the Free State would compensate the British by the lease of a 25 kilometre corridor linking Uganda with Lake Tanganyika and so, theoretically, with northern Rhodesia. Anderson had somehow forgotten that, four years earlier, Britain had accepted German objections to a similar corridor; by reintroducing the idea indirectly he gave Germany as well as France grounds for objecting to the treaty, and so brought the danger of a Franco-German colonial entente perceptibily closer.[24]

An angry German protest, drafted by Kayser, reinforced Harcourt's fulminations inside the Cabinet[25] and persuaded Kimberley to abandon this useless corridor on 22 June; but it was too late to save the rest of the treaty. Belgian politicians also became worried by the danger that Belgian officers in Congolese service might come into conflict with the French; on 14 August they compelled their King to abandon the leases which Britain had granted. The one British consolation was that German and French objections had been separately expressed; the threatened colonial entente did not materialize.[26] Even without German support however French colonialists seized upon the Treaty to mobilize public outrage behind what was hitherto the wild scheme of a minority – the plan to prise the British out of Egypt with the fragile lever of a trans-African expedition. "It is the Egyptian question which opens before you", Etienne told an angry Chamber on 7 June; two days later Delcassé, now a fully fledged Colonial Minister, successfully sought credits of 1 800 000 francs "for the defence of French interests in Africa".[27]

Nevertheless the Treaty also had the effect of making French ministers, and the more rational colonialists, perceive the risks of trying to solve the Nile problem by military expeditions. Monteil's scheme had already been criticized in *La Politique Coloniale* of 6 April: "It is not through the upper Ubanghi and the Bahr-el-Ghazal that the Egyptian question can be solved".[28] Gabriel Hanotaux, plucked from his backroom as Director of Commercial and Consular Affairs at the Quai d'Orsay to become Foreign Minister in Dupuy's government, remained anxious for a diplomatic settlement, and was encouraged when on 5 June Kimberley offered "a general review of all African questions pending between the two governments [Egypt excepted] for the purpose of such an adjustment as would place the relations of the two countries in that continent on a more satisfactory footing". There was a clear need for some new initiative; negotiations on pending African problems were making no progress, and by 29 June the British Ambassador was so worried as to issue the famous warning "that if M. Monteil attempted to act the part of a second Mizon in the Nile valley it would simply mean war between the two countries".[29] Yet both governments firmly intended to avoid such a result. In London Harcourt, still furious about Rosebery's latest escapade, tried to mitigate the damage by amending the Ambassador's record,[30] and on 13 July Monteil, on Hanotaux's insistence, was forbidden to penetrate into the Nile basin "de façon à ce que la question du Soudan égyptien reste entière et complètement réservée".[31] In enforcing this restraint Hanotaux was aided by his old colleague Haussman, Delcassé's own *directeur politique*, who feared that Monteil might create another insubordinate military command like the Soudan.[32] By 14 August, when Leopold abandoned his treaty with Britain, Monteil's assignment had served its purpose. Delcassé, judging that his patriotic zeal might be more prudently directed against Samori, diverted him to the Ivory Coast, with three of his four companies (see above, p. 63); the way was open for a last attempt to settle the Nile problem within a comprehensive African agreement.

Both British and French governments might have been expected to desire this. Not only did African disputes complicate European policy, but prudent colonialists on both sides saw that no practical advantages would be gained from confrontation in the swamps of the upper Nile. Unfortunately the intangible factors of national prestige which since 1882 had complicated the substantive issue of Britain's occupation of Egypt had now extended to the entire Nile basin. When on 16 August the British Ambassador suggested that France should recognize Britain's sphere of influence in the Nile valley in return for assurances that any territory occupied would be held in temporary trust for Egypt, he knew he was asking a lot. Besides reiterating Kimberley's willingness "to settle all pending questions in Africa in a great spirit of conciliation", Dufferin therefore held out the specific inducement of "allowing them to connect their territories on the Niger with the hinterland of Dahomey".[33]

The apparent concession on the Niger originated with Goldie, who hoped it might "satisfy France without sacrificing any material British interests". To secure concessions on the Nile he offered to extend the Dahomey–Lagos boundary of 1889 northwards to reach the Niger at the twelfth parallel: this implied a partition of the indeterminate countries known as Borgu and Gurma, the assignment to France of territories supposedly under the sovereignty of Gwandu, and theoretical opportunities for westward expansion into Mossi and other Voltaic states. In return France was explicitly to recognize British claims, in Bornu as well as Sokoto, to the south of an adjusted Say–Barruwa line. Anderson believed that such an agreement "would be a solid advantage to France and would give M. Hanotaux the prestige to which he aspires";[34] but this was to under-rate the extent to which the colonial party had enlarged its ambitions on both Niger and Nile.

When on 5 September Hanotaux began to examine (with his old sparring partner Phipps) the details of the package which he had welcomed in principle, it proved disappointing. The minor ingredients comprised relatively trivial British concessions over the Sierra Leone boundary and the disposal of claims arising from the Waima incident, the Mizon missions, and the losses of French missionaries in Uganda; the one substantial concession did not include the desired access to the navigable Niger below Bussa, and even those opportunities for northern expansion which Goldie offered were liable to involve conflict with German expeditions from Togo. This did not satisfy Delcassé and his officials, now increasingly attracted by Kayser's hints about a continental entente; instead they suggested a Franco-German protest against the Niger Company's new regulations in terms which would challenge British rights in both Muri and Adamawa. Sensing this mood, Hanotaux concealed Phipps's proposals for two weeks, hoping that if Britain offered more concessions the President and the Prime Minister might agree to present the Colonial Office with a *fait accompli*.[35] But no more concessions came. Anderson, taking Goldie's self-confidence at face value, would not budge over the Niger; and though the Colonial Office would have been willing to throw in the Isles de Los (in which France had shown interest in 1888–9) the Admiralty continued to veto this.[36]

The Prime Minister quickly despaired of any good result from the "dreary dribble" of negotiation.[37] Desperately anxious for a diplomatic triumph, Phipps continued to hope that Hanotaux might force through a settlement; and on 9 October reduced Britain's West African proposals to writing. But even an improved offer would not have induced the French colonialists to make concessions over the Nile.[38] Delcassé's officials now believed that by reorganizing the forces which the civilian Commissioner Liotard already controlled on the upper Ubanghi they could beat the British in Uganda in a race for the Nile.[39] Nothing which Britain was offering could induce ministers under such strong colonial pressure to prohibit this plan. On 17 November the Cabinet decided to suspend comprehensive negotiations and to allow

Liotard to move into the disputed territories.[40] Only the Sierra Leone boundary negotiation survived, to be concluded on 22 January 1895, with discreet French assurances that British trade would not be totally excluded.[41]

* * *

The collapse of these negotiations opened the door on to what was, for Anglo-French relations, the most dangerous phase of the partition. Yet it was nearly four years before this culminated in the Fashoda crisis of 1898. Liotard was unable to advance as rapidly as Delcassé hoped; the Marchand mission did not leave Paris until 25 June 1896, after another attempt to organize a comprehensive agreement between France and Britain (see below, p. 225). The area where the breakdown had its strongest immediate effect lay to the north of Dahomey, in the indeterminate country known as Borgu.

The fall of Abomey opened new opportunities for French expansion northwards; as early as December 1892 Jamais was contemplating sending Binger to forestall British and German claims.[42] But Dodds, still preoccupied with his pursuit of Behanzin, feared that an armed mission might alarm the Mahi and lead them to join the resistance; only on hearing of Carter's journey into Yorubaland did he agree, apparently reluctantly, to such an enterprise. By this time Binger had been appointed to govern the Ivory Coast, and the officer appointed to replace him, Captain H. A. Decoeur, proved a less resolute traveller. Arriving at Cotonou on 16 May 1893 with grandiose plans to secure Borgu by treaty with the ruler of Nikki and to press on towards Say, he complained that the military authorities were unco-operative in the recruitment of porters, and did not leave the advanced French base of Savalou until late December, when the pursuit of Behanzin was reaching its climax. Local rulers were often uncertain how to treat the Frenchman suddenly appearing among them; Decoeur, though escorted by twenty-nine Hausas, became extremely nervous as he moved into Bariba country; he reached only Tchaourou, some eighty miles from Savalou and by 27 January 1894 was back with Dodds, who was openly contemptuous of his meagre achievement.[43]

After Behanzin's surrender the Colonial Ministry restored Dahomey to civilian control, appointing the able and energetic Victor Ballot as Governor. But Decoeur, having returned to spend the rainy season in France, somehow persuaded Delcassé to give him a new independent mission, "to put Dahomey in communication with the Niger and our possessions in the Ivory Coast, to the rear of Togo and the Ashanti country"; and he secured a grant of 10 000 francs from the *Comité de l'Afrique française*. Despite having argued the urgency of forestalling rival British and German expeditions,[44] Decoeur moved even more hesitantly than before. From mid-September to mid-October he remained near Carnotville, an advanced base which Ballot had established on the ninth parallel, his force of a hundred *tirailleurs* and 50 *gardes indigènes* making heavy demands on depleted food supplies. Ballot was exasperated by Decoeur's complaints about desertion by porters (whom he treated badly) and by his excessive nervousness about attacks from "treacherous" chiefs;[45] his lack of enterprise wasted France's advantageous position in what had indeed become a sort of international steeplechase[46] towards the lower Niger, and the unappropriated territories to the north and west.

The first objective of the contestants was Nikki, identified by the French as the Borgu capital. At first the French assumed that Decoeur would have to outpace Captain Bower, who they wrongly believed was intent on pushing rapidly northwards from Ibadan;[47] in fact the challenge came from Lugard, the unemployed hero of British Uganda, who, after venturing to the *Moulin Rouge* to discover Monteil's intentions for the Foreign Office,[48] had in July been quietly recruited by Goldie. His primary aim was to secure treaties which would consolidate the company's dubious claims to Borgu; thereafter he was if possible to push westwards towards Mossi, obtaining *en route* a scatter of treaties in the country "south and west of Say".[49] When Lugard reached Jebba on the Niger on 8 September there was still a faint hope of settling the Borgu question diplomatically, in which case Goldie had contingency plans to send him to confront the problems posed by Rabih's conquest of Bornu; but it quickly became clear that Phipps and Hanotaux were getting nowhere, and on the 19th Goldie was informed that Kimberley "was not prepared to take the responsibility of stopping the expedition on which Captain Lugard had been despatched".[50] Leaving Jebba on 27 September with forty soldiers, Lugard secured on 10 November a treaty by which the "King of Nikki and all Borgu country" appeared to cede jurisdiction over foreigners and control of external relations to the Niger Company.[51] But though Decoeur's timidity had lost the steeplechase, the indoor contest which diplomatists in Europe played with documents had not been settled. When Decoeur reached Nikki on 29 November he claimed that Lugard had dealt not with the authentic ruler, but only the *imam* of the Muslim community; he secured a treaty of his own, which became the subject of much ingenious and heated argument.

Nikki was only the first stage in a much longer and more complex race to raise European flags in unappropriated countries to the west and south of the Niger. All governments now increasingly adopted the practice pioneered by France in the 1880s, of treaty-making expeditions intended less to regulate relations with African collaboraors than to secure title deeds with which their diplomatists could bargain in European. Increasingly too these were entrusted to soldiers who proved less patient negotiators than some of their predecessors, more ambitious to prepare for "effective occupation". Although Lugard failed to pass from Borgu to Mossi, G. E. Ferguson, on his second mission to the upper Volta, had on 2 July 1894 secured the agreement of the Mogho Naba to a treaty of trade and friendship of the old sort (see above pp. 127–8). But diplomatic missions of this sort now proved inadequate; both French and Germans were sending armed parties led by military officers into the disputed area.

With the Sudanese army still recovering from its defeat at Timbuktu in January 1894, the French had at first to rely on resources available in Dahomey. Decoeur, urged on by his impatient subordinates, Lieutenants Baud and Vermeersch (and possibly anticipating the order for recall which Delcassé telegraphed on 17 December) eventually moved energetically northwards from Nikki. By forced marches in December and

January Decoeur managed to forestall a German mission at Sansanne Mango, to secure a treaty purporting to cover the disintegrating state of Gurma, and to reassemble his mission at Say, where France's footing on the Niger was guaranteed by the 1890 agreement with Britain. Further south Ballot, trying to undo the damage caused by Decoeur's earlier hesitation, visited Nikki and Bussa to make his own assessment of the political status of Borgu; Baud went westward through Mamprussi to Wa in an abortive attempt to join Monteil near Kong; the civilian Alby travelled into Mossi, but was unable to see the Mogho Naba.[52]

More immediately disturbing for Britain was a new challenge to Goldie's monopoly. No sooner had the Hanotaux–Phipps negotiation finally collapsed than a naval gunboat, *L'Ardent*, asserted its rights by sailing into the Niger, where it promptly ran aground; and on 17 November Captain G. J. Toutée received instructions to establish or extend relations with riverain populations in regions where France risked being forestalled by the British or Germans. It was originally planned that Toutée should sail up the Niger, but Hanotaux judged this too reminiscent of Mizon; instead he was to follow the Anglo-French boundary up to the ninth parallel and then head east to the river, collecting treaties and making "acts of occupation" which, even if not permanently maintained, might serve as "elements of exchange in future negotiations".[53]

Toutée, accompanied by three French officers, 25 soldiers and twenty Sarakule sailors, found French prestige was strong among the northern Yoruba, as "conquerors of the Dahomean minotaur and master-presumptive of the Baribas"; at Shaki, in the presence of an emissary of the Alafin, he negotiated a treaty which his government had later to disavow as a clear intrusion into the British sphere.[54] On 14 February 1895 Toutée reached the Niger at Bajibo, and secured from the Nupe chief of the left bank permission to build a fort (which he named after D'Arenberg) on a site of twelve square kilometres on the right bank, earlier abandoned by the Nupe to avoid Dahomean raids. From Bida he received greetings and supplies from Etsu Maliki, who, increasingly worried by pressure from the Niger Company and by the dissension which this encouraged among his own subjects, welcomed the prospect of securing French support and French firearms (see vol. I, pp. 102, 107–8).[55] Toutée was soon astonished to discover the fragility of the Niger Company's presence; the nearest European was 250 kilometres downstream at Igga, though there were African agents at Rabba and Jebba. Toutée poured scorn on the claim of Byron Macaulay, a Creole trader upsteam at Leaba, to represent the British empire in Borgu; no company steamer had been seen for seven years. Although the King of Bussa did keep the treaty of 1885 inside his Koran, he had not ceded suzerainty, and regarded the annual payment of cowries by the company as tribute rather than stipend. He welcomed Toutée warmly and provided boats; the French force then sailed up-river beyond Say (thus establishing that, once the twenty-five miles of rapids were passed, this was a viable waterway), and clashed with the Tuareg who were opposing the French army near Timbuktu.

Toutée was an intelligent and discriminating man; although he claimed to have made serious efforts to explain to their African signatories the purpose of the numerous treaties which he brought back from his voyage, he was under no illusion that these should be accepted at face value. "A treaty has value", he argued, "only so far as it results from and is justified by a *de facto* situation". Other French colonialists too were now arguing that negotiating with Africans should be supplemented by more direct exercises of power. If France based her claims on effective occupation, rather than on solemn attempts to construe meaningless treaty-texts, this would enable her to deny British claims to Borgu, retain Fort D'Arenberg, and develop the fertile middle Niger valley as a main route to the Sudan.[56]

Toutée, in his anxiety to check the British, was prepared to encourage the extension of German Togo to the right bank of the Niger. For some years it had been clear that German traders, soldiers and officials were working vigorously to expand this colony, as in Kamerun, and that the diplomacy of partition was becoming a triangular affair. "It is impossible not to be struck by the activity which the Germans deploy for the development of their small colony", wrote the French Resident at Porto Novo in 1891.[57] This expansion usually involved conflict with Britain. Since the 1880s Germans had resented the Gold Coast's refusal to consider including their territory east of the Volta estuary in a colonial exchange; as they pressed inland, friction over trade- routes and custom-houses extended further up the Volta valley, and was not wholly eliminated by the Neutral Zone agreement of 1888 (see vol. I, pp. 213–16, 221–3). In 1893, when the British were planning more vigorous action to forestall the French in the upper Volta region, they would have liked to establish a permanent frontier by partitioning the zone. But by now Vohsen had formed a Togo Committee to defend the colony's interests,[58] and Kayser was reluctant to make an concessions. He did agree that Ferguson, Britain's talented African envoy, might enter the zone and negotiate treaties to preclude any French incursion; and in September 1894 Ferguson held successful negotiations with Issifa, the ruler of Salaga. But Krause, still travelling in the area under the name of Mallam Musa, heard reports which suggested that Issifa had recognized the British as his sole masters; he summoned the young administrator Heinrich Klose, who complained that Ferguson had tricked the ruler into signing a document which violated German rights.[59] Ferguson's zeal provided useful ammunition for Kayser's tactic of exacerbating quarrels with Britain in order to threaten rapprochement with France unless heavily compensated.[60] Although the British Foreign Office readily agreed to eliminate any illegal or objectionable phrases from Ferguson's treaty, Kayser launched another tirade against "the numerous rebuffs [Germany] had received from England for many years back in all matters relating to colonial expansion"; if he read Ferguson's text to the Reichstag, Kayser declared, he would be "blown up on the spot". Yet, he made it clear, it was not the importance of Salaga as such which provoked his anger: "Germany wanted to expand her borders and get in touch with the Niger – if this were agreed to, she would be ready to hand over the Neutral Zone and be ready to fall in with the views of Her Majesty's Government".[61] Togoland, in other words, was directing its expansion to the north-east rather than the north-west, and would be prepared to work with either Britain or France against the other. The *Deutsche Kolonialgesellschaft* – helped, as in Kamerun, by business contributions and government subsidies – had just raised 100 000 marks for an expedition under Dr Grüner which aimed to obtain treaties "especially along the banks of the Niger and its navigable tributaries".[62] If this intrusion into the Niger Company's sphere could secure valid treaties, Germany would have acquired either an important enlargement of Togo, or a highly marketable commodity for exchange.

In fact she got neither. Grüner's party left its advanced base on 6 November, reached Sansanne Mango shortly after Decoeur in January 1895, and pressed on through Gurma to Gwandu, where they obtained a curious Arabic document purporting to be a protectorate treaty signed by the Emir. When the endorsement of this document was translated, however, the Emir's intention was shown to be quite opposite.[63] But although Germany's late start in the steeplechase left her short of treaty claims, Kayser still tried to profit from the growing antagonism between the other two contestants. British officials, though infuriated by Kayser's handling of the Salaga incident, knew that agreement with Germany could provide a trump-card in their dealings with France. In January 1895 Goldie made new approaches to Vohsen; and in March, when Anglo-French rivalry over the Nile was approaching a new peak, Meade even contemplated ceding the Trans-Volta territory "as part of a general political arrangement".[64]

A little later, Germany made her final attempts to enlarge Togoland by threatening to seek agreement with France. This worried the Foreign Office because of its European rather than its African implications; to secure agreement Salisbury, encouraged by Goldie, seemed ready to press a reluctant Colonial Office to offer the trans-Volta triangle, or other substantial concessions.[65] But Wilhelm II's clumsy intervention in the Transvaal destroyed any possibility of an early Anglo-German entente, and the alternative strategy of creating a continental league against the British empire had still not been fully thought through. The diplomatists continued to pre-enact the moves of Sarte's *Huis Clos;* France and Britain both preferred to reconvene the Niger Commission on 15 January 1896. But here once more, diplomacy proved incapable of reconciling the claims presented by impassioned imperialists in Africa. Increasingly it seemed, even to the reluctant British, that steeple-chasing had become a costly and dangerous form of rivalry which would be better settled by effective occupation of the African interior.

THE EXPANSION OF THE GOLD COAST

Since 1890 officials on the Gold Coast had been advocating expansionist policies. One incentive was financial. Palm products, which until 1885 accounted for over two-thirds of the Colony's exports, were seriously affected by unstable prices, though the gap was made up by the extraction of wild rubber, and of gold.[66] In 1889 a Commission of African notables called for the encouragement of new crops (the significance of recent initiatives by African cocoa farmers was not yet apparent), and for better roads.[67] Another solution, favoured by old Coasters like Governor Griffith, was to expand the northern trade. But this would revive the unsettled problem of relations with Asante.

Since the war of 1874 the British had followed no consistent policy towards this state, hoping vaguely that some central authority might emerge in Kumasi which, without becoming too powerful, or expanding too widely, would encourage British trade and influence. The immediate effect of defeat had been to weaken central authority, and increase dissension among chiefs and office-holders. After the death of Mensa Bonsu in 1881 the office of Asantehene became the focus of contending parties, which by 1887 were engaged in civil war. The complex issues at stake have been studied by Wilks and Lewin, and will not be pursued here. Constitutional questions about the proper relationship between the Monarchy, the Kumasi office-holders, the inner ring of *amantoo* states, and the outer provinces, interacted with opposing views on Asante's future relations with the capitalist world. Influential commoners, including entrepreneurs who were supplying the growing market for rubber, wanted an easing of Kumasi's traditional control over economic activity; together with chiefs seeking greater provincial autonomy and exiled groups who had found refuge in the Colony, they supported the candidature of Twereboanna. The rival party, who in March 1888 secured the election by the general assembly known as the *Asantemanhyiamu* of Agyeman Prempe, a teenage grandson of Kwaku Dua I, also wished to encourage foreign trade and modern Asante, but under the firm direction of a "mercantilist" monarchy.[68]

Since the successful "centralizing" party, like its opponents, wished to promote peaceful trade with the Gold Coast, the prospects for collaboration should have been good; indeed, discreet inverventions by British agents seem to have assisted Prempe's election. Despite their former support of secessionist elements, the Travelling Commissioners who shaped British attitudes had come to desire an Asantehene strong enough to enforce order and protect traders. But before long Griffith, possibly influenced by the refugee groups, began to doubt whether Prempe could perform this role. In July 1890 an Asante delegation visited Elmina to seek British help in persuading these dissidents to return; but Griffith felt his gubernatorial dignity affronted by their "presumption and impertinence", and rejected the juridical basis of their claims. He concluded not only that the Asante generally were "artful, unscrupulous, treacherous, untruthful, and utterly unworthy of . . . reliance", but that Prempe's authority was probably not effective beyond Kumasi.[69]

International rivalry further sharpened Griffith's desire to secure control of Asante. Since the war of 1874 Kumasi had continued to import arms through Grand Bassam and Assinie; Prempe's close adviser John Owusu-Ansah actively cultivated a French connection which his father had helped establish.[70] The Colonial Office believed that the 1889 boundary agreement would prevent the French from "coquetting with Ashantee" (and indeed it seems to have done so); yet confidence in scraps of paper was never complete. "I am rather surprised", the same note continued, "that the Ashantees have not endeavoured to play off the French against us".[71] The 1889 partition of Gyaman gave French a footing in those former northern dependencies of Asante where Griffith hoped to find commercial salvation; this seemed all the more alarming as Prempe tried to re-assert control over the new transit markets in the Brong region. Anxious to isolate Kumasi, Griffith found an outstanding agent in George Ekem Ferguson; his first success was a protectorate treaty with the important market centre of Atebubu in November 1890.[72]

In March 1891 Griffith, without authority from London, sent an envoy to Kumasi with a verbose letter inviting Prempe to sign a treaty accepting British protection, with a Resident Commissioner in Kumasi. This, he argued, would reverse the apparent decline of central authority, give the refugees confidence to return home, and, encouraging access by British subjects, promote "steady and progressive improvement throughout the country". After anxious debate among Kumasi office-holders the *Asantemanhyiamu* was convened, and several members, including supporters of Twereboanna and entrepreneurs enriched by the rubber trade, urged acceptance. But eventually Prempe expressed the assembly's decision in a famous letter: "Ashanti must remain independent as of old, at the same time to be friendly with all white men." Since Knutsford, still reluctant to extend his responsibilities, disapproved of the initiative, Griffith could do no more for the present.[73]

Soon however Salisbury's new resolve to resist foreign penetration (see above, pp. 81–2) began to affect relations with Asante. Ferguson's mission of April 1892, authorized to forestall the French, also challenged Kumasi influence in its former dependencies. Prempe, fearing to lose the remaining markets of the northern trade, invaded Nkoranza to assert control of Kintampo, and in September 1893 invited Atebubu to renew its allegiance. British observers differed as to whether this indicated growing strength or increasing desperation, but in each case their conclusions were similar. Sir Francis Scott, head of the Gold Coast Constabulary, veteran of the war of 1874, and commander of the recently successful Ijebu campaign, favoured "doing away with the power of Kumasi", and acting-Governor Hodgson supported this; but though both discounted effective Asante resistance neither could guarantee that British troops would not be needed. In the Colonial Office, John Bramston believed "the time is ripe for a bold stroke such as tells with savages"; but the bellicose euphoria induced by Ijebu had been checked by the return of a Liberal government. Lord Ripon, Gladstone's Secretary of State and a former Viceroy of India, in southern Africa proved ready enough to promote imperial expansion; but he was aware of opposition among his colleagues to tropical commitments, and the Waima tragedy of December 1893 made him wary of constabulary expeditions. "I do not," he wrote, "desire to annex Ashanti in name or in fact and thereby greatly to increase the responsibilities of the Gold Coast government".[74]

Ripon's wishes notwithstanding, the Gold Coast government was effectively committed to stronger policies in the north. A garrison was sent to occupy Atebubu; and in February 1894 this became the starting-point for a new and extremely important journey by Ferguson. After negotiations with Nkoranza and other Brong states where Asante diplomacy was active, Ferguson was instructed to seek a wide range of treaties of friendship and free trade which would inhibit French penetration of the upper Volta. He was first to go to Bouna, Lobi and Wa, then to the kingdoms of Mamprussi and Mossi and such other states as could be identified to the north of the Neutral Zone.[75] (It was during his return from this epic journey that Ferguson enraged the Germans by his excessive zeal at Salaga; (see above, p. 206). And in Asante itself, Ripon was persuaded that increased control, on the new Yoruba model (cf. above, pp. 211–2) was unavoidable. In March 1894 an Afro-Dutch diplomatist, Hendrik Vroom, returned to Kumasi and again proposed to appoint a British Resident to supervise external relations.

Vroom's arrival stimulated new debates, and in June the *Asantemanhyiamu* was reconvened. A few "hawks" favoured trying to force Britain to withdraw from Atebubu; but most participants, whichever side they had taken during the civil war, were aware of the power of modern weaponry and anxious to avoid conflict. Some, particularly those who were prospering through trade in rubber or gold, were positively favourable to British influence and values; but virtually all were apprehensive about British policy towards domestic slavery – an important source of individual wealth and prestige and an integral part of the social structure, in the dissident provinces no less than in Kumasi. Given satisfactory assurances on this and other matters, however, the *Asantemanhyiamu* no longer opposed the acceptance of a Resident.[76] They appeared generally well-disposed towards Queen Victoria, though still highly suspicious of her local representatives. Prempe therefore appointed a delegation of chiefs led by John Owusu-Ansah to negotiate about the proposed Resident's role; this eventually reached Accra in December 1894 and, despite Griffith's attempts at obstruction, proceeded to London in April 1895.

In sending messengers to appeal to Caesar, Prempe seems to have been consciously following Behanzin's example (see above, pp. 175–7); but he was no more successful. Owusu-Ansah proved a provocative choice of envoy. He and his brother Albert, though descended from the great Asantehene Osei Bonsu, were Christians, thoroughly westernized in behaviour and dress, with experience of government employment and private business in the Colony – precisely the type of "educated African" whose claims to speak for their countrymen modern colonial administrators regarded most sceptically. Colonial officers (including Ferguson), fearing that the envoys might appeal over their heads to ill-informed Liberal MPs and philanthropists, vehemently challenged their right to represent Asante. The known connections of both brothers with French businessmen caused additional suspicion.[77] On 28 September 1894 Griffith therefore tried to pre-empt the Owusu-Ansah mission by seeking authority to send a "strong mission" to Kumasi in order "to bring Ashanti into line with humanity, civilization and order".[78]

All the conditions needed to justify colonial imperialism were now assembled. British Chambers of Commerce had for some time been pressing for a resolution of the "Asante problem"; during 1895 the cause was taken up by a new Chamber at Accra (with both African and European members) as well as by the older one at Cape Coast.[79] Fears of French intervention, despite the boundary agreements, gave added urgency; commercial interests and patriotic pride were provided with a moralistic cover. Griffith's assertion that "Kumasis have purchased arms and ammunition from French at Bassam and French Officers have been teaching them how to use arms" was tentatively credited in the Colonial Office. Finally, a barrage of propaganda such as had served to justify the French conquest of Dahomey was directed against Asante. Newspaper reports and despatches written with an eye to publication emphasized the central role of slavery in Asante society, often exaggerating its cruelty; still more prominent were references to human sacrifice, with inflated estimates of numbers. In reality, Asante evidence suggests that most if not all of the victims had been convicted of some offence and that the use of terror as an instrument of control was decreasing under Prempe; the ceremonies at his formal enstoolment in May 1894 did include some sacrifices, but expansionists exaggerated the numbers. Captain Davidson-Houston, a bellicose Constabulary officer, endorsed reports of four hundred casualties and one hundred headless bodies in the streets of Kumasi, ignoring another informant who put the death-toll at forty.[80]

At the end of October Griffith persuaded his Executive Council to endorse the need for "a strong and resolute policy"; in his usual verbose style he urged that Colonel Scott, on leave in England, should be authorized to prepare a military force to back up an ultimatum before the 1895 rainy season.[81] Hemming and other officials favoured giving the commander of the Ijebu expedition the opportunity to repeat his success; but since Imperial troops might be required, Cabinet authority was necessary. The weakening Liberal government was unwilling to give this. Ripon submitted the papers to the Prime Minister with notable lack of enthusiasm:

> You will see that the Governor wants us to send an expedition to Kumasi and force the King to receive a British Resident &c. In this he is supported by Merchants, Missionaries, and other warlike classes.
>
> Myself I greatly dislike the idea of another Ashanti war. It may be a serious business and could not be undertaken without the Cabinet. If the force proposed by the Governor is sufficient and if there is no hitch in the operations the cost of the expedition can be borne by the finances of the Colony. But if anything goes wrong there will be a demand for more troops and for aid from Imperial Funds. . . . My

> policy would be not to make the expedition now but to leave the next Governor to look into the whole question with an impartial eye and report fully when he has done so.

Even Liberal Imperialists did not favour costly military expeditions in West Africa; Rosebery replied through his secretary that he was "not in a position to sanction either small or big wars just now".[82] Ripon therefore thankfully ruled that the question should be deferred for report by a new governor.[83]

W. E. Maxwell, a lawyer experienced in extending British jurisdiction over Malay sultans, quickly resolved to demonstrate the implications of British paramountcy on the Gold Coast by requiring the formal submission of Prempe. On 13 June he expounded the thesis of the "warlike classes" with a clarity which Griffith had never achieved:

> It is necessary for the peace and welfare of this Colony . . . that the neighbouring tribes should be allowed to live unmolested. It is desirable in the interests of humanity that the horrible practice of sacrificing human victims should be stamped out wherever our power can reach. . . . And finally, at a period when the French are advancing inland on both sides of us, it is not, I submit, to be tolerated that the opening up of the interior of this part of Africa to British commerce should be pretentions of a petty despotism from which no decent government is to be expected, on whose protestations no reliance can be placed and whose history is a chronicle of deceit, cruelty, and breach of treaty engagements.

Maxwell concluded that discussions with the Ansahs should be terminated as soon as possible, that a supporting force of Imperial troops should be prepared, and that he himself should present a comprehensive set of demands at Kumasi shortly after the end of the rains.[84]

Approval of this programme fell to be given by Joseph Chamberlain, who after the July elections reversed conventional judgements of ministerial precedence by selecting the Colonial Office as his base within the Unionist coalition from which to educate the public in the importance of Empire. Developing his own political image as a strong leader whose business experience would help to solve Britain's economic problems within an Imperial framework, he early asserted that the West African colonies had a hitherto undervalued role to play in this programme. Chamberlain's celebrated doctrine of "undeveloped estates" referred specifically to prospects in West Africa, and was surely framed with Asante in mind.

> the trade is rapidly increasing, because we are rapidly getting into communication with the interior. No trade is possible as long as native disturbances are taking place, and when hon. Members, animated no doubt by philanthropic intentions, protest against expeditions, punitive or otherwise, which are now the only way we can establish peace between contending savage tribes in Africa, they are protesting against the only system of civilizing and practically of developing the trade of Africa.[85]

Maxwell's proposals therefore received speedy general approval; the only problems concerned the scale and composition of the force behind them, and the form in which they were to be justified to the British public. Although despatches written with an eye to publicity often denounced Asante's attachment to slavery, officials hesitaed to commit themselves to any measures which might actually encourage domestic slaves to leave their masters; this aspect of Asante "savagery" had thus to be played down. Instead Chamberlain directed Maxwell to base his indictment on Asante's breaches of the peace treaty of 1874 – regarding human sacrifice, freedom of trade and the payment of the promised idemnity in gold. The legal basis of these arguments was a little strained; officials recognized that no time had ever been set for the payment of the indemnity, the reference to freedom of trade was highly general, and the former Asantehene had promised only "to use his best endeavours to check the practice of human sacrifice", without setting any period for its abolition.[86] Nevertheless it was on the basis of treaty violations that Maxwell despatched an ultimatum on 23 September 1895 requiring Prempe to accept the appointment of a British Resident.[87]

In August, news of Samori's capture of Bonduku threatened to complicate the *denouement* of Anglo-Asante relations. Bewildered by the sudden re-appearance on their limited horizons of "the Mahdi of West Africa", Colonial officials envisaged two possible developments, each disturbing in itself, each capable of causing new complications with France.[88] At first Maxwell and Ferguson feared that the *Gyamanhene* might be driven back into alliance with Kumasi, that the two states might jointly bring pressure on Nkoranza, and that this alliance "might be interpreted by natives as establishing an understanding between the French and Kumasi".[89] But in September Prempe, after receiving Samori's messengers in Kumasi, despatched a numerous return mission to Bonduku, reportedly with gifts of gold and a request that Samori would "help him to recover all the countries from Gaman to the coast which originally belonged to Ashanti". Some Gold Coast observers now feared an alliance between the two major African rulers of the region, possibly supported by France.[90] But this was never a real possibility; as Samori repeatedly made clear, his primary aim was to re-establish the commercial and diplomatic relations he had formerly enjoyed with Sierra Leone, and he would never jeopardize this for Prempe's sake. Reassured by reports from a Hausa emissary, Maxwell concluded that "Samory's alliance would be of great value to us at the present juncture and that it is worth securing, so long as he can be made to understand that no assistance can be given to him against the French".[91] But although Samori offered Prempe no salvation, his appearance strengthened a general British feeling "that if we don't get control over Ashanti we shall have serious difficulties".[92]

When Vroom and Stewart delivered their ultimatum on 7 October there were the usual divergent responses and disagreements within the *Asantemanhyiamu,* but the terms of the reply no longer mattered: Maxwell, arguing that Asante ascendency meant "hostility to British influence, interference with trade, activity in the seizure and sale of slaves, and the slaughter" of sacrificial victims, was determined to secure "complete submission and proper guarantees".[93] In January

1896 Scott's expedition marched to Kumasi, expecting and even hoping for a fight. But this was to be deferred until 1900. Prempe and his counsellors had already decided to accept the establishment of a British Resident and military garrison in Kumasi; resigned to the inevitability of British ascendency, they still hoped through statecraft to avoid direct British control. Maxwell, however, was determined clearly to demonstrate hegemony by displaying "some signal proof to the people of Kumasi and the surrounding tribes that the paramount influence of Great Britain had been firmly established in Ashanti".[94] He therefore demanded the immediate payment of 50 000 ounces of gold "or a very large portion of it" as the indemnity due since 1874. When Prempe protested that only 700 ounces were available the Governor arbitrarily removed him to the coast, whence he was deported to Sierra Leone, and eventually to the Seychelles.

Maxwell's thunderbolt caused astonishment, not only in Kumasi, but in the Colonial Office. Chamberlain's first reaction was strongly critical.

> [Prempe] has submitted, and as to indemnity, "la plus belle fille ne peut donner que ce qu'elle a", and if he has no money he cannot pay. I do not see at present sufficient justification for his permanent detention as a political prisoner . . .

But when Maxwell provided fuller arguments, the Minister concurred.[95] As recent experience in a very different context with Dr Jameson had shown him, once an armed emissary had been authorized to act in the name of the Empire it was difficult to control the consequences. Moreover – and this conclusion would not have followed in earlier periods – unauthorized acts of Imperial force, if successful, could prove highly popular with sections of the public to whom Chamberlain sought to appeal. George Baden-Powell MP echoed the euphoria which his brother Robert experienced as one of Scott's officers. Not only did the expedition open "a new market which, if properly organized, should take within a few years probably from two to three million pounds' worth of British produce each year"; but

> in thus setting up strongly and definitely the Queen's power over this great native area, in place of the degrading demoralizing and pauperizing regime hitherto dominant, we shall be bringing to perhaps four or five millions of natives all the advantages of peaceful industry and commerce and those high principles of law, order, justice, and goodwill for all men, which are, after all the guiding lessons taught by our firm national religion.[96]

Similar Imperial zeal was expressed by Kipling; his *Song of the English,* published in 1896, might have served as Maxwell's epigraph:

> Clear the land of evil, drive the road and bridge the ford . . .
> By the peace among Our peoples let men know we serve the Lord.

The expedition of 1896 could be presented as an exemplary demonstration of how moral satisfaction as well as commercial advantage might be secured by resolute use of national power.

In the short term, reports of Asante seemed to justify such optimism. Many office-holders and wealthy traders, in Kumasi as well as in the *amantoo,* were ready to collaborate in opening the country to missionary education and coastward commerce; though Prempe's removal provoked astonishment, there was no immediate wave of anger. Only as soldiers and officials imposed new demands for labour, and as traditional social bonds began to weaken, did the exiled ruler become the focus for those conservative and national forces which eventually joined in the insurrection of 1900. For the immediate future Maxwell had consolidated a base from which his officers could engage in more active rivalry with French and Germans for control of the upper Volta basin.

THE COMPLETION OF THE FRENCH EMPIRE

French plans for the consolidation and development of the West African empire after the fall of Segou centred on the occupation of the vast, ill-defined and little-known region which they called *le boucle du Niger*. During 1893 Archinard, on his final West African campaign, had occupied Jenne and Bandiagara and imported Ahmadu's disloyal half-brother Aguibou to control Macina province. In January 1894 his successor, Lieutenant-Colonel Etienne Bonnier, occupied Timbuktu, advancing in defiance of instructions from Delcassé, who in an attempt to restrain the expansion of military expenditure and military control had appointed a controversial civilian, Albert Grodet, as Governor of the Sudan. When Bonnier perished, with ten French officers and seventy men, in a Tuareg night attack on a fighting patrol the advance down the Niger was temporarily halted. In 1895 all the French colonies except Dahomey were joined in the administrative Federation of *Afrique Occidentale française*, under a civilian Governor-General. But, as Archinard and Borgnis-Desbordes had always realized, the logic of an imperial position made it impossible to stand still. While the conquest of Macina gave the French a still somewhat precarious control of the northern flank of their empire, the Colonial Ministry became increasingly pre-occupied by threats from the south.

As British and German contestants in the steeplechase moved towards the upper Volta the French became anxious to secure Mossi and the neighbouring kingdoms which Binger had located. Although the treaties secured by Ballot and Decoeur might serve to bar Lugard's route from the Niger, Ferguson's second mission of 1894 seemed highly dangerous. But any attempt to forestall him from the Ivory Coast would have to reckon with Samori, who, having disengaged his forces from combat with the Sudanese army on the upper Niger, had by early 1894 relocated his court and military headquarters in Djimini, south of Kong. Samori was anxious to avoid direct conflict with Europeans and had indeed sent messengers to seek a stable peace settlement with Grodet; but as Marchand had discovered (see above, p. 63) his power and influence remained strong enough to block the northern expansion of the Ivory Coast and to neutralize French influence at Kong.

Although Delcassé generally favoured civilian policies of peaceful penetration, he could not ignore the military argument that Samori would respond only to armed force.

When the government decided in August 1894 not to send a battalion towards the Nile, the instrument for a compromise policy seemed at hand; Monteil, with three companies of *tirailleurs*, was diverted to the northern Ivory Coast. His instructions were first to occupy Kong; it was hoped that Samori would then recognize the necessity of submission, in which case he might be permitted to retain a limited territorial base under close French control. Monteil could then proceed to secure treaties which would frustrate foreign challenges from Togo and the Gold Coast and consolidate France's colonies into a compact whole.[97] But this plan broke down in its first, military, phase. Monteil first encountered unexpectedly fierce resistance from Baule villages in the Bandama valley (where he made heavy requisitions of porters and provisions), and then suffered heavy casualties in combat with Samori's forces. French politicians, even though better disposed towards the idea of colonial expansion, recoiled from the prospect of financing a new military command in the Sudan; Monteil's column was recalled in March 1895.[98]

Meanwhile the French were exploring alternative routes towards the Upper Volta. While the missions of Baud and Alby from Dahomey were largely unsuccessful (see above. p. 204), Grodet sent Captain Destenave south from Bandiagara in the Sudan. In Wahiguya Destenave found an aged and drunken ruler willing to accept a French protectorate, and so decided to treat with the state of Yatenga independently of Mossi.[99] Not unnaturally, this increased his difficulties in Wagadugu; when he arrived there on 29 May 1895 Destenave, like Alby the previous February, was refused audience by the Mogho Naba, and told that Mossi needed no assistance from white men with evil motives. During the nine years since receiving Krause, their first European visitor, the rulers of this kingdom had grown increasingly suspicious of Europeans; and the French attack on Ahmadu had roused particular hostility in the influential and well-informed Muslim community. Binger, after being ordered to leave Wagadugu in 1888, had placed great hopes on the friendly attitude of the heir-apparent; but once enthroned under the name of Wobogo the same man had treated Crozat and Monteil with great reserve.[100]

The French now resolved to over-ride Wobogo's resistance before they were forestalled by the British. On 1 July 1894 Ferguson had arrived, with a small escort, including a Mossi interpreter; this reassuringly pacific and tactful envoy from the region to which Mossi's exports of cattle were largely directed was able – to the subsequent fury of the French – to secure a treaty of peace and friendship, and to present Wobogo with a Union Jack.[101] Archinard, now directing the colonial army from Paris, wanted to pre-empt any diplomatic compromise by military action; this was eventually authorized by André Lebon, a staunch expansionist who secured the Colonial Ministry in the Méline government of April 1896. On 1 September 1896 Wagadugu was occupied by 250 troops under Captain Voulet, an aggressive young officer determined to write his name on the map of French imperial expansion. After a brutal campaign against determined Mossi resistance Wobogo was declared deposed on 20 January 1897 and replaced as Mogho Naba by a more compliant brother.[102]

The conquest of Mossi brought the French back into contact with Samori on a new front, where European rivals were also involved. Having established control of Kong in April 1895 and occupied Bonduku in July, Samori sent his son Sarankenyi-Mori towards the valley of the White Volta; he invaded western Gonja in December 1895, moved north into the small kingdom of Wa (both states which had accepted Ferguson's treaties) and began to intervene in the complicated politics of Gurunsi.[103] The over-riding need was contact with oceanic ports, in Togo or the Gold Coast. Hoping to re-establish at Accra the entente he had once enjoyed with the British at Freetown, Samori offered to become a collaborator in imperial expansion: "I am now British Commissioner on every British land here."[104] But even the most sympathetic officials could not meet his need for modern armaments without violating the Brussels treaty, and the moral obligation to maintain European solidarity against Africans excluded any serious though of allying with Samoir against France.

The new British ministers were indeed prepared to take greater risks to extend the West African empire. Lord Selborne, Chamberlain's Under-Secretary and Salisbury's son-in-law, favoured new attempts to incorporate Togo and

Dahomey by negotiated exchanges, and to exend the Gold Coast's "hinterland" to the Niger.

> I do not understand how it is that the hinterland doctrine always works against us. If the French or Germans have a strip of coast they claim, and claim successfully, everything behind it to the North Pole. But with us it is quite different. The French are allowed to cut off all the hinterland of an old colony like the Gold Coast. . . . Why did we let all this back country slip through our fingers? What is our policy in this respect now (i) as to saving anything which yet remains to be saved (ii) as to asserting our claims against France and Germany where we both claim the same territory (iii) as to remedying by exchange the worst consequences of past neglect?[105]

Chamberlain largely sympathized, and after the fall of Kumasi British military forces began actively to assert British claims against France in the northern territories. But this brought no reprieve for Samori. Military officers sent to follow up Ferguson's diplomacy began to demand military action against the slave-raiding forces whom they found in occupation of western Gonja and Gyaman; in their moralistic strictures, the spirit of Lendy rose again and precluded anything more than temporary and local collaboration.[106]

Samori's hopes of survival thus rested on some form of accommodation with the French; to avoid conflict he withdrew his forces from Gurunsi as soon as Voulet began to move southwards from Mossi. But the chances of France conceding even a limited, Ethiopian-style, independence were not good. Since withdrawing to the east Samori no longer tried to enforce Islamization, but his state now consisted essentially of a predatory army living off occupied territory. To obtain horses from the Niger valley, the few firearms which got through from the coast, and even the provisions needed for subsistence in a time of famine, his *dyulas* had little to offer but slaves; neither the moral principles of his European neighbours nor their own manpower strategies would have allowed them to tolerate such an economy for long. In the short run however Binger and the civilian officials of the Ivory Coast were anxious to develop trade with the north and to avoid imposing on their subjects the burden of further military operations; and they were supported by civilian colonialists in Paris, who attached greater priority to forestalling the British than to increasing the battle-honours of imperialism. In March 1896 Guieysse, colonial Minister in Bourgeois's radical government, responded to overtures from Samori by offering to recognize his control – under a French protectorate, represented by a Resident and garrison – of a limited territorial base.[107] Unfortunately he entrusted negotiations, not to the Ivory Coast civilians but to the high-handed Captain Braulot, who sent African interpreters ahead with a peremptory message. Samori received them politely, displayed the work of his gunsmiths, but returned a reply which Braulot rejected.[108]

For the rest of 1896 Samori had little contact with Europeans; their preoccupation with the race to occupy land in the upper Volta region allowed him some vestigial freedom of manoeuvre. Even after March 1897, when Captain Henderson and his Gold Coast Constabulary were driven out of Wa (which they had occupied to forestall the French) and taken prisoner by Sarankenyi-Mori, Chamberlain refused to authorize an offensive against the *sofas*, and the French organized one more peace mission from the Ivory Coast, this time under the civilian administrator Nebout. But meanwhile in the Sudan the military reacted to Samori's destruction of Kong in May 1897 and his subsequent sanguinary advance towards Bobo-Dioulasso. Braulot, sent with a hundred *tirailleurs* to forestall a British occupation of Bouna, found Sarakenyi-Mori in occupation. Though Samori seems to have been willing to leave the town to the French, negotiations between these two old antagonists took place in a tense atmosphere; on 20 August Braulot and half his force were murdered, in circumstances still obscure. Samori, angered by this disaster, still tried to salvage the negotiations with Nebout; but it was now inevitable that the French would launch a final offensive once their other commitments allowed.[109] The young Lieutenant Demars may have anticipated orders by occupying Kong in January 1898, but there was little doubt that more sustained action would follow.

One necessary preliminary was the reduction of the Senufo state of Kenedugu. Babemba, who in 1893 had succeeded his brother Tieba, Samori's great antagonist, had become increasingly aware that the gravest threat to his independence would come from his French "protectors"; by 1896 the historic feud with Samori had given way to tacit co-operation. Early in 1898 Audéoud, now acting Governor of the Sudan, resolved to leave no potential enemies in his rear during the coming campaign; on 1 May Sikasso fell, after a prolonged and costly siege, and Babemba was killed. Samori took the warning, and at the end of May began a last great *hegira*. Perhaps 100 000 people, 12 000 of them armed, 4 000 with modern weapons, began slowly to move into the forested hinterland of Liberia. The French government, having at last settled its West African frontiers with the British (see below, p. 234), authorized its soldiers to carry out harassing operations during the rainy season; soon the retreating forces were devastated by famine and disease, and began to desert in large numbers. When Samori was finally tracked down and captured on 29 September 1898 he had already decided to surrender to the French. Denied his wish to return with his family to Sanankoro, Samori was honourably exiled to Gabon, where he died in 1900. His ashes were returned to Guinea in 1968.

THE ANGLO-FRENCH CONFRONTATION

Between 1896 and 1898 there was for the first and only time real danger that the apportionment of territory in tropical Africa might cause armed conflict between the French and British empires. This danger bore no relation to the intrinsic economic or strategic value of the disputed lands; Professor Sanderson perceptively uses as epigraph for his study of the Fashoda crisis the Norwegian captain's lines:

> We go to gain a little patch of ground.
> That hath in it no profit but the name.
> To pay five ducats, five, I would not farm it.

The commercial prospects of the Niger valley may have been

better than those of the Bahr-el-Ghazal, and the risks of war were probably never quite so great; but it is impossible to read the records of this period without a similar sense of disproportion and irrationality. In both Britain and France, as wiser statesmen knew, the ship of state was in danger of being overbalanced by the superstructures of imperial mythology which certain politicians were using to launch their own careers. Although there is little evidence that democratic electorates knew or cared anything about Bonduku or Borgu, the colonial lobbies had decided they were important, and political figures like Joseph Chamberlain and André Lebon felf constrained to satisfy them.

* * *

The French Foreign Ministry embarked upon confrontation with the British empire only reluctantly. Edward Grey's famous warning of 28 March 1895 that French encroachments on the Nile (by which he may or may not have meant the Niger) "would be an unfriendly act" possibly caused Hanotaux to hesitate; more important was his perception of the danger of becoming over-dependent on the new alliance with Russia.[110] In June he persuaded the Cabinet to abandon Toutée's provocatively sited Fort D'Arenberg,[111] and in October to re-open detailed negotiations on the middle Niger frontier. During the winter of 1895–6 the French and British governments seem to have been tentatively moving towards a general entente on international policy. But this was checked in March 1896, when the British decision to commence reconquest of the Egyptian Sudan rekindled strong prejudices among French politicians.[112]

Even before this the colonial party had succeeded in re-imposing its views on Marcellin Berthelot, the distinguished elderly scientist, during his undistinguished tenure of the Quai d'Orsay in Leon Bourgeois's radical government. When the Niger Commission reconvened in February 1896 its French members declined to recommence where Phipps and Hanotaux had left off; they refused to accept Ferguson's treaties on the extraordinary ground that negotiations conducted by an African had no international validity; most alarmingly of all, they challenged the hitherto accepted interpretation of the Say–Barruwa line of 1890. Pressure from colonialists (including the *Compagnie française de l'Afrique Centrale*, an offshoot of Tharel's *Syndicat*)[113] persuaded the uncomprehending Berthelot to argue that France was free to penetrate any lands south of that line not clearly dependent on Sokoto, including Bornu. Some of their arguments were doubtless advanced as bargaining counters, but what emerged clearly was their determination to challenge the Niger Company's monopoly by securing territorial access to the navigable Niger below Bussa. Direct negotiations between Salisbury and Courcel, the French Ambassador, failed to break the deadlock before Bourgeois's fall.[114]

The new government, headed by the protectionist leader Jules Méline, was to enjoy more than two years in office, during which its Colonial Minister, André Lebon, had much success in persuading Hanotaux and the Quai d'Orsay to endorse intransigent policies. Lebon, as a young graduate, seems to have been converted by Gambetta to the need for colonial expansion; subsequently he became connected with a number of overseas business enterprises, mostly after his tenure of the Colonial Ministry,[115] Convinced that "only those nations are respected which command respect", Lebon resolved to confront Chamberlain's imperialism head-on. When the Marchand Mission, originally approved by Guieysse, finally left Paris in June 1896, Lebon had already suspended negotiations in the Niger Commission in order to strengthen France's bargaining position by effective occupation.[116] According to Yves Person it was principally to help the new Governor-General of *Afrique Occidentale française* co-ordinate opposition to Britain that Lebon visited Dakar, Saint Louis and Kayes in October 1897 – the first visit to tropical Africa by any Minister of a European government.[117]

The opportunities for French penetration of the Niger valley were re-emphasized, between January and November 1896, by Lieutenant Hourst. From Timbuktu Hourst established a French post on an island near Say and sailed down to the Bussa rapids, travelling on to Leaba without finding any trace of effective British influence. This stimulated a new series of missions from Dahomey. This colony, not yet incorporated into AOF, was developing its own impetus for northern expansion; Mante *frères* and the Deputy Charles-Roux were planning a railway company of which Lebon would eventually become a director.[118] Lebon's priority was to secure the territorial connection with the Sudan (a process which aroused some fierce resistance among the Bariba); but when in February 1897 Lieutenant Bretonnet exceeded his instructions by occupying Bussa he was permitted to remain there, thus reviving the threat to break into the Niger Company's sphere on the Niger.[119]

Another initiative by an enterprising officer soon presented a new threat to the Nigerian sphere of interest about which the British had been so long complacent. In February 1897 French ministers endorsed a plan by the *Comité de l'Afrique française* to strengthen their long-cherished Chad plan. Starting from Dahomey, Captain M. G. Cazemajou was to reconnoitre the Say–Barruwa line; at Hanotaux's insistence he was instructed to avoid any territory dependent upon Sokoto. But in January 1898 Cazemajou arrived in Argungu, an emirate east of the Niger, which Monteil in 1891 had found in open revolt against the Caliph; arguing, like Monteil and Hourst, that it had effectively established its independence, he signed a protectorate treaty. Lebon regarded this initiative, like Bretonnet's, as strengthening France's effective bargaining position; while not endorsing Cazemajou or ratifying the treaty he refused to disown him. This apparent threat that France might work for the dismemberment of the Caliphate alarmed the British; (but still more the Caliph, who was probably responsible for Cazemajou's murder at Zinder in May 1898).[120]

The most solid French achievement of 1897 was to end the growing danger of frontier conflicts with the Germans of Togo. On 23 July Commissioners, including Binger and Vohsen, reached a comprehensive boundary agreement; France made concessions in the coastal sector (which would lead to the commercial decline of Aghwey) but in return Germany renounced Togolose expansion towards the Niger.[121] Diplomatically, this increased the pressure on Britain. Increasingly, French colonialists found their hostility towards Germany modified by a sense of common interest; the growing frontier tensions with Britain made that continental league which had been mooted to Monteil in Berlin (see above, p. 193) just a little less improbable. A recent study of Franco-German relations sees "The Perspective of the Continental Entente" emerging most strongly during the years 1897–1900.[122] It never actually materialized; it was always clear that the Germans were unwilling to meet France's price by committing themselves against the British empire in Egypt, still less by any concession over Alsace-Lorraine. But the evident growth of Anglo-German antagonism gave French diplomatists additional confidence during the closing stages of the partition.

French incursions finally obliged the British government to reassess its policy of using the Niger company as an economical agent for reserving Hausaland for the Empire. Goldie, despite his protestations of imperial statesmanship and his perceptions of historical unities within Sudanic Africa, had always given priority to maintaining the commercial monopoly on which, he could fairly claim, the whole structure depended. But as Lagos expanded northwards the complaints of British and African competitors were authoritatively reinforced by frustrated officials of that colony. In May 1896 Chamberlain finally insisted that the company should either enforce the control it claimed over the Yoruba emirate of Ilorin or allow Governor Carter to intervene directly. Obliged to mount a major military expedition, Goldie decided first to coerce the new Etsu of Nupe, whose authority, and willingness to continue collaborating with the company, had been further weakened since Toutée's incursion. Early in 1897 Goldie personally led five hundred troops, armed with six Maxims and a twelve-pounder gun, in a hard-fought attack on the Nupe capital of Bida, before proceeding to chastise the Emir of Ilorin. Unfortunately the Foreign Office, by publicly assuring France that this force would not enter disputed territory in Borgu, had encouraged Bretonnet to do precisely that. It was now clear that they would have to deal directly with French encroachments which it had unwittingly encouraged; and that in the process the basis of their compact with the Niger Company would be fundamentally changed.[123]

The subsequent Anglo-French confrontation has been described many times, and will only be summarized here. Chamberlain now resolved to remove the ambiguities concerning the extent of British authority in West Africa without delay, both by applying pressure to the Niger Company which would eventually lead to the abrogation of its Charter and by reacting in kind to French attempts to claim "effective occupation" by military patrols. This could be done more speedily in the northern Gold Coast than on the Niger. On 4 June 1897 Maxwell was instructed to seek "a satisfactory arrangement" with Samori, despite the humiliation at Wa, and to concentrate on extending his military occupation "as a material guarantee for dealing with the French seizures of Mossi and Boussa, when negotiations are resumed".[124] Even Bonduku was temporarily occupied, despite French protests, and in October Lieutenant-Colonel H. P. Northcott was appointed Commissioner for the Northern Territories, in command of a strengthened force. In a sense this was shadow-boxing; no European officer intended to become involved in conflicts from which only Samori could benefit, and Voulet's occupation of Wagadugu had given France a decisive local advantage. Ferguson's diplomacy, and the subsequent constabulary operations, had secured most of Asante's former northern dependencies for Britain, but Chamberlain could have secured Mossi and Gurunsi only by concessions on the Niger which he did not intend to make. Borgu would be the critical area. In July Chamberlain and Selborne (an even more intransigent imperialist) resolved to strengthen their position there by raising a new colonial army, the West African Frontier Force; the command was offered to Lugard, a choice acceptable to Goldie but provocative to the French.

Even Lugard, briefed by Chamberlain in November on his return from the Kalahari, was taken aback by the risks inherent in Chamberlain's proposed "chessboard policy", of occupying posts alongside the French. But when he expressed military doubts and advised diplomatic compromise,

> J.C. scouted the idea vehemently and angrily, said he would *never* be a party to giving up our country in order to get what

> is already ours . . . we could always have more money behind us than the French and hence spend double and have a larger force till they gave in – the Birmingham "Screw Policy"![125]

Chamberlain, convinced that Imperial interests demanded a resolute display of force to the French, was equally anxious that the British public should observe it. In Bagehot's phrase, he was announcing Imperial texts in order that the "scribes in the newspapers" should write the sermons, as they had just done on the occasion of the Diamond Jubilee.[126] Chamberlain even suggested that Salisbury should provide an exceptionally prominent pulpit by appointing him Commissioner to conduct the Paris negotiations in person.[127] The objective of the Screw Policy remained a diplomatic compromise, on terms not evidently favourable to France; war for Bussa or Mossi would have made little sense even to Chamberlain's strongest supporters.[128] But for nearly a year his apparent readiness to back dubious legal claims by military force alarmed prudent diplomatists of the old school, notably Sir Edmund Monson, the patrician Ambassador in Paris.

Even diplomatists of long experience, however, shared Chamberlain's conviction that prestige had become a primary consideration in the Niger crisis; as Francis Bertie argued at a later stage, it would be disastrous "to lose face with the natives generally; to give to France and other Powers the impression that we can always be squeezed".[129] Salisbury's own appreciation, of political pressures at home as well as of international implications, led him to insist that France should withdraw from Bussa, and concede to Britain the extensive Nigerian "hinterland" to which she had always believed herself entitled; to this extent Dr Uzoigwe is right to emphasize that the two Ministers "differed only as to means, not ends".[130] But Salisbury knew than the disputed areas in Borgu would never be of intrinsic economic value; he had for some time been ready to abandon the monopoly so stridently defended by Goldie (who at times seemed "hardly sane");[131] he was aware of large gaps in the legal and moral briefs which his Commissioners were required to defend when the Paris negotiations resumed in October 1897. Most important of all, he had a broader view than Chamberlain of Nigeria's place in the foreign relations of the British Empire.

Although the prospect of a Continental League had made little concrete progress, the perils of Britain's isolation were clearer by 1898 than ever before. She had been unable to intervene effectively in the Near Eastern crises of 1895–7; she was obliged in March 1898 to acquiesce in Russia's occupation of Port Arthur, and to participate herself in the first stages of a Chinese partition; during the following summer, while the expected confrontation with France on the Nile drew closer, she reluctantly purchased German complaisance in southern Africa by envisaging a partition of the Portuguese colonies.[132] When Chamberlain compared the stakes in Nigeria to those in eighteenth-century India, Salisbury delicately corrected his perspective:

> if we are to send British or Indian troops, in the hope of fighting another Plassey with Lugard as our Clive, and Sokoto as our Bengal, the prospect becomes much more serious. Our Clive will be in no danger of being astonished at his own moderation. There is no loot to get except in Goldie's dreams.[133]

He never lost sight, as Chamberlain sometimes did, of the necessity of ultimately finding a diplomatic solution.

One possibility, which both Ministers contemplated in November 1897, was to merge the Niger problem in a wider diplomatic compromise, embracing the Gambia, Dominica, Newfoundland – perhaps even Egypt.[134] But the French would not be ready for such an entente until Marchand had completed his mission, for good or ill. Until such time, Salisbury sought to disengage the issue of national prestige from the possession of particular places, and to seek ways of reconciling the concrete issues at stake. Interestingly, the old patrician had a longer economic view than the Birmingham businessman. As he commented when Chamberlain raised belated arguments about the commercial importance of Ilo, "the doctrine of the immutability of trade routes has been . . . a little over done".[135] Boundary lines certainly had to be drawn:

> the intentions of the Powers assembled at the Conferences of Berlin and Brussels, and their efforts for the welfare of the African races, can only be fulfilled if the Powers territorially interested in that continent agree to work in separate spheres for the common end, arranging those spheres by mutual concession.[136]

But Britain's primary intention at Berlin had been to secure access, not control, and the details of the disputed boundaries which Salisbury reviewed in this celebrated despatch would be of less importance than the future commercial relations between the partitioning powers.

Salisbury had sketched the strategic goals of his African policy at the Lord Mayor's Banquet of 9 November 1897; (the same words might have served for his objectives in China):

> We do not wish to take territory simply because it may look well to paint it red upon the map. The objects we have in view are simply business objects. We wish to extend the commerce, the trade, the industry and civilisation of mankind. We wish to throw open as many markets as possible, to bring as many producers and consumers into contact as possible; to throw open the great natural highways, the great waterways of this great continent; we wish that trade should pursue its unchecked and unhindered course on the Niger, the Nile and the Zambezi.[137]

When shortly afterwards the French emphasis began to shift from territorial sovereignty to commercial access to the lower Niger Salisbury – having already decided to terminate Goldie's monopoly – was prepared to meet their practical needs by amending the navigation regulations and by guaranteeing access to transit and warehousing facilities such as Britain had in 1891 leased from Portugal at Chinde on the Zambezi. In return, on 31 January he suggested protecting *Britain's* practical interests by establishing a uniform tariff structure for the French and British colonies – a move towards the sort of West African customs union which a deputation from the Chambers of Commerce was later to press on him.[138] If France would accept such terms, Salisbury would ensure that

Chamberlain's attachment to such places as Bouna and Ilo did not prevent agreement.

But securing French acceptance involved composing a package which Hanotaux could impose upon the imperialist Lebon and the protectionist Méline. And though all the needs of foreign policy pointed towards early settlement, Hanotaux himself was genuinely worried when British forces in West Africa began to act as provocatively as French expeditions had done, with increasingly vocal public support. When Emile Zola's famous article re-opened the Dreyfus case in January 1898 the contemptuous comments of British newspapers at first strengthened his resolution; Salisbury's initial proposal that tariffs should be equalized in *all* West African colonies (including Senegal) seemed to Hanotaux a *proposition de rupture*, and he gloomily contemplated war.[139] But such comtemplation could only be discouraging. War would involve dependence on the Russian alliance – and on those army officers who were now openly displaying profound hostility towards the democratic Republic. Despatches from London suggested that militant imperialists would welcome the opportunity for some *coup d'audace* to compensate for the setback over Port Arthur; the power of the British empire, Courcel feared, was no held in check only "by the wisdom of a Queen who will shortly be senile and a [Prime] Minister weakened by sickness and age".[140] The more important confrontation pending on the Nile also suggested a need to settle the Niger question; *patriotes mégalomanes* in Britain were anxious to keep it open as a source of compensation (though this was not in fact Salisbury's view).[141] So when in mid-February Salisbury offered substantial territorial concessions and commercial access to the Niger in return for an equalization of tariffs restricted to the southern colonies only, Hanotaux was relieved to glimpse the outline of an honourable compromise.

Time, and nerve, were still needed to complete the details. In March news of Cazemajou's incursion into Argungu: in April, British intervention at Kishi in support of an engineered "Native rising":[142] in May, the arrival of Lugard's force on the Borgu chessboard: all inflamed patriotic tempers. Méline and his protectionist supporters were reluctant to accept the vital commercial provisions, which would indeed be of more practical value to the British than to the French. The re-drawing of the Say–Barruwa line raised new problems, though it did bring the French explicit recognition of their treasured claims north and east of Lake Chad. But in May the French election warned Méline's Ministry that its days were numbered, and a Convention was finally signed on 14 June 1898, its last day in office. Besides defining the boundaries of Nigeria and the Gold Coast on lines roughly corresponding to the local balance of colonial forces, it marked out a wide area (incorporating that already covered by the 1889 Agreement on the Gold and Ivory Coasts) within which British and French would enjoy "the same treatment in all matters of river navigation, of commerce, and of tariff and fiscal treatment and taxes of all kinds".[143] Taken in conjunction with arrangements which both governments had already made with the German in Togo, this offered some partial guarantee that existing trade patterns would not be immediately shattered by protective tariffs, and that (except in Senegal and the Sudan) the large European trading houses which were now forming would be able to continue to operate across new colonial boundaries.

CONTROL AND CONSOLIDATION

The agreement of 14 June 1898 virtually completed the partition of West Africa so far as European governments were concerned; it remained only for Britain and Germany to divide Dagomba, and the rest of the Neutral Zone, as part of a wider colonial agreement of 14 November 1899 centred on Samoa.[144] Afro-European relations were another matter. Ijebu and Dahomey, Asante and Benin, had been conquered; authorities in Opobo and Porto Novo, Assinie and Abeokuta, had made their own compromises with European power; but – as the insurrections of the Temne and the Mende were currently demonstrating – effective European control would in many areas still take time, and strong coercion, to enforce. Most immediately, the British had to enforce the sovereignty they claimed over Sokoto and Bornu; and the French, besides their final campaign against Samori, had numerous Muslim opponents to deal with before their Chad Plan was complete.

Although the British always claimed that the Say–Barruwa agreement of 1890 placed Bornu in their sphere of influence, they could do little to implement this after its conquest in 1893 by the formidable armies of Rabih Fadlallah. The risk therefore remained that the French would either try to use Rabih as "a sort of Menelik, to be turned against the British"[145] (an unlikely project, given his known attitude towards Europeans), or would conquer him and claim Bornu together with his other territories. The 1898 Convention not only removed these dangers, but conveniently ensured that it would be the French who, hastening to establish control in Chad, undertook the inevitable battle which destroyed Rabih's empire on 22 April 1900.

Sokoto might still present serious military problems. Since 1894 its rulers had been growing increasingly apprehensive about the armed bands of Europeans who seemed to be converging from all sides, and their suspicions of Goldie were naturally intensified by his military campaigns of 1897 in the south-western emirates. But Caliph 'Abd Al-Rahman was in no condition to challenge the British directly. Although feeling against the Nasare'en seems to have been growing among the population, the Emirs increasingly acted in accordance with local interests rather than instructions from Sokoto; and in the east they gave priority to the even more acute threat from Rabih and his Mahdist followers. Moreover, the arrival near Say in 1894 of Ahmadu bin 'Umar, Al-Bouri Ndiaye, and other fugitives from the West reminded the Caliph that the French were Islam's most dangerous enemies. All these weaknesses pointed towards accommodation with the British. In 1900 Lugard was able to take up his duties as High Commissioner in peace, and to proceed to extend military control over the Caliphate by instalments over the next three years.[146]

* * *

In 1897–8 the French government, working with leaders of the colonial party, were planning three armed expeditions to converge on Lake Chad. At a time when it was still possible to hope for results from Marchand's mission, success would not only effect the junction of France's existing African colonies but reinforce their thrust towards the Nile. Already in 1897 Emile Gentil had reached the lake through the Chari valley, securing the protectorate of Bagirmi en route; he now returned prepared to deal with the problem of Rabih, by force if not as formerly hoped by diplomacy. While Captains Foureau and Lamy were crossing the Sahara from Algeria, Captain Paul Voulet and his close friend Julien Chanoine, who had won repute by their speedy and brutal conquest of Mossi, renewed the approach from the west. Since Cazemajou's death had shown that African opposition was likely, their force consisted of six hundred well-armed fighting men. It would clearly be difficult to provide food and water for such an expedition through *sahel* country, especially since Delcassé (now Foreign Minister) insisted that they should keep to the north of the recently defined frontier; Sudanese military experts had grave doubts about this project. By January 1899, when the column assembled on the middle Niger, the Fashoda crisis was over and the eastern boundary of Chad was about to be assured by a new Anglo-French Convention of 21 March; nevertheless the tripartite plan was under way and Voulet's force duly set out.[147]

In April one of its officers returned to Paris and confirmed reports that it was behaving with exceptional violence and brutality. In retrospect Voulet's methods seem to have differed in degree, rather than in kind, from those employed by other European forces, including some led by his critics. *Tirailleurs* and African auxiliaries commonly expected booty and slaves as part of their emoluments, and under-financed columns in remote areas had to depend on the country for labour and supplies. In this case, Delcassé's instructions to avoid British territory (though sometimes disregarded) obliged Voulet to lead his large force through regions of the *sahel* where recent famine had rendered water and supplies particularly scarce, All these considerations, as well as the personalities of the leaders, indicated the systematic use of terror as a means of control; Voulet carried this "unsound method" to excess. But with the Dreyfus affair approaching its climax, the French cabinet was desperately anxious to avoid renewed conflict with Britain coupled with a colonial scandal; Lieutenant-Colonel Arsène Klobb, an upright and devout Christian, was sent to take command of the party. Once he came within range Klobb, outraged by the evidence of savage slaughter of suspected dissidents and wholesale burning of villages, launched an angry ultimatum; Voulet, now pathologically intent on personal glory, rejected this and murdered Klobb – an act which caused a greater sensation in France than the atrocities against Africans. This did not affect the political outcome; Voulet and Chanoine were in turn killed by their demoralized *tirailleurs*; the remnant of the force was re-organized under Lieutenant Joalland, occupied Zinder, and eventually joined Gentil and Foureau in time to take part in the defeat of Rabih and the occupation of Chad. But this gruesome climax allowed the French public to assume that Voulet and Chanoine were madmen, thus leaving the colonial conscience and the myth of the *mission civilisatrice* untainted by their behaviour. Having settled their international disputes, European governments were free to evolve their own methods of controlling their new subjects.

* * *

Voulet's experience showed that problems could be created for colonial rulers (as well as Africans) when boundaries were drawn in Europe with rulers and compasses; but apart from such minor adjustments as could be accepted on the spot by boundary Commissioners, diplomatists made few attempts to change them. In the *Entente Cordiale* agreement of 8 April 1904 the northern Nigerian boundary was adjusted to improve French lines of communication,[148] and the British Admiralty at last agreed that France should have the Isles de Los; but a renewed French attempt to secure the Gambia ended with a minor adjustment of its eastern border, intended to allow Senegal to make greater use of river transport. In subsequent years the idea of a Gambia exchange was regularly revived, and equally regularly failed because the French counterpart was never sufficient to outweigh the attachment of British imperial sentiment to this tiny (but generally viable) colony (*Prelude*, pp. 347–8) The diplomatic compromises of the 1890s hardened into rigid boundaries. In 1911 the border between Sierra Leone and Liberia was redrawn, on lines which substantially rewarded the efforts of a British-protected ruler to re-unify Luawa chiefdom;[149] but this was an isolated example. Indeed, this negotiation proved that, despite apparent threats to her independence posed at different times by France, Germany and Britain, even Liberia's boundaries were becoming definitively established; the advantages which any of these powers might derive from extending colonial control would be greatly outweighed by the international complications.[150]

Apart from some inter-colonial boundary adjustments within *Afrique Occidentale française* there was one major change of boundaries. After the First World War the German empire was re-partitioned between France and Britain,[151] and twenty years later a still wider repartition was discussed in the context of attempts by France and Britain to appease the appetites of Hitlerite Germany.[152] But by this time the attachment to colonial boundaries which the inhabitants of Bathurst had shown in the 1870s had spread more widely. African leaders now aimed to focus national energies, in the first place at least, within the partition lines, and strongly resisted any idea of being bartered to different colonial masters. In November 1938 Governor Bourdillon reported grave alarm about rumours that Nigerian territory might be transferred to Germany; this he declared would "blacken our name all over Africa".[153] Colonial rule, however arbitrary or oppressive, tended to bond its subjects into new political entities. These bonds were strong enough to survive the processes of decolonization; only in south-west Cameroon did people choose on independence to alter the political map of 1919, and that was to revert partially to that of 1885. It is one of the ironies of history that the boundaries established by foreigners during their partition of West Africa are those which the governments of independent Africa have solemnly guaranteed by the OAU Charter of 1963.

NOTES

1. ANSOM, Afrique IV/38/a, Aperçu, géographique.
2. ANSOM, Dahomey III/2/b, Proposal of 11 December 1890.
3. E. M. Chilver "Paramountcy and Protection in the Cameroons," P. Gifford and W. R. Louis, *Britain and Germany in Africa* (New Haven, 1967) pp. 479–91.
4. R. Kaeselitz, "Kolonialoberung und Widerstandskampf in Süd Kamerun", in H. Stoecker, *Kamerun unter deutscher Kolonialherrschaft*, II (E. Berlin, 1968) pp. 13–26.
5. FO 64/1316, Minute by Anderson on RNC to FO, 26 May 1893, encl. correspondence with Vohsen; Flint, *Goldie* pp. 180 ff.
6. H. Stoecker, H. Mehls, E. Mehls, "Die Eroberung des Nordostens", in Stoecker, *Kamerun*, II, pp. 62–3; S. Passarge, *Adamaua* (Berlin, 1895) pp. v–vii.
7. A. H. M. Kirk-Greene, "Von Uechtritz's expedition to Adamawa, 1893", *JHSN*, I, 1957, pp. 86–98 gives a precis of Passarge's published account.
8. Flint, *Goldie*, pp. 180–4. For the Agreement, Hertslet, *Map of Africa* III, pp. 913–15. Marschall defends it against possible colonial criticism in GP, VIII, no. 2021, Report to Wilhelm II, 16 November 1893.
9. DDF X, nos 232, 233, Herbette to Develle, 9, 11 May 1893; no. 308, Marschall to Herbette, 15 July, no. 334, Herbette to Develle, 12 August.
10. Rudin, *Germans in the Cameroons*, pp. 88–90, DDF X no. 455, d'Estournelles to Develle, 1 December 1893.
11. DDF X no. 434, Herbette to Develle, 18 November 1893.
12. DDF X nos 471, 474, Herbette to Casimir-Périer, 15, 17 December 1892; H. Labouret, *Monteil*, pp. 173–81; Roberts, "Railway Imperialism" pp. 146 ff.
13. G. N. Sanderson, *England, Europe and the Upper Nile* (Edinburgh, 1965) pp. 106–8; DDF X no. 478, Herbette to Casimir-Périer, Tel. 21 December 1893; DDF X1, no. 3n quoting Note by Monteil, January 1894. H. Labouret, *Monteil*, pp. 181–5; P. L. Monteil, *Souvenire Vécus* (1924) pp. 94–100. For text of the Agreement, Hertslet, *Map of Africa*, II, pp. 657–60.
14. Flint, *Goldie*, pp. 185–6.
15. T. A. Bayer, *England und der Neue Kurs* (Tübingen, 1955) ch. v and pp. 117–20 (Malet to Kimberley, 7 March 1894); GP, VIII, 2023, Marschall to Hatzfeldt, 17 April 1894. See also P. Grupp, *Deutschland, Frankreich und die Kolonien* (Tübingen, 1980) pp. 89–91.
16. Labouret, *Monteil*, p. 170.
17. A. Neton, *Delcassé* (1952) pp. 105–8.
18. Majority of 260–239, 15 May 1893: Neton, *Delcassé*, p. 125.
19. E. Rabut, "Le dessein colonial des milieux d'affaires implantés en Afrique noire", in *Etudes africaines offertes à Henri Brunschwig* (1982) p. 178; H. Brunschwig, *Mythes et Réalités*, pp. 124–37; S. M. Persell,

"Joseph Chailley-Bert and the Importance of the *Union coloniale française*" (1960), *HJ*, xviii, 1974, pp. 176–84.
20. Person, *Samori*, III, pp. 1487–89; Kanya-Forstner, *Conquest* pp. 209–14.
21. J. Stengers, "Aux origines de Fachoda: l'expedition Monteil". Extrait de la *Revue Belge de Philologie et d'Histoire*, XXXVI, 1958, pp. 436–50; XXXVIII, 1960, pp. 366–404, 1040–65. Sanderson, *England, Europe*, ch. VII; M. Michel, *La Mission Marchand* (1972) ch. 1.
22. See H. C. G. Matthew, *The Liberal Imperialists* (1973).
23. W. Roger Louis, "Sir Percy Anderson's Grand African Strategy, 1883–1896", *EHR*, LXXXI, 1966, pp. 305–11.
24. The best and latest account of this much-discussed treaty is Sanderson, *England, Europe*, ch. VIII (and maps); Louis, op. cit. pp. 305–11.
25. R. R. James, *Rosebery* (1963) pp. 348 ff.
26. A. J. P. Taylor, "Prelude to Fashoda: The Question of the Upper Nile, 1894–5", *EHR*, LXV, 1950, p. 62; Sanderson, *England, Europe*, pp. 171–80.
27. G. N. Sanderson, "The European Partition of Africa: Coincidence or Conjuncture?" in E. F. Penrose (ed.) *European Imperialism and the Partition of Africa* (1975) pp. 34–5; Sanderson, *England, Europe*, p. 170.
28. *La Politique Coloniale*, 6 April 1894, quoted by M. Michel, *La Mission Marchand*, p. 23.
29. Taylor, "Prelude to Fashoda", pp. 61–5; DDFXI, 129, Decrais to Hanotaux, 5 June; 178, Note by Hanotaux, 29 June 1894. The best discussion of Hanotaux's role is C. M. Andrew and A. S. Kanya-Forstner, "Gabriel Hanotaux, The Colonial Party and the Fashoda Strategy", in Penrose, *European Imperialism*. See also R. G. Brown, *Fashoda Reconsidered: The Impact of Domestic Politics on French Policy in Africa, 1893–98* (Baltimore, 1969) ch. I; P. Grupp, "Gabriel Hanotaux, Le personnage et ses idées sur l'expansion coloniale", *RFHOM*, LVIII, no. 213, 1971.
30. Stengers, "Aux origines", pp. 1044–52.
31. DDF XI, no. 191, Delcassé to Monteil, 13 July 1894, with Minute by Hanotaux.
32. Michel, *Mission Marchand*, pp. 23–4, quoting Haussmann to Hanotaux, 22 August 1894.
33. DDF XI, no. 218, Hanotaux to Decrais, 17 August 1894; FO 27/3186, Dufferin to Kimberley, 209 Af 16 August 1894.
34. FO 27/3208, Memo by Goldie, 10 July 1894, with minute by Anderson.
35. FO 27/3186, Phipps to Kimberley, 223 Af, 5 September; 232 Af Conf. 13 September 247 Af 22 September 1894; cf. ANSOM, Afrique IV/38/a, Delcassé to Hanotaux, 18 Sepember 1894.
36. FO 27/3208, Minutes of Cardew to Ripon, Conf. 38, 23 May 1894; FO 27/3186, Phipps to Anderson, Pte 14 September 1894; FO 27/3187, Minute by Anderson, 10 October on Phipps 266 Af Conf: "The French colonial party may have 'ambitions', but we have possession."
37. Rosebery Papers, 88, Rosebery to Kimberley, 15 September 1894.

38. FO 27/3186, Phipps to Kimberley, 256 Af 29 September; FO 27/3187, Phipps to Kimberley, 260 Af Most Conf., 4 October; 266 Af Conf., 9 October, minutes by Anderson and Kimberley.
39. DDF XI, no. 260, Note by Hanotaux, 30 October 1894.
40. DDF XI, no. 285, Note by Hanotaux, 17 November 1894. P. Renouvin, "Les Origines de l'expédition de Fachoda", *Revue Historique*, 1948, p. 186; Andrew and Kanya Forstner, "Gabriel Hanotaux", pp. 63–4. For fuller accounts of these negotiations, Sanderson, *England, Europe*, ch. IX: Taylor, "Prelude to Fashoda", pp. 68–75.
41. Hertslet, *Map of Africa*, II, pp. 757–64. C. W. Newbury, "The Tariff Factor in Anglo-French West African Partition", Gifford and Louis, *France and Britain in Africa*, pp. 247–9.
42. ANSOM, Dahomey I/8/d, Jamais to Dodds, Tel. 23 December 1892; Cornevin, *Dahomey*, pp. 367–9.
43. ANSOM, Missions 23, Decoeur proposals, approved by Delcassé, 27 February 1893; Decoeur to Deloncle, Pte 18 May; Decoeur report, 29 August 1894. Dahomey V/11/b, Journal de marche, February 1894, f. 34–5. Cornevin, *Dahomey*, p. 372.
44. ANSOM Missions 23, Decoeur to Minister of Marine [?*sc* Colonies] (copy) 9 July; Rapport by Haussmann, approved by Delcassé, 24 July 1894; Dahomey III/4/b, Decoeur to Chautemps, 17 June 1895.
45. ANSOM, Dahomey III/4/b, Ballot to Delcassé, Conf. 7 November 1894; Cornevin, *Dahomey*, pp. 374–7.
46. H. Brunschwig, "Scramble et 'Course au Clocher' ", *JAH*, XII, 1971, 139–41 shows that the French term, though often applied to the events described here, had been used as early as 1884.
47. ANSOM, Soudan III/2, Delcassé to Toutée, 17 November 1894; Dahomey III/4/b, Ballot to Delcassé, Conf. 7 November 1894.
48. Perham, *Lugard*, I, 466–7.
49. Goldie to Lugard, 24 July 1894, in M. Perham and M. Bull (ed.) *The Diaries of Lord Lugard*, IV (1963) pp. 55–61.
50. FO 83/1315, Note by Anderson, 19 September 1894.
51. This brief summary is based on Perham and Bull, *Diaries*, and Flint, *Goldie*, pp. 220–7.
52. ANSOM, Dahomey III/4/a, Ballot to Chautemps, Parakou, 17 February 1895; III/4/b, Note du Bureau d'Afrique, 16 April 1895. Cf. Cornevin, *Dahomey*, pp. 381–8; Obichere, *West African States*, pp. 164–70.
53. ANSOM Soudan III/2, Delcassé to Toutée, Conf. 17 November 1894 (copy); cf. G. J. Toutée, *Dahomey, Niger, Touareg* (1897) p. 18.
54. My source for Toutée's mission, except where otherwise indicated, is the *Notes Politiques* which he compiled in Paris on 23 January 1896 (ANSOM, Soudan III/2).
55. Soudan III/2, Toutée to Chautemps, Yauri, 26 April 1895; Michael Mason, "The Nupe Kingdoms in the Nineteenth Century: A Political History" (Ph.D. thesis University of Birmingham, 1970). I am grateful to Dr Mason for showing me a revised version of his thesis.

56. ANSOM, Soudan III/2, Toutée, *Notes Politiques*, f. 35; cf. Afrique IV/38/a, Aperçu geographique.
57. ANSOM, Dahomey I/6/c, Ehrmann to Ballay, 8 May 1891. For British reactions see, for example, Hemming's minutes of 6 March, 18 June 1890 on FO to CO, 5 March, 14 June, CO 96/213.
58. K. Vietor, *Geschichtliche und Kulturelle Entwicklung unserer Schutzgebiete* (Berlin, 1913) pp. 52 ff.
59. J. A. Braimah and J. R. Goody, *Salaga: The Struggle for Power* (1967) print translations of Krause's letters (pp. 150–6) and of extracts from H. Klose, *Togo unter deutsche Flagge* (Berlin, 1899).
60. Cf. Bayer, *England und der neue Kurs*, pp. 88–90, quoting Gosselin Memo 30 August 1894 and Kimberley minute, 7 September.
61. FO 64/1334, Malet to Kimberley, 2 December 1894, encl. Gosselin, Memo of conversation with Kayser, 1 December; and Minutes.
62. W. Markov and P. Sebald, "The Treaty between Germany and the Sultan of Gwandu", *JHSN*, IV, 1967, p. 142; cf. R. Cornevin, *Histoire de Togo* (1959) pp. 139–49.

62 Markov and Sebald, "The Treaty", pp. 147–53. For hopes built on this expedition by German imperialists, see the map enclosed in FO 64/1358, Malet to Salisbury, 117 Af, 3 October 1895.

64. Flint, *Goldie*, p. 228. CO 96/248, Minute by Hemming on Griffith, Secret, 28 September 1894; CO 96/264. Minute by Hemming on FO, 1 March 1895; Meade to Maxwell, Pte, 14 March 1895.
65. For Colonial Office fears, CO 96/265, minutes on FO to CO, 5 September; 30 October, 21 December, 1895; cf. J. D. Hargreaves, "*Entente manquee*", *CHJ* XI, 1953, p. 77.
66. See Table A. I, p. 256. cf. R. E. Dumett, "British Official Attitudes in Relation to Economic Development in the Gold Coast, 1874–1905", Ph.D. thesis, University of London, 1966.
67. PP 1890, XLVIII, C 5897–40, *Economic Agriculture on the Gold Coast, 1889*.
68. I. Wilks, *Asante in the Nineteenth Century* (Cambridge, 1975) esp. ch. XIII; T. J. Lewin, *Asante before the British: the Prempean Years* (Lawrence, 1978). For indications of how historians are now seeing such conflicts in relation to "a seismic shift in values and beliefs", see T. C. McCaskie, "Accumulation, Wealth and Belief in Asante History", *Africa*, 53, 1983.
69. PP 1896, LVIII, C 7917, no. 9, Griffith to Knutsford, 8 September 1890, pp. 19, 29; Lewin, *Asante*, pp. 145–50 summarizes the negotiations.
70. Wilks, *Asante*, pp. 613–15, 637–8.
71. CO 96/217, Minute by Meade, 16 July 1891, on Griffith to Knutsford, 179, 3 June 1891.
72. His report is reprinted in K. Arhin (ed.), *The Papers of George Ekem Ferguson* (Leiden, 1974) pp. 4–24; cf. Lewin, *Asante*, pp. 168–74. On the Atebubu and Kintampo markets, see K. Arhin *West African Traders in Ghana in the Nineteenth and Twentieth Centuries* (1979).
73. PP 1896, LVIII, C 7917, nos 13, 16, Griffith to Knutsford, 19 May, 3 June 1891; cf. Lewin, *Asante,* pp. 155–63; W. Tordoff, "Brandford Griffith's Offer of British Protection to Ashanti", *THSG*, VI, 1962.

74. CO 96/238, Hodgson to Ripon, Conf. 13, 14, 18, 22 November 1893 (partially printed in C 7917, nos 42–5), with Minutes, (Bramston, 21 December; Ripon, 15 January 1894). Lewin, *Asante*, pp. 168–82 gives the Asante version.
75. CO 879/38, CP African 448, no. 88, Hodgson to Ferguson, 9 January 1894.
76. This analysis follows Lewin, *Asante*, pp. 183–9.
77. On the Owusu-Ansah, see Wilks, *Asante*, pp. 632–54. (For the Asante's inconclusive Paris contacts in August 1895, CO 96/271, Maxwell to Chamberlain, Secret, 19 March 1896).
78. CO 96/248, Griffith to Ripon, Conf. 28 September 1894 (extracts in C 7917, no. 96).
79. For the British Chambers, Hynes, *Economics of Empire*, pp. 121–2; some of their representations of 1894 may be found in C 7917. CO 96/257, Maxwell to Ripon 211, 23 May 1895 (Accra C of C); CO 96/259, Maxwell to Chamberlain, 358, 27 August 1895 (Cape Coast C of C).
80. CO 96/248, Davidson-Houston (Kwahu) to Griffith, 6 October 1894. For the Asante evidence, Lewin, *Asante*, pp. 180–3 (and cf. p. 196).
81. CO 96/248, Griffith to Ripon, Conf. 31 October 1894, with encs; cf. C 7917 no. 100.
82. Rosebery Papers, National Library of Scotland, 46, Ripon to Rosebery, 20 February 1895; Note by J. H. Murray (Rosebery's secretary), 24 February.
83. CO 96/255, Minutes by Hemming, Wingfield, Ripon on Griffith to Ripon, Tel 12 February 1895.
84. CO 96/258, Maxwell to Chamberlain, Conf. 13 June 1895 (extracts in C 7918, no. 45), Maxwell to Hemming, Pte, 14 June.
85. Hansard, 4th series, 36, 22 August 1895, 640–5. Cf. Robinson and Gallagher, *Africa and the Victorians*, pp. 395–402. A. N. Porter, *Origins of the South African War*, p. 49.
86. CO 96/258, Chamberlain to Maxwell, 6 September 1895. This is based on discussion in the Minutes on Maxwell, Conf. 13 June, including an outline "Indictment" drafted by Chamberlain on House of Commons notepaper. The terms of the Treaty of Fomena, 1874, may conveniently be consulted in C. W. Newbury, *British Policy towards West Africa*, I, (1965) pp. 333–5.
87. CO 96/260, Maxwell to Chamberlain, Secret, 26 September 1895.
88. CO 96/259, Maxwell, Tel., 17 August and Minute by Antrobus, 19 August.
89. Ibid., Maxwell to Chamberlain, Conf. 19 August 1895, encl. Ferguson, 31 July.
90. CO 96/262, Maxwell to Chamberlain, Conf., 28 October 1895; CO 96/263, Maxwell, Tel., 13 December 1895; cf. Wilks, *Asante*, pp. 302–3. The tradition recorded by Lewin, *Asante*, p. 192 is clearly erroneous.
91. CO 96/260, Maxwell to Chamberlain, Conf., 6 September; Conf., 26 September; C 096/263, Conf., 10 December; Conf., 17 December 1895. Cf. Person, *Samori*, III, p. 1804.

92. CO 96/259, Minute by Hemming, 16 September on Maxwell, Conf., 19 August.
93. CO 96/263, Maxwell to Chamberlain, Conf., 23 December; Maxwell to Hemming, Pte, 23 December 1895. For the Asante traditions, Lewin, *Asante*, pp. 195–7.
94. CO 96/270, Maxwell to Chamberlain, Conf., 20 January 1896.
95. CO 96/270, Minute by Chamberlain, 21 January, on Maxwell, Tel.; cf. his and other minutes on Maxwell, Conf., 20 January 1896.
96. G. Baden-Powell, *Policy and Wealth in Ashanti* (1896), appendix to R. S. Baden-Powell. *The Downfall of Prempêh* (1896).
97. ANSOM, Afrique III/26/b, Delcassé to Monteil, 24 September 1894 (copy).
98. Person, *Samori*, III, pp. 1652–70; Weiskel, *Baule Peoples*, pp. 56–76; Labouret, *Monteil*, pp. 193–275.
99. ANSOM, Afrique III/26/a, Destenave to Governor, Wahiguya, 19 May 1895.
100. For fuller references, John D. Hargreaves, "West African States and the European Conquest", in L. H. Gann and P. Duignan, *Colonialism in Africa*, I (Cambridge, 1969), pp. 203–4.
101. Ferguson, almost immediately called to other duties, wrote only a brief report, which is reprinted in K. Arhin, *The Papers of George Ekem Ferguson* (Leiden, 1974) pp. 143–4. A French informant provided a circumstantial account of his visit and dated it as December 1894 (ANSOM, Afrique III/26/b, Note by Lt. Chanoine, 2 September 1896). But Ferguson's original treaty was sent to London in Griffith, Secret, 28 September 1894 (CO 96/248).
102. Obichere, *West African States*, pp. 195–9.
103. Person, *Samori*, III, pp. 1685–1711.
104. CO 96/270, translation of letter from Samori encl. in Maxwell to Chamberlain, Conf., 22 February 1896.
105. CO 96/265, Minute by Selborne, 6 December 1895, on FO to CO, 4 December. Cf. Minutes by Selborne and Chamberlain on FO to CO, 21 December.
106. CO 96/275, Hodgson to Chamberlain, Conf., 20 July 1896 encl. report by Capt. Davidson-Houston. Cf. Person, *Samori*, III, pp. 1807 ff.
107. ANSOM, Côte d'Ivoire IV/5/d, Guieysse to Chaudié, 18 March 1896.
108. Person, *Samori*, III, pp. 1767–71.
109. My interpretation of Samori's policy in this final phase rests essentially on Person's masterpiece. The evidence for the conflict at Bouna is in vol. III, pp. 1886–97.
110. Edward Grey, *Twenty-Five Years*, I, (1925) pp. 18–20; Sanderson, *England, Europe and the Upper Nile*, pp. 212–18.
111. Obichere, *West African States*, p. 174.
112. J. D. Hargreaves, "*Entente Manquée*: Anglo-French Relations, 1895–1896", *CHJ*, XI, 1953, pp. 65–92.
113. Roberts, "Railway Imperialism", pp. 258–62; Kanya-Forstner, *Conquest*, pp. 169–70.

114. The best concise account is C. Hirschfield, *The Diplomacy of Partition: Britain, France and the Creation of Nigeria, 1890–1898* (The Hague 1979) pp. 83–8. See also G. N. Uzoigwe, *Britain and the Conquest of Africa* (Ann Arbor, 1974) pp. 103–10.
115. For details of Lebon's interests, see C. M. Andrew, P. Grupp and A. S. Kanya-Forstner, "Le mouvement colonial français et ses principales personnalités, 1890–1914", *RFHOM*, LXII 229, 1975, p. 667; and the unpublished appendix to L. Abrams and D. J. Miller, "Who were the French Colonialists?", *HJ*, 19, 1976.
116. A. Lebon, *La politique de la France en Afrique, 1896–1898* (1901). pp. x, 66.
117. Person, *Samori*, III, pp. 1917–18.
118. Roberts, "Railway Imperialism", pp. 250, 265 ff.
119. Hirschfield, *Diplomacy of Partition*, pp. 109–10; Obichere, *West African States*, pp. 200–7; J. Ganiage, "Un épisode du partage de l'Afrique: Les affaires du bas Niger, 1894–98", *Revue Historique*, CCLIV, 1975.
120. Hirschfield, *Diplomacy*, pp. 142–8; R. A. Adeleye, *Power and Diplomacy in Northern Nigeria, 1804–1906*, pp. 194–5.
121. Cornevin, *Histoire du Dahomey*, pp. 395–400. On Aghwey, cf. P. Manning, *Slavery, Colonialism and Economic Growth in Dahomey, 1640–1960* (Cambridge, 1982) p. 166.
122. P. Grupp, *Deutschland, Frankreich und die Kolonien* (Tübingen, 1980) esp. pp. 92–7.
123. Flint, *Goldie*, pp. 230–63. See also Mason, "The Nupe Kingdom and the Europeans", and Adeleye, *Power and Diplomacy*, pp. 179–88.
124. CO 879/48. CP African 529, no. 265, Chamberlain to Maxwell, Conf., 4 June 1897.
125. Lugard's diary, 13 March 1898 (relating to 12 November 1897); M. Perham and M. Bull (ed.) *The Diaries of Lord Lugard*, IV (1963) pp. 332–5.
126. A. N. Porter, *The Origins of the South African War* (Manchester, 1980) ch. II; cf. above, pp. 104.
127. Hirschfield, *Diplomacy of Partition*, pp. 112–16.
128. Chamberlain seems to have contemplated this possibility in moments of irritation, for example, to Selborne, 28 and 29 September 1898 (J. L. Garvin, *Life of Joseph Chamberlain*, III, pp. 208, 211). For Chamberlain's desire for an ultimate entente with France, see A. E. Papiers Hanotaux, 20, Courcel to Hanotaux, 23 August 1895 (reprinted in *Revue Historique*, 212, 1954), 10 December 1897.
129. Minute of 22 May 1898, quoted Uzoigwe, *Britain and the Conquest of Africa*, pp. 133–4.
130. Uzoigwe, pp. 137–8; cf. Robinson and Gallagher, *Africa and the Victorians*, p. 408.
131. Minute of September 1897, quoted Uzoigwe, p. 118; cf. Flint, *Goldie*, pp. 270–8.
132. The best general accounts of the international context are still W. L. Langer, *The Diplomacy of Imperialism* (NY, 1935) and A. J. P. Taylor, *The Struggle for Mastery in Europe* (Oxford, 1954).

133. Salisbury to Chamberlain, 3 June 1898; Garvin, *Chamberlain*, III, p. 220.
134. Hirschfield, *Diplomacy of Partition*, p. 126.
135. Salisbury to Chamberlain, 2 June 1898; quoted Uzoigwe, p. 135.
136. FO 27/3335, Salisbury to Monson, Africa 259, 7 September 1897.
137. Quoted by Obichere, *West African States*, pp. 224–5.
138. Obichere, *West African States*, p. 237; cf. *The Times*, 23 February 1898.
139. DDF XIV, Hanotaux to Courcel, 1 February 1898; cf. R. G. Brown, *Fashoda Reconsidered* (Baltimore, 1970) p. 70; Obichere, *West African States*, p. 231.
140. DDF XIV, nos 47, 80, 176. Courcel to Hanotaux, 9 February, 12 March; Geoffray to Hanotaux, 30 April 1898.
141. DDF XIV, no. 32, Courcel to Hanotaux, 28 January 1898; cf. Sanderson, *Britain, Europe*, pp. 322–3.
142. Hirschfield, *Diplomacy of Partition*, pp. 171–4.
143. Hertslet, *Map of Africa*, II, pp. 785–96.
144. Hertslet, *Map of Africa*, III, 919–20.
145. Terrier to Cazemajou, 25 March 1896; cit. Roberts "Railway Imperialism", p. 307.
146. These paragraphs are chiefly based on R. A. Adeleye, *Power and Diplomacy in Northern Nigeria, 1804–1906*, ch. VI. For the final British conquest, see also M. Perham, *Lugard: The Years of Authority, 1895–1945*, (1960) and D. J. M. Muffet, *Concerning Brave Captains* (Douglas, 1964).
147. This interpretation largely follows Finn Fuglestad, "A propos de travaux récents sur la mission Voulet-Chanoine", *RFHOM*, LXVII, 1980, pp. 73–7; see also J. Suret-Canale, *Afrique noire* (1958) pp. 236–45. A more highly coloured reconstruction of thsi mission which nevertheless makes effective use of archive material where available is J. F. Rolland, *Le Grand Capitaine* (1976). On the broader French strategy, Roberts, "Railway Imperialism", chap. VIII.
148. J. C. Anene, *The International Boundaries of Nigeria* (1970) pp. 275–81.
149. M. McCall, "Kai Londo's Luawa and British Rule", DPhil thesis, University of York, 1974, ch. IV.
150. Cf. J. D. Hargreaves, "Liberia: The Price of Independence", *Odu*, n.s. 6, 1971, pp. 16–17; D. M. Foley, "British Policy in Liberia, 1862–1912", Ph.D. thesis, University of London, 1965.
151. W. R. Louis, *Great Britain and Germany's Lost Colonies* (Oxford, 1967).
152. W. R. Louis "Colonial Appeasement, 1936–38", *Revue belge de philologie et d'histoire*, XLIX, 1971.
153. PRO Prem I/47, Bourdillon to Macdonald, Secret and Personal, 22 November 1938.

12 West African Colonialism and the History of Imperialism

Europeans of the early twentieth century commonly regarded the establishment of colonial rule in regions like West Africa as the natural climax of historical interaction; political control, shared among the nation-states of western Europe in rough proportion to their political vitality, seemed to have become the necessary means for the extension of civilization, for the penetration of archaic economies by modernizing capitalism. The living nations, in a memorable phrase by Salisbury,[1] would inevitably encroach upon the dying nations; the important questions concerned the effects of this process on relations among themselves. For the ideologues of colonial empire – as also for its critics – partition and conquest were so clearly a product of the logic of history that it seemed hardly worth subjecting the details to close scrutiny.

By the 1960s the logic of history, and the relationship it implied between the secular expansion of European power and the imposition of colonial control, began to appear more complex. When in 1963 the Organisation of African Unity endorsed existing boundaries the only West African countries not yet independent were The Gambia (for two more years only), and Guiné-Bissao, where Portuguese control already seemed precarious. But it was clear that freedom from colonial rule would not necessarily bring freedom from want and fear, or end the subordination of Africans within the international community. Immiseration and control were evidently not the same thing; and historical studies began to confirm the complexity of their relationship. Imperialism – a word now commonly used in the broadly inclusive sense of manipulation and control of weak peoples by the rich and powerful – had clearly both pre-dated and survived the brief colonial period.

These new perspectives compelled reconsideration of simple reductionist explanations of the initial partition; to say that European governments went to West Africa to exploit seemed no more adequate than to say they went to civilize. Marxists who defined imperialism as the highest stage of capitalism found themselves in special terminological difficulties. Having by definition tried to exclude the term from exercises of power by military castes or merchant adventurers before the later nineteenth century, they found that banks and monopolies showed little interest in tropical Africa even within that period. To maintain the purity of their axiom they had to devise such concepts as *colonisation pré-impérialiste*.[2]

Even this ingenious phrase raises problems of dating. In the region most readily accessible from Europe and America, Senegambia, such *colonisation pré-impérialiste* had begun in the seventeenth century. But experience here had not been very encouraging, and elsewhere the British and French governments (as their Treaty of 1783 provided – *Prelude*, p. 93) preferred to seek access to African resources of labour, minerals and vegetable products, and to African markets, without assuming the responsibilities of political control. As European industrialization proceeded, soap-boilers seeking supplies of vegetable oil, exporters of cheap cottons and spirits, ambitious young officers, missionaries and accountants, all sought to realize some of their ambitions in Africa; and governments responsive to their needs were occasionally persuaded to use naval or military force to compel Africans to collaborate with them. But nobody who exercised decisive power or influence in Europe was yet ready to pay the price of trying to assert direct control over the hostile African environment; if capitalist Britain had a consistent African policy it was that expressed by the Parliamentary Committee of 1865 (*Prelude*, pp. 64–78). The century after 1783 might indeed be labelled a period of *impérialisme pré-colonialiste*; but it seems more profitable to distinguish the modes by which power was exercised than to try to encapsulate complex relationships in a single phrase. All forms of imperialism depend on some combination of force with collaboration; until the 1890s most Europeans emphasized the second component wherever possible.

The purpose of this study has been to explain how this informal imperialism of collaboration gave way to colonization, with European governments driving purposefully to control specific blocs of territory by force. The immediate answer has been found in short-term conjunctures within the European nation states. The period of hiatus in capitalist development known as the Great Depression was also the period when ruling elites in western Europe were facing the problems of addressing greatly expanded electorates. Whereas some ministers reacted by increased nervousness about the financial and human costs of overseas expansion (noting the fates of both Ferry and Gladstone in 1885), other politicians gradually perceived how old-fashioned Palmerstonian patriotism might be channelled towards colonial empire and made a useful political weapon. Meanwhile in Africa the short-term movement of produce prices, or resistance to foreign influence from conservative or patriotic elements, began to precipitate crises in local systems of collaboration which had been worked out between European traders and missionaries and their African hosts and landlords. But there was still nothing automatic about the methods by which European governments reacted or began to assert colonial control; while the Ijebus received fire from the Maxim gun, the Egbas secured a Treaty guaranteeing limited independence. Old-fashioned *histoire événementielle*, presented in the context of longer-term changes, provides the only satisfactory approach to historical explanation.

* * *

Prelude to the Partition ended with European governments first scrambling to secure juridical claims on African coasts and rivers, then gathering in conference at Berlin to impose some sort of regulation on their own rivalries. Territorial partition was not yet their aim; they were still more interested in access than in control. Since the collaborative arrangements on which they had hitherto relied were beginning to break down, they hoped to regulate, and therefore limit, the conditions on which force might be applied on the coasts and rivers (*Prelude*, pp. 334–8; vol. 1, pp. 40–2). Their diplomatic manoeuvres, more influenced by European than by African considerations, ended with a sort of self-proclaimed mandate to promote commercial access, linked with a vaguer commitment to the improvement of the continent.[3]

Behind these immediate pre-occupations were complex forces of longer duration. Professor Sanderson, seeking to explain these from the point of view of relations among European governments, has analysed the disappearance of "stabilizing factors" which were essentially political in character;[4] in the wider perspective of "a global confrontation between the developing and the underdeveloped countries", the effects of unstable terms of trade and the uncertainties of the Great Depression seem more fundamental (cf. above, pp. 9–13).[5] But on either view, the crisis in Afro-European relations proved too serious to be controlled by the Berlin provisions. Europeans were beginning to leave the enclaves on the sea-coast where they had been tolerated and protected and to try to solve their economic problems by securing more direct or favourable access to interior markets. When independent-minded rulers like Lat-Dior and Jaja tried to defend their existing rights, state power was invoked to coerce them; the conflicts of the "loaded pause" made neighbouring peoples increasingly suspicious. Proclaiming protectorates on the coast in itself did little to increase the authority of European governments; on the contrary, their attempts to meet the cost by imposing customs duties provoked reprisals from both European rivals and African customers. Everywhere the presence of foreign traders and missionaries – let alone Consuls and customs-men – produced contradictions and confrontations among Africans concerning the threat which these strangers posed to traditional interests and values. Already in the 1880s those Dahomeans, Ijebus and Asantes who would eventually opt for armed resistance can be observed expressing their anxieties.

By about 1890, therefore, European governments who claimed protectorate rights on the coast were finding that continued access to the interior would require increased control. But the Berlin agreement offered no method of determining who should control which territories. There was much talk of a possible doctrine of "hinterland", but this offered no basis for international consensus. Apart from the mathematical impossibility of delimiting segments of territory equivalent to sections of an irregular coastline, any attempt to do so would have been totally out of touch with actual relationships among the peoples to whom access was sought. From the early 1880s the French had begun to place much greater emphasis upon claims based on treaties with African rulers – treaties which not only provided, as hundreds of those in British possession already did, for friendly collaboration, free trade and intercourse, and the mutual protection of strangers, but appeared to confer exclusive control of foreign relations by acceptance of a "protectorate".

Since learned European jurists inconclusively debated the meaning of this term, it is hardly surprising that African office-holders who affixed their crosses to the treaties should interpret them in different ways. For years colonial governments had been claiming that protectorates over "uncivilized peoples" could imply rights of internal intervention, thus practising a form of "jurisdictional imperialism";[6] by 1895 the British Colonial Office had advanced so far as to argue that:

> the existence of a Protectorate in an uncivilised country carries with it a right on the part of the Protecting Power to exercise within that country such authority and jurisdiction, in short such of the attributes of Sovereignty, as are required for the due discharge of the duties of a Protector for the purpose not only of protecting the natives from the subjects of civilised powers and such subjects from the natives and from each other, but also for protecting the natives from the grosser forms of ill-treatment by their rulers, and from the raids of slave dealers and marauders.[7]

But such comprehensive authority might not be readily acknowledged by the *protégé*; arguments and conflicts ensued which could offer European rivals opportunities to contest the initial claim. Although diplomatists approached their rivals' treaties cynically, they knew that their own treaties were equally vulnerable; until the mid-1890s it was convenient to maintain the fiction that the grubby texts solemnly scrutinized by Boundary Commissioners provided evidence that sovereignty had been willingly conceded (vol. I, pp. 195–6; above, p. 71). But thereafter pressures to assert national control and raise the national flag reached such a pitch that French, German and British governments in turn moved on to the doctrine of "effective occupation" and began to engage in the dangerous sport of international steeplechasing.

The critical questions for students of the West African partition concern the origin of these pressures and the conditions which favoured their success – the rise and application to West Africa of a specific form of imperialism directed to the extension of colonial control. This "new imperialism" clearly has some continuity with much older expansionist tendencies within European states, which had already been sporadically directed towards West Africa under Palmerston and Napoleon III. How it should be related to the rise of finance capitalism, and so to Marxist terminology, is more problematic.[8] This study suggests that its essential elements, compounded in varying proportions according to conditions and national culture in the three states chiefly concerned, were commercial anxiety, patriotic zeal, and an overlying ethos of moral superiority.

Examples of each may be found throughout this book. Commercial anxiety, it should be re-emphasized, extended more widely than the provincial merchants – Régis, Woermann, Hutton – whose own modest fortunes were at risk. Their fear of doors being closed by foreign tariffs or African middlemen, their hopes of expanding business if railways could be pushed inland (preferably at public expense) were diffused through Chambers of Commerce, echoed periodically in the newspapers, and accentuated by contemporary uncertainties about the prospects for continuing capitalist expansion. Sometimes it is possible to observe worried businessmen seizing an opportunity to identify their own concerns with a wider national interest (for example, *Prelude*, pp. 183–95, 317–21; vol. 1, pp. 111–21; above, pp. 79–81). At others, their general anxieties converged with the desire of politicians or publicists to respond to, or to mould, the fund of patriotic sentiment which they perceived in the recently enlarged electorates. Because the local crises in Lagos and Dakar, in Opobo and Porto Novo, coincided with – indeed, derived more or less directly from – a more general crisis of the capitalist economy, the expansionists found opportunities to identify their own ambitions with real or imagined needs of their nation. And by about 1892, hard-headed politicians found it expedient to use moralistic arguments which they would formerly have cynically discounted. Expeditions to occupy African territory or destroy African armies were now marketed to match the ideals of philanthropists, economic modernizers, patriots – and even pacifists. "La colonisation est la solution pacifique d'un problème economique dont la guerre est la solution violente", Monteil argued when he turned his patriotic energy to electoral politics.[9]

The 1890s, it remains clear, marked the apogee of a new form of imperialist ideology. As its spokesmen supplemented their claims that colonial expansion would help ensure employment and prosperity at home with the moralizing rhetoric against "fiendish practices" which accompanied the conquest of Ijebu, Dahomey and Asante, "Social imperialism" became a serviceable political technique. Professor Gallagher discounted imperialist opinion as an actual cause of expansion;[10] he may be right, but not because it emerged too late to affect the course of events. The lines of partition were far from complete in the 1890s, and during that decade expansionists were able to mount public campaigns which anti-imperialists like Gladstone and Harcourt, or cautious diplomatists like Hanotaux, Marschall and Salisbury, ignored at their peril. It took a real national crisis such as France faced at Fashoda to demonstrate that most of the apparent colonial fever was only skin deep.[11]

Once the race for "effective occupation" of the interior was under way, the dialectic of Afro-European relations, as well as the inter-European rivalry, made it impossible to stop. As Salisbury obliquely indicated in his despatch of 7 September 1897 (see above, p. 232), partition was becoming necessary to guarantee access. Although the origins of the partition must be sought in Europe, its speed, and the methods by which it was implemented, were largely regulated by interactions on the frontiers. European demands tipped the balance, in the political process of Ijebu and Dahomey, in favour of those who favoured armed resistance. Even when the military forces engaged in the steeplechases aimed to operate with the consent and collaboration of African rulers, their demands for food supplies and porters quickly led to tension, often to fierce conflict. Peaceful penetration by the methods of *colonisation moderne* often ended similarly. The more committed the new governors were to improving transport and communications, the higher their demands for taxes and forced labour; the more sincere their detestation of slavery and other "fiendish practices", the more likely they were to provoke violent reactions.[12]

Conflicts with Africans may however have helped to sublimate some of that patriotic zeal which in the mid-1890s threatened to change the structure of inter-state relations in Europe. Although finance ministers sometimes lost control of what colonialists were up to in Africa, the foreign ministries never did so completely. That great Continental League against the British Empire which Courcel and Kayser periodically envisaged (vol. I, p. 36; see above, p. 228) might conceivably have materialized if the rulers of Russia, France and Germany had managed to concert their respective aims in China, Egypt and South Africa; but the interests and issues at stake in the West were never weighty enough to change the Eurocentric priorities of official minds. In the final settlements they imposed a certain crude rationality on the colonial enthusiasts, at the expense of African populations, who on the whole received progressively less consideration in successive boundary agreements. Men like Salisbury knew that in the long run access would prove more important than colonial control, and that it could be better secured on an international than a national basis; hence those fiscal provisions which allowed international capital continuing access to African resources across the new colonial boundaries.

In retrospect, colonial control of African territory, which ideologues believed would provide their countries with opportunities to prove themselves worthy heirs of Imperial Rome, may appear as merely one temporary and local manifestation of the force of secular imperialism. Even from the point of view of West African history, some writers now question the importance of the colonial period.[13] But control did allow the new rulers to change many things. Railways were built, taxes imposed, production more thoroughly commercialized, new forms of education introduced; on these foundations the independent African states of the 1960s were to be constructed. And for the colonial masters themselves, control did offer certain preferences in access to markets and supplies, to opportunities for investment and employment, so making modest contributions to their national prosperity, and rather more significant ones to their capacity to wage international war. In some cases these contributions have diminished as, with independence, the former colonial powers have had to rely for access on collaboration rather than force, and in fiercer competition with other states and corporations. But there have been few traumatic breaks in continuity; the colonial partition has left enduring marks, not only on the map of West Africa but on the lives of its peoples.

NOTES

1. *The Times*, 10 November 1898.
2. J. Bouvier, R. Girault, J. Thobie, *La France Impériale, 1880–1914* (1982) pp. 168–9.
3. W. R. Louis, "The Berlin Congo Conference", in Gifford and Louis, *France and Britain*, pp. 217–20.
4. G. N. Sanderson, "The European Partition of Africa", in E. F. Penrose (ed.), *European Imperialism and the Partition of Africa* (1975).
5. A. G. Hopkins, *An Economic History of West Africa* (1973) pp. 164–6.
6. R. Ross Johnston, *Sovereignty and Protection: a Study of British Jurisdictional Imperialism in the late Nineteenth Century* (Durham NC, 1973); cf C. H. Alexandrowicz, "The Partition of Africa by Treaty" in K. Ingham (ed.), *Foreign Relations of African States* (1974).
7. CO 96/264, Ripon to Griffith, Conf., 11 March 1895.
8. For pointers, see Robin Law, "Imperialism and Partition", *JAH*, XXIV, 1983, pp. 103–4.
9. H. Labouret, *Monteil* (1937) p. 282.
10. J. Gallagher, *The Decline, Revival and Fall of the British Empire* (Cambridge, 1982) pp. xiii, 80.
11. M. Michel, *La Mission Marchand*, pp. 223–5.
12. Cardew's governorship of Sierra Leone provides good examples; cf J. D. Hargreaves, "The Establishment of the Sierra Leone Protectorate and the Insurrection of 1898", *CHJ*, XII, 1956.
13. J. F. Ajayi, "Colonialism: an Episode in African History", in Gann and Duignan, *Colonialism in Africa*, I, pp. 497–508.

Appendix

Table A.1 *Export trade of the Gold Coast, 1882–96*

Year	Palm Oil		Palm kernels		Rubber		Gold		Cocoa		Total value
	Gall (million)	Value	Tons	Value	lbs	Value	oz	Value	lbs	Value	of Exports
1882	2.9	£178 508	8 151	£50 316	70	12/6	17 098	£61 552	—	—	£340 019
1883	2.6	£208 721	7 428	£61 542	57 913	£2 371	14 565	£52 435	—	—	£363 868
1884	3.6	£282 398	8 930	£76 530	223 827	£13 619	18 386	£66 189	121	£6	£467 228
1885	4.0	£284 391	4 991	£52 823	NA	£30 234	NA	NA	—	—	£496 318
1886	3.1	£155 978	9 426	£47 829	1 549 121	£69 911	20 709	£74 829	—	—	£406 539
1887	3.0	£143 395	8 022	£41 613	1 306 252	£62 430	22 547	£81 168	—	—	£372 446
1888	3.4	£150 361	13 330	£68 525	878 387	£38 048	24 031	£86 510	—	—	£381 619
1889	2.9	£137 283	10 919	£62 542	1 241 629	£55 198	28 667	£103 200	—	—	£415 926
1890	2.9	£144 378	12 650	£78 433	3 361 055	£231 281	25 460	£91 657	—	—	£601 438
1891	2.9	£192 852	12 928	£89 959	2 946 913	£198 901	24 476	£88 112	—	—	£684 348
1892	3.6	£178 954	15 846	£103 295	2 663 020	£166 660	27 446	£98 806	—	—	£665 064
1893	3.4	£183 910	12 041	£8 072	3 395 990	£218 162	21 972	£79 099	3 460	£94	£722 167
1894	4.2	£237 623	17 136	£112 373	3 027 527	£232 550	21 332	£76 796	20 312	£547	£850 344
1895	4.3	£231 415	15 560	£93 385	4 022 355	£322 070	25 416	£91 947	28 906	£470	£877 804
1896	2.4	£126 857	13 046	£85 349	3 735 439	£313 827	23 940	£81 186	86 754	£2 276	£792 111

Source *PP*, 1897, xcvii, C8605, Statistical Abstract for the general Colonial and other Possessions of the UK, 1883–97; supplemented by annual *Blue Books*.

A Bibliographical Note

Since this work has been annotated sufficiently copiously to enable interested scholars to identify the sources on which it has drawn, I have not attempted to list all the works I have used. What follows is conceived as a general guide to the routes my research has taken. The first section gives a general account of the primary evidence I have used, more or less intensively. For fuller guides to manuscript sources students are referred to such works as the *Guide to the Sources of the History of Africa South of the Sahara*, published by the International Council of Archives (Zug) – especially vols 3 and 4 relating to French sources – and N. Matthews, *Material for West Africa in the archives of the UK* (1973). The second section lists books and articles by twenty historians whose work has influenced, in part, the arguments of this book. This may provide a basis for interested readers to follow up some of the issues raised. The third section lists the unpublished theses which I have been privileged to use.

I SOURCES

My major source has clearly been the colonial archives of the French and British governments, consulted respectively in the Archives Nationales, Section d'Outre-Mer, Paris, and in the Public Record Office, Kew. It is now well-known that these contain rich material concerning not only the making of "policy" but the interaction between colonial governments and their African neighbours. It is my impression that they often contain more extensive and reliable recordings of African oral traditions than those made later, whether by colonial officials with historical interests or by modern scholars. I have consulted these colonial archives fairly intensively for the later 1880s, more selectively for the period 1890–4, only occasionally thereafter. In some cases I began with the British series of Confidential Prints; in this period these frequently reproduce the bulk of the material on Afro-European relations, though the absence of minutes limits their value for the study of policy formation. The archives of the two Foreign Offices (respectively housed in the Ministère des Affaires Etrangères and in the PRO) have also been used selectively; those of the Ministère de la Marine, at Vincennes, only for the period of the military campaigns in Dahomey. German policy was studied chiefly through secondary works; and I have not attempted to deal with Portuguese policy in Guiné-Bissao.

The scale of my work did not permit any comprehensive study of archives in Africa. The importance of these, as well as the facility of consultation, appears to be variable. Although over the years I have derived great profit from the study of the records of the Native Affairs Department in the Sierra Leone National Archives, by 1890 a fairly large proportion of this material was being copied to the Colonial Office. The Archives of AOF (fully described, for this period, in the *Répertoires* prepared by C. Faure and J. Charpy) are well cared-for in the Archives Nationales du Sénégal, Dakar; microfilms are now in the Archives d'Outremer at Aix-en-Provence. There are clearly rich possibilities for local or regional studies based on such resources, but these would be unlikely to change general interpretations of the partition very drastically.

The private papers of European statesmen like Salisbury, Rosebery and Hanotaux contain a little relevant evidence, proportionate to the place which West Africa occupied in their world view. (There is a little more in Joseph Chamberlain's papers in Birmingham University, but largely on topics outside the design of this study). For the study of African attitudes, missionary archives can provide invaluable evidence. I have made some use of microfilms from the Church Missionary Society archives (in Aberdeen University Library), and rather more of the archives of Missions Africaines, formerly of Lyon, now at the Society's headquarters in Rome.

The major printed collections of European public records are well-known. The British series of Parliamentary Papers (conveniently rearranged, for students of West Africa, in the reprint published by Irish Universities Press) is informative on some areas (for example, Asante in the 1890s), almost silent on others. It has no real equivalent in France or Germany, but a fair amount of official documentation – including agents' reports as well as legislative documents and statistics – may be located, with diligence, in the *Journal Officiel* or in the semi-official *Revue Maritime et Coloniale*. Official and semi-official texts may also be found in the *Bulletin du Comité de l'Afrique française* or the *Revue française de l'Etranger et des Colonies et Exploration*. For texts of treaties, see E. Hertslet, *The Map of Africa by Treaty* (I have used the third edition of 1909, reprint of 1967) and E. Rouard de Card, *Les Traités de Protectorat conclus par la France* (1897). Among the collections of diplomatic documents published after 1919, there is more of relevance to West Africa in *Documents Diplomatiques français* (first series) than in *Die Grosse Politik* or the *British Documents on the Origins of the War*. The most useful modern historical anthology is C. W. Newbury (ed.), *British Policy Towards West Africa* vol. II (1875–1914) (Oxford, 1971).

It will be clear from the notes that I have found valuable evidence in very many other sources. These include contemporary periodicals of many kinds; biographical or autobiographical publications, from pot-boiling memoirs to modern editions of private papers; works by travellers, traders and officials, notably the *apologiae* of literary French soldiers such as Binger, Frey, Gallieni and Péroz; and miscellaneous contemporary works. This residual category ranges from polemical books and pamphlets, which often unwittingly illuminate the intentions of their authors, to informative works of local reference, such as *Annales Sénégalaises* and J. Otonba Payne's invaluable *Lagos Almanacks*. African newspapers are one such source which I could happily and profitably have explored more deeply had time allowed.

II THE CONTRIBUTIONS OF MODERN SCHOLARSHIP

In place of a full bibliography, which would have added greatly to the weight of this volume without in any way being comprehensive, this section attempts to provide sufficient information to enable my readers to follow up the principal issues of African and Imperial history which have been raised. Section A lists seven collaborative volumes; the contributions, though clearly of variable value and relevance, contain some useful and even seminal essays. Section B is an annotated list of works by the twenty modern historians from which I have gained most insight into aspects of my study. Selection was difficult; a scrutiny of footnotes will show some excellent monographs from which I have derived more information, often with less dissent. But these are the works to which I would in the first place direct enquirers.

Section A

i M. Crowder (ed.), *West African Resistance: the Military Response to Colonial Occupation* (1971).
ii L. H. Gann and P. Duignan (eds.), *Colonialism in Africa, 1870–1960*, vol. I, *The History and Politics of Colonialism, 1870–1914* (Cambridge, 1969).
iii P. Gifford and W. R. Louis (ed.), *Britain and Germany in Africa: Imperial Rivalry and Colonial Rule* (New Haven, Conn., 1967).
iv P. Gifford and W. R. Louis (ed.), *France and Britain in Africa: Imperial Rivalry and Colonial Rule* (New Haven, Conn., 1971).
v R. Owen and B. Sutcliffe (ed.), *Studies in the Theory of Imperialism* (1972).
vi E. F. Penrose (ed.), *European Imperialism and the Partition of Africa* (1975).
vii University of Edinburgh, Centre of African Studies, *The Theory of Imperialism and the European Partition of Africa* (Seminar Proceedings, 1967).

Section B

Adeleye, R. A. *Power and Diplomacy in Northern Nigeria, 1804–1906* (1971).
"Rabih Fadlallah 1879–1893: Exploits and Impact of Political Relations in Central Sudan", JHSN, v, 1970, pp. 223–42.
Shows exemplary skill in combining the use of Arabic and European sources for the study of inter-state relations in the Sudan.

Ajayi, J. F. Ade, and Smith, Robert, *Yoruba Warfare in the Nineteenth Century* (Cambridge, 1964).
Ajayi, J. F. Ade, *Christian Missions in Nigeria 1841–1891* (1965).
"The Continuity of African Institutions under Colonialism", in T. O. Ranger (ed.), *Emerging Themes of African History* (Nairobi, 1968)
(with R. A. Austen) "Hopkins on Economic Imperialism in West Africa", *Econ. HR*, xxv, 1972, pp. 303–12.
(Also in A (ii) above.)

Smith Robert, *Kingdoms of the Yoruba* 2nd edn. (1976).
Warfare and Diplomacy in Pre-Colonial West Africa (1976).
The Lagos Consulate, 1851–1861 (1978)
(Also in A (i) above).

Though it is convenient to bracket them under the title of their collaborative work, these two authors have little in common except the way their Yoruba interests are combined with much broader perspectives on modern African history.

Andrew C. M., and Kanya-Forstner, A. S., "The French Colonial Party: Its Composition, Aims and Influence, 1885–1914", *HJ*, xiv, 1971.
"The *Groupe Colonial* in the French Chamber of Deputies, 1892–1932", *HJ*, xvii, 1974.
"Gabriel Hanotaux, the Colonial Party and the Fashoda Strategy", *JICH*, iii, 1974.
(with P. Grupp) "Le Mouvement colonial français et ses principales personnalités, 1890–1914", *RFHOM*. lxii, 1975.
"French Business and the French Colonialists", *HJ*, xix, 1976.
France Overseas: The Great War and the Climax of French Imperial Expansion (1981).

Andrew, C. M. *Theophile Delcassé and the Making of the Entente Cordiale* (1968).
"The French Colonialist Movement during the Third Republic: the unofficial mind of Imperialism", *TRHS*, 5th series, xxvi, 1976.

Kanya-Forstner, A. S. *The Conquest of the Western Sudan: A Study in French Military Imperialism* (Cambridge, 1969).
"French African Policy and the Anglo-French Agreement of 5 August 1890", *HJ*, xii, 1969.
(Also in A (i) (iv) (v) (vi) (vii) above)

While each of these authors has made important individual contributions to, respectively, the study of foreign policy and of military imperialism, they have been closely associated in their careful studies of the French colonial party. These lead them to the conclusion that "Before the First World War French imperialism, in the Leninist sense, and French colonialism, went, more often than not, in different directions" ("French Business", p. 997). They have been criticized by L. Abrams and D. J. Miller ("Who were the French colonialists?", *HJ*, xix, 1976) for under-estimating the importance of business interests; though not, in my view, very effectively.

Asiwaju, A. I. *Western Yorubaland under European Rule, 1889–1945* (1976).

Though the scope of this study goes beyond my own, I include it as a good example of a comparative study which successfully crosses colonial boundaries. Professor Asiwaju has continued to work on this topic and has edited a forthcoming volume entitled *Partitioned Africans*.

Ayandele, E. A. *The Missionary Impact on Modern Nigeria, 1842–1914* (1966).
Holy Johnson (1970).
The Educated Elite in the Nigerian Society (Ibadan, 1974).
Nigerian Historical Studies (1979).
African Historical Studies (1979).

Professor Ayandele deals perceptively with the historical interaction of African and European cultures. Fuller publication of his important studies of Ijebu is expected shortly.

Brunschwig, Henri, *Mythes et réalités de l'impérialisme colonial française, 1871–1914* (1960).
L'avènement de l'Afrique noire (1963).
Le partage de l'Afrique noire (1971).
Noirs et Blancs dans l'Afrique noire française (1983).
"Politique et economie dans l'empire français d'Afrique noire 1870–1914", *JAH*, XI, 1970, pp. 401–17.
"Notes sur les technocrates de l'impérialisme française en Afrique noire", *RFHOM*, LIV, 1967, pp. 171–87.
"Le docteur Colin, l'or du Bambouk et la 'Colonisation moderne' ", *CEA*, XV, 1975, pp. 166–88.
"French Expansion and Local Reactions in Black Africa in the Time of Imperialism (1880–1914)", in H. L. Wesseling (ed.), *Expansion and Reaction* (Leiden, 1979).
"L'Afrique noire atlantique et l'Europe", *Itinerario* (Leiden) 1980–1, pp. 129–36.
(Also in A (ii) (iv) (vi) above.)

The short book of 1960 by this distinguished pupil of Bloch and Febvre re-opened the study of the *parti colonial*. Sceptical of simple theories of imperialism, Brunschwig sees nineteenth century Africa as undergoing a process of *s'occidentalisation*, through collaborative relationships in which Africans as well as Europeans took initiatives.

Coquery-Vidrovitch, Catherine, *Le Congo aux temps des grandes compagnies Concessionaires* (1972).
"La fête des coutoumes au Dahomey: Historique et essai d'interpretation", *Annales*, XIX, 1964.
"De la traite des escalves à l'exportation de l'huile de palme et des palmistes au Dahomey", in C. Meillassoux, *Development of Indigenous Trade and Markets in West Africa* (1970).
"La mise en dépendance de l'Afrique noire: essai de périodisation, 1800–1970", *CEA*, XVI, 61–2, 1976, pp. 7–58.
"L'impact des interêts coloniaux: SCOA et CFAO dans l'Quest africain, 1910–1965", *JAH*, XVI, 1975.
(Also in A (ii) above.)

Since her early researches on Dahomey and the Congo, Professor Coquery has become a leading specialist in modern African economic history, and a notable theorist of imperialism.

Diké, K. Onwuka, *Trade and Politics in the Niger Delta* (Oxford, 1956).
Though it is now beginning to date, the publication of this book marked an epoch in modern African historiography.

Flint, John E. *Sir George Goldie and the Making of Nigeria* (1960).
Nigeria and Ghana (Englewood Cliffs, 1966).

"Economic Change in West Africa in the Nineteenth Century", in J. F. Ajayi and M. Crowder, *History of West Africa,* II, 1974, pp. 380–401.
"Britain and the Partition of West Africa", in J. E. Flint and G. Williams (eds.), *Perspectives of Empire* (1973) pp. 93–111.
(Also in A (ii) above.)
The debt this book owes to Flint's pioneer study of the Niger Company is obvious.

Fyfe, C. H., *A History of Sierra Leone* (1962).
Africanus Horton (NY, 1972).
"European and Creole Influence in the Hinterland of Sierra Leone before 1896", *SLS,* n.s.6, 1956, pp. 113–23.
"Race, Empire and Post-Empire", The Africanus Horton Memorial Lecture (Freetown, 1979).
(Also in A (vii) above.)
Besides his unequalled contribution to the social history of Sierra Leone, Christopher Fyfe has contributed considerably to the subject of this book, and to the education of its author.

Gallagher, J., *see under* Robinson.

Hopkins, A. G., *An Economic History of West Africa* (1973).
"Economic Imperialism in West Africa: Lagos, 1880–92", *Econ. HR,* 2nd series, XXI, 1968, pp. 580–606.
"Imperial Business in Africa", *JAH,* XVIII, 1976, pp. 29–48, 267–90.
"Property Rights and Empire Building: Britain's Annexation of Lagos, 1861", *Journal of Economic History,* XL, 1980, pp. 777–98.
(with P. J. Cain) "The Political Economy of British Expansion Overseas, 1750–1914", *Econ. HR,* 2nd series, XXXIII, 1980, pp. 463–90.
Professor Hopkins's distinguished work emphasizes, and holds in balance, two essential, though simple, insights: that the long-established skills of African entrepreneurs merit serious analysis by economic historians, and that the internal development of Africa has been increasingly affected by the "global confrontation between the developing and the underdeveloped countries".

Kanya-Forstner, *see under* Andrew Newbury *and under.*

Lewin, T. I., *Asante before the British: the Prempean Years* (Lawrence, 1978). As a contribution to the internal history of Asante, this must take second place to Ivor Wilks' massive *Asante in the Nineteenth Century* (Cambridge, 1975); but it is essential reading for the period of the partition.

Newbury, C. W., *The Western Slave Coast and its Rulers* (Oxford, 1961).
(ed.), *British Policy Towards West Africa:* Select Documents I, 1786–1874 (1965); II, 1875–1914 (1971).
"Credit in early nineteenth century West African Trade", *JAH,* XIII, 1972, pp. 81–95.
"North African and Western Sudan Trade in the nineteenth century: a re-evaluation", *JAH,* VII, 1966, 233 ff.

"The Protectionist Revival in French Colonial Trade: the Case of Senegal", *Econ. HR,* XXI, 1968.
with Kanya-Forstner, A. S., "French Policy and the origins of the scramble for West Africa", *JAH,* x, 1969, 253 ff.
(Also in A (ii) (iv) above.)
All students of the periods are indebted to Dr Newbury's researches on the relations between tariffs, trade and politics.

Obichere, B. I., *West African States and European Expansion: the Dahomey-Niger Hinterland, 1885–1898* (New Haven, Conn, 1971).
Though rather inadequately prepared for publication, this book contains a great deal of thorough research covering a wide area.

Person, Yves, *Samori: Une Revolution Dyula,* 3 vols (Dakar, 1968–75).
"Samori et la Sierra Léone", *CEA,* VII, 25, 1967, pp. 5–26.
"L'aventure de Porèkèrè et le drame de Waima", *CEA,* v, 18–19.
(Also in A (i).)
Despite its lack of maps and references Person's massive study remains the most impressive achievement of modern West Africanist scholarship, and is fundamental to an understanding of the modern history of the region.

Robinson R, and Gallagher J., *Africa and the Victorians* (1961; new edn., 1982).
"The Imperialism of Free Trade", *Econ. HR,* VI, 1953, pp. 1–15.
"The Partition of Africa", in *The New Cambridge Modern History,* XI (Cambridge, 1962) pp. 593–640.

Robinson, R., "Imperial Problems in British Politics, 1880–1895", in *The Cambridge History of the British Empire,* III, (Cambridge, 1959) pp. 127–80.
(Also in A (v).)

Gallagher, J., *The Decline, Revival and Fall of the British Empire* (Cambridge, 1982).
Though not normally at their best on West African affairs, Robinson and Gallagher have done more than any other writers to compel the re-assessment of received opinions about modern British imperialism.

Smith, Robert, *see under* Ajayi.

Wehler, Hans-Ulrich, *Bismarck und der Imperialismus* (Köln, 1969).
"Bismarck's Imperialism, 1862–1890", *Past and Present,* no. 48, 1970.
(Also in A (v).)
A major attempt to interpret German imperialism in the context of modern German history; but compare the interpretation of, for example, C. Eley, *Reshaping the German Right* (New Haven, Conn., 1980).

III UNPUBLISHED THESES

Aderibigbe, A. A. B., "Expansion of the Lagos Protectorate, 1863–1900", PhD, University of London, 1959.

Akpan, M. B., "The African Policy of the Liberian Settlers, 1841–1932", PhD, University of Ibadan, 1968.

Amenumey, D. E. K., "The Ewe People and the Coming of European Rule", MA, University of London, 1964.

Awe, B., "The Rise of Ibadan as a Yoruba Power, 1851–93", DPhil, University of Oxford, 1964.

Balogun, S. A., "Gwandu Emirates in the Nineteenth Century, with Special Reference to Political Relations", PhD, University of Ibadan, 1971.

Dumett, R. E., "British Official Attitudes in Relation to Economic Development in the Gold Coast, 1874–1905", PhD, University of London, 1966.

Ekoko, A. E., "British Defence Policy in Western Africa, 1878–1914", PhD, University of Aberdeen, 1976.

Etheridge, N., "The Sierra Leone Frontier Police", MLitt, University of Aberdeen, 1967.

Folayan, K., "Egbado and Yoruba-Aja Power Politics, 1832–94", MA, University of Ibadan, 1967.

Foley, D. M., "British Policy in Liberia, 1862–1912", PhD, University of London, 1965.

Garcia, Luc, "La France et la Conquête du Dahomé, 1875–1894", Doctorat d'Etat, Paris-I, 1983 (Not read).

Jeng, A. A. O., "An Economic History of the Gambia Groundnut Industry, 1830–1924: the Evolution of an Export Economy", PhD, Birmingham, 1978.

Lassissi-Pinto, Joelle, "La France et le Libéria de 1880 à 1918: la Bataille pour un Territoire", Mémoire de Maitrise, Paris-I, Nov. 1978.

McCall, M., "Kai Lundu's Luawa and British Rule", DPhil, University of York, 1974.

Mason, M., "The Nupe Kingdoms in the Nineteenth Century", PhD, University of Birmingham, 1970.

Pallinder-Law, Agneta, "Government in Abeokuta, 1830–1914: with Special Reference to the Egba United Government, 1898–1914", University of Göteborg, 1973.

Pogge von Strandmann, H., "The Kolonialrat: its Significance and Influence on German Politics from 1890 to 1906", DPhil, University of Oxford, 1970.

Roberts, T. W., "Railway Imperialism and French Advances towards Lake Chad, 1890–1900", PhD, University of Cambridge, 1973.

Ross, D. A., "The Autonomous Kingdom of Dahomey, 1818–1894", PhD, University of London, 1967.

Senkomago, N. S., "The Kingdom of Porto Novo, with special reference to its external relations, 1872–1908", PhD, University of Aberdeen, 1976.

Index